Security to the North

Canada-U.S. Defense Relations in the 1990s

Security to the North

Canada-U.S. Defense Relations in the 1990s

by Joseph T. Jockel

Michigan State University Press
East Lansing
1991

Copyright © 1991 by Joseph T. Jockel

All Michigan State University Press Books are produced on paper
which meets the requirements of American National Standard of
Information Sciences — Permanence of paper for printed materials
ANSI Z39.48-1984.

Michigan State University Press
East Lansing, Michigan 48823-5202

Printed in the United States of America

Library of Congress Cataloging-in-Publication Data

Jockel, Joseph T.
    Security to the north: Canada-U.S. defense relations in the
1990s/Joseph T. Jockel
        p.   cm. — (The Canadian series ; #1)
    Includes bibliographical references and index.
    ISBN 0-87013-293-8 : $22.00
        1. Canada — Defenses. 2. Canada — Military relations — United
States. 3. United States — Military relations — Canada.   I. Title.
II. Series: Canadian series ; #1.
UA600.J63   1991
355'.033071 — dc20   91-52910
                                                          CIP

CONTENTS

Acknowledgments

My thanks go to many people and institutions in the United States and Canada.

With the generous financial support of a Senior Fellowship in Canadian Studies from the Government of Canada, I began work on this book as a visiting scholar at the Center of Canadian Studies of Johns Hopkins University's Nitze School of Advanced International Studies in Washington, D.C. I am grateful to the center's director, Prof. Charles Doran, and its program coordinator, Elaine Férat, for welcoming me back to the most engaging spot in the United States for following Canada-U.S. relations.

I completed the first draft as a Fellow of the Woodrow Wilson International Center for Scholars, which is also located in Washington and which, thanks to its wonderful staff, its setting at the Smithsonian, and the other Fellows while I was there, I can only describe as America's academic paradise. I will never have it so good again.

John Anderson, Charles Doran, Louis Dupont, Peter Haydon, Barry Lowenkron, Douglas Murray, Francis McHugh, Joel Sokolsky, and Wayne Thompson provided helpful and often extensive comments on various drafts. My special thanks to all of them.

I was in a quandary as to how to thank properly the many officials of the U.S. and Canadian governments, especially of the U.S. Department of Defense and the Canadian Department of National Defence, who agreed to be interviewed. About half of these men and women asked not to be named. Seeing that among the others none seemed to attach any importance at all to having his or her name mentioned in an academic study, I will simply say that I am grateful to all I talked to in Washington, Ottawa, Norfolk, Halifax, and Colorado Springs.

Prof. Victor Howard of Michigan State University, editor of the new series on Canada in which this book appears, was judicious in his comments and very fast in providing them.

With so much help one would think that in the end I would get every-thing right. But just in case, I should emphasize in closing that respon-sibility for the content of this work is solely my own.

This publication was prepared in part under a grant from the Woodrow Wilson International Center for Scholars, Washington, D.C. The state-ments and views expressed herein are those of the author and are not necessarily those of the Wilson Center.

I
Introduction

"A VERY IMPORTANT PIECE OF REAL ESTATE"

The United States and Canada are essential to each other's security, and Canadians tend to be more vividly aware of this than are Americans. This remains the case even in today's promising new era of East-West relations, the "post-post war period" that dramatically emerged in late 1989 with the collapse of communist regimes in eastern Europe.

The United States possesses the strategic nuclear deterrent, while Canada lies between the United States and the Soviet Union. Since the Soviet Union first acquired the capability to strike at North America with nuclear weapons—a capability which it will retain for the foreseeable future—U.S. security has been dependent upon at least a minimum of strategic defensive or surveillance operations undertaken in Canada by Canadian or U.S. forces. This has made Canada, as John Foster Dulles once put it, "a very important piece of real estate."[1]

Americans were once well aware of the significance of Canadian territory and airspace, and of the Canadian air force. During the 1950s and early 1960s, the era of the intercontinental bomber, the United States and Canada built a vast air defense system which included thousands of fighter aircraft, hundreds of surface-to-air missiles, and several great radar networks stretching across the North American continent, including the Distant Early Warning (DEW) Line in the high Canadian and Alaskan Arctic.

Beginning in the 1960s, as the intercontinental ballistic missile (ICBM) and the submarine-launched ballistic missile (SLBM) supplanted the manned bomber as the main means whereby, the Soviet Union could deliver nuclear weapons to North America, Canada and the United States pruned their air defenses. The pruning accelerated when the United States decided to forego the erection of an antiballistic missile (ABM) system and to rely on deterrence for its protection against nuclear attack. Why maintain thick air defense "walls" when there was to be no ABM "roof"?

When the United States deployed a variety of ground- and space-based sensors which could detect and track ballistic missiles approaching North America, none of these systems was located on Canadian soil or operated by the Canadian Armed Forces. However, the remnants of the once-vast continental air defense system have always remained essential in preventing Soviet bombers and now long-range cruise missiles from being able to attack, without warning, the United States strategic deterrent. In the 1980s Prime Minister Pierre Trudeau could still accurately tell the Canadian House of Commons, "we contribute an element of priceless value: the airspace above our vast land."[2]

In the 1990s, the importance to U.S. security of Canadian "real estate" and of defense cooperation with the Canadian Armed Forces will in all probability not diminish, and could well modestly increase in importance, depending upon certain technological developments and strategic choices faced by both the United States and the Soviet Union. This is unlike the case in Europe where the stunning decline in the Soviet threat is leading to dramatic reductions in armaments. Three aspects stand out:

• The heart of Canada-U.S. defense cooperation is air defense. The aging North American air defense system, including its elements on Canadian territory, is being modernized to cope with new Soviet nuclear-armed, long-range air- and sea-launched cruise missiles. It may, before the decade is out, require further enhancement to cope with "stealthy" cruise missiles and bombers. Ironically, a new strategic arms reduction agreement, now pending between the United States and the Soviet Union and leading to cuts in the number of ballistic missiles, will substantially shift strategic nuclear arsenals towards weapons carried in bombers. This could accelerate the development of air-breathing systems and thus increase the importance of the North American air defense system.

• The U.S. Strategic Defense Initiative (SDI), a research program begun in 1983, holds out the prospect that the United States may deploy a ballistic missile defense system. Ronald Reagan's dream of the all but leakproof system of ballistic missile defense that could make nuclear weapons "impotent and obsolete" is gone. But the Bush administration or its successor may still opt, before the decade is out, for the deployment of a system with limited capabilities. Regardless of whether the elements of such a system may require the use of Canadian territory, a ballistic missile defense "roof" could lead to the strengthening of the air defense "walls" which certainly must involve Canada. In any event, close coordination between missile defense and air defense operations, including those in Canada, would be a necessity.

• Antisubmarine warfare operations in the waters off North America will remain necessary to help protect North America against nuclear attack, especially as longer-range Soviet sea-launched cruise missiles, carried in submarines, continue to enter the Soviet inventory, and to keep sea lines of communication between North America and Europe open in a crisis. As the United States draws down its forces in Europe, it will shift towards a defense posture based in part on the ability to reinforce Europe in an emergency with forces sealifted and airlifted from North America. Canadian Arctic waters may have become important for U.S. Navy antisubmarine warfare operations. These waters may also be relied upon by the U.S. Navy as secondary transit routes into the Arctic Ocean and by the Soviets as secondary routes into the Atlantic.

The United States will continue to take the lead in deciding how North America can best protect itself. But Canadians will want to determine the ways in which their armed forces cooperate with the United States and, to the extent possible, how their territory, airspace and waters are used.

To be sure, the two countries maintain a decades-old partnership of unparalleled intimacy between their armed forces for warning of, and assessing, and to a limited extent actively defending against Soviet nuclear attack on North America. If deterrence ever were to fail, the first warning and integrated assessment of an attack Washington and the Strategic Air Command would receive could very well be issued on the instructions of a Canadian general at the Colorado Springs, Colorado combat operations center of the binational North American Aerospace Defense Command (NORAD), which the two countries established in 1957. The Canadian and U.S. navies have also continued their cooperative efforts to monitor the movements of Soviet missile-carrying submarines near North America, and their joint preparations to destroy those submarines should war ever come.

Nonetheless, within such a close relationship between two countries of such disparate power and global security commitments, differences have been inevitable. Canadians tend to grow irritated when Americans overlook this fact. As a Canadian secretary of state for external affairs (and later prime minister), Lester B. Pearson, felt compelled to tell an American audience during a 1954 address on Canada-U.S. defense relations, in what has become a classic statement of Canadian grievance, "It would be a big mistake to think that, because our countries are so close, so alike in so many ways, we are identical in all things; that we always operate as nations, and as governments in the same way; or that Canada shall always and automatically agree, in the realm of foreign or domestic affairs, either with what you do or how you do it."[3] While Canadians share fundamental defense interests with the United States, they also incessantly worry about being overwhelmed by an American defense agenda.

A leading Canadian newspaper columnist recently observed that his countrymen once "remained blissfully unmoved by the imperatives of thinking hard about—let alone acting upon—the exigencies of defense in the modern age."[4] Yet unexpectedly, Canadians have found themselves since the early 1980s in the midst of public debate over the implications for their security and their sovereignty over a host of developments—real and hypothetical—related to the air, sea, and missile defense of North America. This debate has revealed, as Joel J. Sokolsky of the Royal Military College of Canada concluded, "that the future of Canada-U.S. defense relations will be more complex politically and strategically than in the past."[5]

That debate has thus far been inconclusive. Today Canada faces some fundamental defense choices. In fact, it is no exaggeration to say that since the spring of 1989 Canadian defense policy has been in disarray. That disarray has only been heightened by the dramatic changes in Europe, which came later that year and by the deployment of three Canadian ships (two destroyers and a supply vessel) and a squadron of fighter aircraft to the Persian Gulf in 1990, the first commitment of Canadian forces outside the North Atlantic Treaty area (except for peace-keeping) since the Korean War.

The Progressive Conservative government of Prime Minister Brian Mulroney, which came to power in 1984 pledging to overhaul and rearm the country's underfunded, undermanned and underarmed defense efforts, released in June 1987 a controversial white paper on defense, the first such policy statement issued by a Canadian government in sixteen years. That document, entitled *Challenge and Commitment*, outlined a fifteen-year plan intended to reverse the effect of years of confusion and financial neglect, especially during the Trudeau years in the 1970s, that had plagued the Canadian Armed Forces. Canada's contributions to the defense of both North America and to the North Atlantic Treaty Organization (NATO) in Europe, the Mulroney government proclaimed in its White Paper, were to be strengthened.

The Mulroney program had two centerpieces. The small Canadian air and army contributions to the defense of Germany were to be strengthened through the commitment to Germany of Canada-based reinforcement units previously earmarked for Norway. Second, to the consternation of the U.S. Navy and of many Canadians as well, the Canadian navy was to be equipped with ten to twelve nuclear-powered, (but not nuclear-armed) attack submarines (SSNs) for security and sovereignty protection operations in Atlantic, Pacific, and North American Arctic waters. The SSN program was but an indication of the emerging complexities of the Canada-U.S. defense relationship, for an important (although not the sole) motivation behind it was to give the Canadian navy the ability to know about otherwise secret U.S. submarine movements in Canadian Arctic waters.

The Progressive Conservatives were returned to power in a bitter November 1988 election fought over the new Free Trade Agreement with the United States. Canada's allies, much of the Canadian public, and above all the Canadian Armed Forces expected the government, once reelected, to proceed with the implementation of *Challenge and Commitment.* But in an April 1989 budget, the Mulroney government announced draconian cuts in defense spending and programs, stunning the Canadian Armed Forces. Far from providing the funds necessary to reverse years of decline, growth in defense spending would scarcely match inflation. "The recent budget," lamented the Canadian Institute of Strategic Studies, "destroyed the 1987 Defence White Paper's plans to rebuild the Canadian Forces. . . . With the destruction of the White Paper the Canadian Forces (are) banished to the incoherent wilderness of the 1970s."[6]

Accompanying the April 1989 budget was a sobering list of specific program cuts, affecting the long-term posture of the Canadian Armed Forces, among them the abandonment of the SSN program and the gutting of the strengthened military presence in Germany. Taken together, the cuts led to the start of a national reassessment of Canada's defense posture, which has continued in the wake of the recent changes in Europe. Indeed, the government announced in 1990 a small cutback in the Canadian presence in Germany which is bound to be the precursor to a much larger cut, if not a complete withdrawal.

An entirely unexpected factor in the debate over the future of the Canadian Armed Forces has been the January 1991 commitment of Canadian forces to the Gulf War against Iraq after its seizure of Kuwait. Canadians will have to decide whether this is the first instance of a new, post-Cold War world order to which they will want to again contribute armed forces as the need arises, or a singular event.

The United States has a significant interest in the outcome of that reassessment. As the leading member of NATO it will, of course, follow and attempt to influence the future of whatever minor commitment to NATO Europe the Canadians will be able to make. Nonetheless, the token Canadian presence in Europe has for decades been marginal to Western security and will be all the more so in the Europe that is emerging. Similarly, the military contribution that Canada has made in the Persian Gulf, while welcome, is very small. But on this side of the Atlantic, what a Canadian prime minister, John Diefenbaker, once called the "irresistible dictates of geography"[7] entail that the United States will be more directly affected by Canadian policy towards North American defense.

Thus the United States has an interest that extends beyond the resolution of the current defense muddle in Canada. Not only do Canadians own "real estate" of long-term importance to U.S. security but, as will be argued in the following pages, it is becoming increasingly unlikely that Canada will be mounting more than an extremely limited token effort in Europe. If this is the case, Canadian attention will be focussed more than ever on what occurs at home, on this continent.

ORGANIZATION OF THE STUDY

This is an assessment of how, and how not, Canada and the United States may continue to cooperate into the beginning of the next century in the protection of the continent they share. It is written by an American, with two purposes in mind. The first is to outline how Canadian approaches to the defense of North America may affect the programs the United States may want to adopt over roughly the next two decades to protect itself against nuclear attack. It includes therefore an attempt to predict: (1) the potential roles Canadian territory, waters, airspace, and the Canadian Armed Forces may play, in cooperation with the United States, in the security of North America and (2) the policies the Canadian government can be expected to pursue towards such future roles. It also includes suggestions for U.S. policy towards Canada.

The second purpose is to inform Canadian readers of recent technological and strategic trends affecting the future of North American defense and thereby to outline what proposals the United States realistically may have in store for them in the 1990s, as well as what U.S. motivations may be.

Canadians often proclaim that they are well informed about events in the United States and complain that Americans ignore what occurs north of the border. Yet it cannot be said that recent defense debates in Canada have been illuminated by a deep understanding of the challenges the United States faces in setting its policy for the defense of North America. This has especially been the case concerning the evolution of U.S. nuclear strategy.

It should be stressed that this is a work about the 1990s, a period of transition in world affairs, one in which the United States and its allies will seek prudently to take advantage of the enormously promising changes in the Soviet Union and Central Europe. During this decade the Soviet Union will not only still possess strategic nuclear weapons capable of threatening North America, but will retain nuclear and conventional forces (albeit reduced) which will still need to be offset if Europe is to feel secure. What lies ahead in the next century is largely beyond the scope of this treatment. The Chairman of the U.S. Joint Chiefs of Staff, General Colin Powell, has taken to quoting both Winston Churchill and Casey Stengel on the dangers of making long-range predictions: "I always avoid prophesying beforehand, because it is much better policy to prophesy after the event has already taken place," said Churchill. "Forecasting is a very risky business," said Stengel, "especially about the future."[8]

The first part of this study reviews Canadian defense policy—and the seemingly intractable difficulties Canadian governments continue to have in setting one. In chapter II, the three chief causes of the Canadian defense dilemma are outlined: the U.S. "involuntary guarantee" of Canadian security, U.S. challenges to Canadian sovereignty, and the "pull" on Canada between North America and Europe. In chapter III the collapse of the "Mulroney solution" to Canada's defense dilemma and where that collapse now leaves the Canadian Armed Forces and Canadian defense policy are considered, with special emphasis on the division of Canadian efforts between North America and the new Europe.

The subsequent chapters deal specifically with North American defense issues—the area in which Canada will always feel compelled to deploy armed forces.

The protection of North America rests, in the final analysis, on the credibility of the U.S. strategic nuclear deterrent. Strategic surveillance and defense activities undertaken in North America by Canadian and American forces are intended to protect that credibility. Yet Canadians and Americans tend to hold differing attitudes towards nuclear weaponry and strategy. These differences—which have often lead to great confusion in Canada and form a backdrop to Canadian debates over functional defense cooperation with the United States—are introduced in chapter IV.

The functional areas of Canada-U.S. strategic defense cooperation, current and potential, are the subjects of the next four chapters. Chapter V concerns the possibilities for ballistic missile defense which may affect Canada-U.S. defense relations, chapter VI outlines current and future strategic air defense efforts, long the heart of Canada-U.S. defense cooperation, chapter VII details the joint NORAD arrangements which, often ignored in the United States, have a much higher and sometimes controversial profile in Canada, and chapter VIII discusses the problems between the two countries arising from strategic antisubmarine warfare preparations in the North American Arctic.

Chapter IX briefly deals with a matter that in 1990 suddenly returned to the North American agenda: the potential implications for North American defense should the Canadian province of Québec become an independent country.

Chapter X, the conclusion, briefly summarizes and includes suggestions for U.S. policy towards Canada, with a view towards how the United States can best secure future defense cooperation in North America with the Canadian Armed Forces.

NOTES

1. Leonard Mosley, *Dulles: A Biography of Eleanor, Allen and John Foster Dulles and Their Family Network* (New York: The Dial Press/James Wade, 1978), 329.
2. Canada, House of Commons, *Debates* (9 February 1984), 1211.
3. The Hon. Lester B. Pearson, Secretary of State for External Affairs, "A Look at the New Look," Canada, Department of External Affairs, *Statements and Speeches* 54, no. 16 (15 March 1954).
4. Jeffrey Simpson, "Canada Roused by Military Plan," *Bulletin of the Atomic Scientists* 43, no. 8 (October 1987): 9.
5. Joel J. Sokolsky, *Defending Canada* (New York: Priority Press Publications, 1989), 2.
6. "The 1989 Federal Budget—The Death of Defence?" *Strategic Datalink,* no. 12 (May 1989), Canadian Institute of Strategic Studies.
7. "Statement by Prime Minister on Air Defence Policy," (20 February 1959); Canada, Department of External Affairs, *Canadian Weekly Bulletin,* (5 March 1958), 6.
8. As quoted in address by General Colin Powell, "NATO in the 1990s: New Initiatives and New Solidarities," before the North Atlantic Treaty Association, 23 October 1989. Text, Office of the Joint Chiefs of Staff.

II

The Origins of the Canadian "Commitment-Capability Gap"

Canada spends very little on defense, yet has felt compelled to retain a range of military commitments in both North America and Europe.[1] The result has been what the Mulroney government itself called, in its 1987 defense White Paper, "a significant commitment-capability gap," admitting that "Canada has not been able to meet even its limited commitments on either side of the Atlantic fully and effectively.[2]

This chapter explains the three factors producing that gap. The first is the "involuntary American guarantee" of Canadian security, which frees Canada from the burden of a substantial defense effort. The other two place simultaneous demands on Canada's small and underfunded defense establishment. These are the protection of Canadian sovereignty at home and pursuit of Canadian interests in Europe.

The following chapter describes the deepening gap after the Mulroney government tried with its White Paper to close it—and two years later abandoned the attempt. It also predicts how Ottawa will be coping with the gap in the 1990s, especially in the light of the changes in Europe.

DEFENSE SPENDING AND THE "INVOLUNTARY AMERICAN GUARANTEE" OF CANADIAN SECURITY

For over forty years, the central organizing principle of U.S. defense policy has been to provide armed forces to meet the Soviet threat, especially in Europe. Until very recently, that threat, again especially in Europe, has been substantial. Consequently, the level of U.S. defense spending has been high. With the Cold War now won, Americans and Europeans are preparing to enjoy their "peace dividends." How much the U.S. defense budget, now running roughly US$300 billion safely can be cut in the 1990s is still not clear, and subject to considerable debate. There is no doubt, though, that there should be, and will be, very substantial cuts in the U.S. defense establishment of over two million uniformed personnel. For the greatest danger mankind has faced for roughly forty years, that of a standing start, or near standing start assault by the Warsaw Pact on NATO Europe escalating to the level of a strategic nuclear exchange between the Soviet Union and the United States, has evaporated in a matter of months, along with the Warsaw Pact itself.

Canadians, as they follow world events and the debate in the United States, are yearning for a peace dividend, too. As they contemplate their mountainous fiscal deficits and their high tax rates, slashing the defense budget will be all the more tempting. So new defense cuts may come in Canada, too. But the situation is different there. Canadians have been enjoying their peace dividend long before there was peace. Or put differently, "to have a dividend you must first risk capital . . . the amount of capital Canadians have risked in defence over the past twenty years has not guaranteed much of a dividend."[3]

The simple truth is that Canada spends very little to defend itself because it does not have to spend more. Geography obliges the United States to protect Canada. Ironically, that protection often threatens Canada's sense of sovereignty.

"The principal direct threat to Canada continues to be a nuclear attack on North America by the Soviet Union," observed the Progressive Conservative government in the White Paper, *Challenge and Commitment.*[4] That remains true today. The principal instrument protecting Canada against that threat also remains the strategic nuclear arsenal of the United States.

America's Western European allies have in the past worried whether the umbrella of nuclear deterrence provided by the United States leaked to the point that it might no longer be relied upon to keep them dry. But, as a committee dominated by Europeans of the North Atlantic Assembly (the organization of parliamentarians from NATO countries) once concluded with more than just a touch of envy after a trip to Canada, "Canadians are probably the only non-American members of the Alliance to have no doubts whatsoever about the American nuclear umbrella."[5]

Canadians do in fact worry about the stability of the nuclear balance, given that a nuclear attack on the United States would severely affect Canada. (These concerns are outlined in chapter IV.) Being "decoupled" from the U.S. strategic arsenal, though, has never been a Canadian concern. Canadians know that almost to the very extent nuclear deterrence protects the United States, it protects them. They profit from what R. J. Sutherland, an official of the Canadian Department of National Defence, called almost thirty years ago in what is now a classic work on his country's defense policy, the "involuntary American guarantee" of their security.[6]

Canada has never had nuclear weapons. As a junior partner of the United States and the United Kingdom during the Second World War

—10—

in the development of the atomic bomb, and as a country with a sizable supply of uranium, it could have relatively easily, at any time since the war, put together at least a modest arsenal of its own. While Canadians sometimes refer to their country as having been the first to "renounce" the acquisition of nuclear weapons, there apparently never was a clear-cut decision by Ottawa not to acquire them. Rather, it has never really seriously occurred to the Canadian government that an alternative to reliance on the American strategic arsenal was ever necessary,[7] although amid considerable controversy the Canadian government did in the early 1960s equip Canadian forces with the capability, now terminated, to use American-owned and controlled air defense nuclear weapons in North America and tactical nuclear weapons in Europe. Certainly the United States, more than content to retain the strategic nuclear decision-making for North America in its own hands, has never encouraged Canada to do otherwise. Canada did put its nuclear skills and resources to use for nonmilitary purposes. Today it has one of the most advanced nonmilitary nuclear industries in the world.

The conventional forces Canada does deploy are very small. (These are described in the next chapter.) Here, too, the "involuntary guarantee" has its effects. The great premise of Canadian strategy was once coolly articulated by the political scientist and historian of his country's defense policy, James Eayrs: "We would be as safe from attack by any conceivable aggressor with no armed forces at all, as with the armed forces we now have, or any combination of armed forces we may care to have."[8] For in addition to supplying the nuclear weapons, the United States can be counted upon, in the final analysis, to do whatever else is necessary for the protection of North America against Soviet attack, whether that entails just the deployment of surveillance and detection systems or the provision of active defenses.

While from time to time various groups have pointed out the short-comings in Canada's defense efforts, there is no even remotely influential domestic constituency in Canada clamoring with effect for expansive defense budgets. As *Challenge and Commitment* put it, "Few Canadians feel militarily threatened and most have difficulty imagining anyone as an enemy."[9] The dramatic decline in East-West tensions can only heighten this indifference.

The effect on Canada's defense efforts of "the involuntary American guarantee" is evident. Since 1969 Canada has not spent more than 2.2 percent of its gross domestic product (GDP) on national defense. After years of neglect, especially under the Liberal Party government of Prime Minister Pierre Trudeau, who held power from 1968 to 1984, (except for a brief period in 1979–1980), the Canadian Armed Forces are in bad shape. For three years the defense budget was frozen. Inflation in personnel and operating costs eroded the provisions for capital expenditures, forcing the military to retain rapidly aging weapons systems. Spending dropped in 1981 to 1.7 percent of GDP (see Figure 2.1).

1988 BILLIONS (CDN)$ PERCENT OF GDP

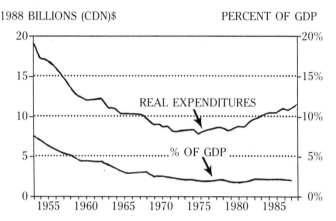

Source: Director of Costing Services, Department of National Defence. Reproduced with permission.

FIGURE 2.1
CANADIAN DEFENSE EXPENDITURES
(Historical Trends)

Modest increases thereafter, begun in the late Trudeau years and continued under the Mulroney government, brought spending back above the level of 2 percent of GDP, but only for several years. In 1987–1988 with 2.1 percent of its GDP or a defense budget of C$10.8 billion (about US$ 8.05 billion) Canada maintained armed forces of 84,600 men and women. Despite the increases, Canada spends the lowest percentage of GDP in NATO except for Luxembourg and Iceland (the Icelanders maintaining no armed forces at all) (see Table 2.1). In recent years, the United States has spent well above 6 percent, while the NATO European average expenditure has been well above 3 percent.

By almost every other measure, Canada's share of the allied burden has been light. Canada has had no conscription since the Second World War. There are no nuclear weapons, no foreign bases and, today, hardly any foreign troops on Canadian soil. By only one traditional measure, per capita defense expenditures, does Canada stack up well against its allies (see Table 2.2). But this reflects Canada's wealth and limited population more than a commitment to defense. It has the fifth largest per capita income in the world and the world's tenth largest GNP. "Canada can hardly plead poverty for cutting defence costs," observed the executive director of the Canadian Institute for International Peace and Security.[10]

TABLE 2.1
DEFENSE EXPENDITURES AS PERCENTAGE OF GDP
AMONG NATO COUNTRIES, 1988

Greece	6.6
United States	6.1
United Kingdom	4.5
Turkey	4.3
France	3.8
Norway	3.3
NATO Europe average	**3.3**
Portugal	3.2
F.R. Germany	3.0
Netherlands	3.0
Belgium	2.9
Italy	2.4
Denmark	2.2
Spain	2.2
CANADA	**2.1**
Luxembourg	1.3
Iceland	0

Source: Government of Canada, National defence 1990-91 estimates

TABLE 2.2
PER CAPITA DEFENSE EXPENDITURES (US$)
AMONG NATO COUNTRIES, 1987

United States	1114
United Kingdom	448
Norway	433
France	376
F.R. Germany	327
CANADA	**292**
Netherlands	275
Belgium	273
NATO Europe average	**256**
Denmark	254
Greece	234
Italy	166
Spain	124
Luxembourg	107
Portugal	61
Turkey	46
Iceland	0

Source: *Challenge and Commitment.*

It has been during the Mulroney years that American officials responsible for relations with Canada have had it brought home again to them how little incentive there is for any Canadian government to spend substantial funds for defense. U.S. expectations were high in September 1984 as Mulroney lead the Progressive Conservative Party to victory. Mulroney and his colleagues had bitterly criticized the Liberals for having allowed the armed forces to decay. Mulroney himself had even exclaimed on the campaign trail that "Pierre Trudeau and his Liberal pals have done the ultimate disservice to Canada by running down our armed services."[11] There was talk by prominent Progressive Conservatives of annual increases in defense spending of up to 6 percent in real terms which would, over a period of several years, bring Canada up to the NATO average in terms of GDP share.

But the new government faced a monstrous, inherited budget deficit, proportionately greater than the one in the United States, as well as absolutely sacrosanct social programs paid for by the state, and demands for new ones. "Which do we want?" asked a newsmagazine, "submarines or day-care?"[12] Knowing that it would hear very few calls from the public to substantively increase the defense budget, the new government, during its first few years in office managed to spend no more than the Liberals were planning to, had they held on to power.

Even so, few Canadians or allied officials were expecting the Progressive Conservatives to treat the Canadian Armed Forces more harshly than the Liberals had. For this reason, the Mulroney government's April 1989 budget, in which it attempted to come to grips with the country's fiscal deficit years before the next general election must be held, was a bitter shock to the Canadian defense establishment. The Chief of the Defence Staff, General Paul Manson, loyally put on a brave face, calling for it to be "clearly understood" by the members of the Canadian Armed Forces that they had a "solemn obligation" to join in the attack on the deficit. "The problem is so serious," he went on, "that unless something is done, Canadian society as we know it would be at risk in a few short years. It is clearly in our own interest, and in the interest of Canada's national security, to reduce the enormous budget of debt."[13]

But the armed forces are still reeling from the announcement that planned defense spending would be cut C\$2.74 over the next five years, meaning that there would be no real growth in the defense budget. Indeed, the 1989–90 defense budget of C\$11.3 billion, released at the same time, included an increase of less than 2 percent in nominal terms over the previous year (see Table 2.3). With inflation running above 4 percent in Canada, the budget obviously meant a loss in purchasing power for the Department of National Defence. The U.S. Defense Department estimated that loss at 2.6 percent. According to estimates made by the

Canadian Institute of Strategic Studies, the GDP share of defense spending will soon fall to as low as 1.7 percent.[14]

TABLE 2.3

CANADIAN DEFENSE SPENDING IN THE MULRONEY YEARS

Fiscal Year	Nominal Expenditure		Real Expenditure (1981 Dollars)		GDP Percentage
	Amount	Percent Increase	Amount	Percent Change	
1985–1986	9,094	3.8	7,454	0.6	1.9
1986–1987	9,993	9.9	7,969	6.9	2.0
1987–1988	10,769	7.7	8,221	3.2	2.0
1988–1989*	11,025	2.4	8,113	−1.3	1.8
1989–1990**	11,210	1.7	7,905	−2.6	1.8
1990–1991**	11,995	7.0	8,215	3.9	1.9

Amounts in C$ billions

*Preliminary figures
**Projected figures

Source: U.S. Department of Defense

Officials in the U.S. Departments of State and Defense were also surprised by the extent of the cuts. Circumstances and national interest have cast the United States in the role of the nag of the Western Alliance, constantly urging its allies to spend more on their contributions to collective defense. The United States has every reason to nag Canada on this score, for in a number of areas, Canada could undoubtedly make a much larger contribution to the collective defense of the West. This too will not change in the 1990s. As the United States sheds a good deal of the defense burden it has carried for forty years it will still want to share the remaining burden, especially with an ally whose burden has been very light.

U.S. officials, including the president, the secretary of state and the secretary of defense have frequently taken the occasion to impress upon their Canadian counterparts U.S. concerns over the persistently abysmal level of Canadian defense spending. But U.S. officialdom knows very well that the "involuntary American guarantee" deprives them of leverage. The ultimate sanction which the United States could vaguely invoke in discussions with the European members of the alliance was an American pullout from Europe. There has never been an equivalent sanction at home in North America.

The nature of the Canada-U.S. relationship minimizes recourse by Washington to two other possible forms of leverage: public chastisement and linkage. Public chastisement of Canada for its failure to do more is simply pointless. No Canadian government can afford the impression that it is being pushed around by the pushy Yanks. Thus, with a few recent exceptions which are most notable for their lack of productive results and the storms of public resentment they produced in Canada, American officials have avoided public criticism of Canada's often meager defense efforts.

Linking Canada's defense effort to other areas of Canada-U.S. relations such as trade, or environmental concerns is a tricky game in which both sides could get badly hurt. The bilateral agenda is usually long and complex, with domestic interest groups to be found on every issue. For every additional billion dollars Canada spends on defense, what would be the appropriate reduction in acid rain-causing emissions in the Ohio Valley or the appropriate reduction in U.S. agricultural subsidies, both Canadian grievances? Could any U.S. administration be expected to explain to Ohioans that their electric bills were going up, or to American farmers that their subsidies were going down because Canada had agreed to buy more ships, or tanks, or aircraft? Moreover, "linkage works, if it works at all, only if it is practiced on one side at a time. If it is attempted simultaneously on both sides, especially when the issue area at stake is tied to completely different issue areas on opposite sides of the border, linkage becomes a recipe for chaos."[15] As a result of these inherent difficulties, Canada-U.S. relations have been characterized by few attempts on the part of either Washington or Ottawa to link issues.

Canada and the United States maintain a series of Defense Development/Defense Production Sharing Arrangements (DD/DPSA), which are intended to allow Canadian defense contractors to compete on an equal footing with American firms in bidding for most U.S. defense work, even those involving classified technology, and for joint governmental investment in selected research and development projects. These arrangements, which are extended to no other ally, were put in place in the 1950s and 1960s as a means of helping Canada bear the burden of defense spending. It might be thought that Washington could threaten to curtail DD/DPSA in view of Canada's poor performance in defense spending. Such a step would not appear to violate the "rules" of Canada-U.S. relations proscribing linkage across issue areas.

Yet curtailing DD/DPSA would be counterproductive for the United States. The arrangements benefit the United States by giving it access to competitive Canadian defense technology and by maintaining a defense industry in Canada which contributes to the overall North American defense industrialization base. Denying Canadian firms access to U.S. contracts would also eventually drive up the cost of the defense goods the Canadian government buys at home, further limiting the effectiveness of Canada's already meager defense efforts.[16]

Hypothetically, still another option would be for Canada's NATO allies to exact a political price for Ottawa's continuing failure to pay what are in effect the country's membership dues in the Western Alliance. This could entail asking the Canadian government to cease sending representatives to NATO's Defense Planning Committee and Nuclear Planning Group, and temporarily excluding Canada from certain allied consultations, held on the staff level, concerning arms control and other major strategic issues. Canada could also be asked to reduce its military personnel at NATO's military and civilian headquarters. In the long run, this is probably the only available approach which would have some promise of eliciting a greater Canadian effort. NATO membership is Canada's ticket to the big league discussions of East-West security issues, now more important than ever. Cutting Ottawa off from that access would hurt. However this is an approach to the Canadian spending problem that is unlikely to be turned to by the allies. Playing tough on such issues has never been the NATO way.[17] As NATO sheds armaments in the 1990s it will have no interest in adopting such an approach.

U.S. CHALLENGES TO CANADIAN SOVEREIGNTY

The Canadian government could take up Eayrs' hypothetical option of spending nothing at all on defense and being just "as safe from attack by any conceivable aggressor." To do so, however, would result in an intolerable loss of Canadian sovereignty to the United States.

To be sure, regardless of the level of defense spending, worrying about being overwhelmed by the United States is a staple of Canadian national life. The relationship with the United States is *the* central concern in Canadian foreign and commercial policies and figures heavily in debates over domestic policy. There is hardly an aspect of Canadian national life that is not affected in some way economically or culturally by the behemoth to the south. Resisting, or at least restricting, or at the very least trying to organize the pervasive impact of the United States on Canadian life while at the same time taking advantage of what the American presence has to offer Canada—military protection, a gigantic market for Canadian exports, and capital for development, as well as enticing opportunities for the investment of Canadian capital, and the cultural and intellectual products of an exuberant neighbor—this always is the trick for Canada. Ottawa once described it in a white paper on foreign policy as "the complex problem of living distinct from but in harmony with the world's most powerful and dynamic nation, the United States."[18]

Canada is and always has been a trading country. Today 73 percent of its exports by value go to the United States and 67 percent of imports come from the United States. At the same time, Canada is by far the most important trading partner of the United States, buying from it twice as much as its second most important partner, Japan, and as much as the entire European Community. The province of Ontario alone buys more American products than Japan. Canada has also become an important source of foreign capital for the United States. Still, Canada accounts for only 24 percent of U.S. exports, and 18 percent of U.S. imports, underlining the asymmetry in the economic interdependence of the two countries. Even more significantly, Canadian exports to the United States constitute 19 percent of Canada's GDP, while U.S. exports to Canada constitute less than 2 percent of U.S. GDP.

The new Canada-United States free trade agreement will result in even greater flows of goods and capital across the border. The agreement, however, was only approved after one of the most bitter election campaigns in Canadian history, during which the two opposition parties charged the Mulroney government with selling out fundamental Canadian interests to the United States. The Progressive Conservatives ratified the agreement after having won, on 21 November 1988 a new majority of the seats in the House of Commons, but with only a minority of the popular vote.

Eighty percent of the Canadian population lives in a long, thin band a scant 100 miles wide, running along the U.S. border, meaning that Canadians, especially the majority of the population which is English-speaking, have ample access to American culture, access Canadians make full use of. The bulk of television programs watched, books and magazines read, and movies seen in Canada are American. Partially because of the pervasive American presence, the sense of overarching Canadian national identity is underdeveloped.

Worry about the Canadian national identity is intensified by linguistic and regional divisions. About a quarter of all Canadians speak French as their mother tongue. Most are located in Québec, where well over 80 percent of the population is French speaking, and where the preservation of the language and of the distinctiveness of Québec society in a sea of English speakers is the dominant political theme. Meanwhile, Atlantic Canada and especially Western Canada nurse historic economic grievances against Central Canada, which consists of the industrialized provinces of Ontario and Québec. Under all these circumstances, "Perhaps the most striking thing about Canada is that it is not part of the United States."[19] And, as will be discussed in chapter IX, keeping the country together may prove impossible in the 1990s.

The key buzzword in contemporary Canadian political discourse about relations with the United States, one that was endlessly invoked during the 1988 election, is "sovereignty." It is a word to conjure with, possessing a general utility akin to the words "national security" in the United States. Extensive use of both these terms have battered whatever precision they may ever have had right out of them, without at all degrading their popularity.[20] Canadians are determined to protect, and accuse their countrymen (especially members of other political parties) of neglecting to protect not just their country's legal and political sovereignty, and its sovereign right to an independent foreign policy but its economic, cultural, and territorial sovereignty, especially in Canada's northern and Arctic regions. In all cases, when the word sovereignty is invoked, it means that in some fashion the speaker fears that a necessary element of control is about to pass out of Canadian hands, and in almost all cases into American ones.

Concern about Canadian sovereignty being affected by the U.S. military is an amalgam of several anxieties. Many center on the NORAD command arrangements, which are discussed in chapter VII. Most viscerally emotional and widely held, though, is the fear that the country will lose control to American forces over portions of its territory and waters, above all those in the Arctic.

There is nothing at all extraordinary about a state wanting to retain full control of what it considers its national, sovereign territory. Many a war has been fought over it. Yet Canadian attitudes towards the north are at least seemingly contradictory, somewhat bewildering—and sometimes (but not always) fiercely held.

The Canadian historian Frank Underhill grumpily remarked a half century ago that, "The artistic cult of the North is, as a matter of fact, pure romanticism at its worst and bears little relation to the real life of Canada. Far from seeking inspiration among the rocks and winds, the normal Canadian dreams of living in a big city where he can make his pile quickly and enjoy such urban luxuries as are familiar to him in the advertising columns of our national magazines."[21] Today, most Canadians do live in large or big cities. In fact, stereotypes to the contrary, the average Canadian is slightly more likely to be an urban dweller than his or her American counterpart. Turned loose in Tuktoyaktuk in the Northwest Territories, the average Torontonian would be at as much of a loss as a New Yorker. Very few Torontonians even try. It is too far away and too cold.

Infrequently visited, the high Canadian north is extremely sparsely populated. While the north includes over 40 percent of Canada's land mass, only about one quarter of 1 percent of the country's population lives there. The Yukon has but 23,000 inhabitants and the immense Northwest Territories only 51,000.

Economic development in the north has been equally sparse. Industrial activity accounts for less than one-fiftieth of 1 percent of the Canadian total. There is little agriculture. Natural resource development is minimal. Expectations have been high for decades that the Arctic's oil and gas reserves would be tapped extensively. Low world energy prices during the 1980s left these expectations thus far unfulfilled. The prospect for economic development in other fields remains quite poor.[22]

In the absence of much of a direct military threat to the Canadian Arctic region itself, the Canadian military presence there has been scant. No ship or submarine of the Canadian navy is capable of operating in ice-covered or even moderately ice-infested waters, barring them from operations in high Canadian Arctic waters. Sixteen or seventeen northern patrol flights for visual observation by Aurora or Arcturus aircraft (Canadian versions of the U.S.Navy's P-3), based at Comox, British Columbia or Greenwood, Nova Scotia are conducted each year. Northern Region Headquarters (NRHQ) of the Canadian Armed Forces is located at Yellowknife in the Northwest Territories and is responsible for the largest military district in the world. Yet it has a staff of only seventy-seven and no military units under its direct command, except for a detachment of two Twin Otter search and rescue aircraft and the Canadian Rangers, a paramilitary reserve force of about 700, largely Inuit (Eskimo) hunters. Over the next five to seven years the force will be increased to 1000 Rangers. There is a small communications station at Alert, on Ellesmere Island ("the most northerly military installation in the world"). Once or twice a year the army conducts a battalion-sized exercise in the north.

Beyond that, there are the minimally manned and unmanned stations of the North Warning System, replacing the old American-operated DEW Line. New Forward Operating Locations (FOLs) will be constructed in the north for fighter aircraft, primarily CF-18s, but this entails relatively small scale upgrading of existing civilian airfields.[23] In short, as Harriet Critchley of the University of Calgary has pointed out, "Canada's defence capabilities in the north are quite modest. . . . Nonetheless, given the cutbacks in manpower, resources, equipment, and defense budgets over the past two decades, the provision of even such a modest capability places a noticeable strain on the overall defense capabilities of the Canadian Armed Forces and Department of National Defence."[24]

The Mulroney government did announce in 1988 that "detailed planning studies" had begun to establish a Northern Training Centre for the Canadian Armed Forces at Nanisivik, on Baffin Island. This would entail a substantial augmentation of the Canadian military presence in the high north. About 100 military instructors and their families would be stationed for two-year tours at the center, which is planned to be operational in 1992–93. Roughly 500 personnel a year would undergo one-month courses in Arctic warfare at the center.

Rarely visited, sparsely populated, underdeveloped, with little prospect for much development, and with a scant military presence; it would be logical to conclude from this evidence that Canadians just do not care about their northland. Yet that would be a mistake. "Canadians," Claude Bissell, literary critic, biographer, and past president of the University of Toronto once said "move slowly, but when they are aroused they move with remarkable speed."[25] U.S. challenges to Canadian Arctic sovereignty are an issue which in recent years has aroused them.

Canada, like the United States, pushed back a frontier in its national development. Images of the north evoke for Canadians their great national achievement of building a second transcontinental country on the continent's less hospitable half. The Canadian north is still frontier, and as such still represents for many Canadians their country's future. For all the disappointments of the past, for all the times that the "Age of the Arctic" has been proclaimed to have at long last arrived, Canadians know that there is a tremendous amount of oil and gas in the Beaufort Sea region and that someday an increase in world prices could touch off the long-awaited boom. According to Robert Page, a scholar of Canada's policy towards its north, Canadians "have had difficulty viewing the North with detachment because their future hopes have always involved the exploitation of its resource riches. Yesterday it was the yellow gold of Bonanza Creek; today it is the black gold of the Beaufort Sea. . . . Our great expectations of northern wealth never seem to materialize."[26] Perhaps that is just as well, for as long as it remains undeveloped, the north still holds out a national challenge and the promise of a distinctive future.

The Arctic is inextricably wrapped up in the whole question of the Canadian national identity, that often elusive bundle of characteristics which both binds the citizens of a very disparate country together and distinguishes them from the United States. For many Canadians, there are "intangible but vital links between the Arctic and the self-image of Canadians as a people."[27] Some of these links are obvious, and also can strike the outside observer as just a bit too nationalistically facile. The Arctic contributes to a northern mythology whereby Canadians can mark themselves as a tough, vigorous nation, the people, in the words of the Canadian national anthem, of the "True North strong and free." One such observer, Thomas Barnes of the University of California at Berkeley warns of the limitations of what he calls Canadian "borealism," which he defines as "a fixation with the North and northerness amounting to an ideology of nationalist definition."[28]

Ownership of Arctic territories unquestionably does establish Canadians as custodians of one of the most starkly beautiful and environmentally fragile regions of the world. It is a responsibility many Canadians take very seriously, especially faced with the possibility the Arctic may eventually become an important source of oil and gas. In national mythology, this responsibility for the Arctic marks Canadians as an environmentally sensitive and caring folk, in contrast with their more rapacious, acid rain-emitting neighbors south of the border.

Many Canadians insist that beyond this lies something deeper. Canada's greatest literary critic, Northrup Frye, suggests that "the largest river in Canada, the Mackenzie, pouring slightly into the Arctic Ocean at what seems the end of the earth is a symbol of the terra incognita in Canadian consciousness, or what Rupert Brooke called the 'unseizable virginity' of the Canadian landscape." Frye also invites his reader to consider the observation of a British visitor to Canada, Windham Lewis, that "this monstrous, empty habitat must continue to dominate this nation psychologically and so culturally."[29]

Whether this, too, is just more boreal mythmaking is irrelevant from the perspective of Canada-U.S. political and military relations. As long as Canadians believe—and many fervently do believe—that their culture and national identity are in large part derived from their Arctic territories, they will be incensed at external challenges.[30] Thus, no Canadian government can afford to be seen as failing to protect the Arctic (and, of course, the related national identity). "Accepting the loss of Canadian control in the high Arctic, whether over the territorial land mass, the islands, or the waters between the Arctic islands, is perceived by both senior officials and the leaders of all political parties as intolerable and a certain defeat for any government in office."[31]

In other words, Canadian attitudes towards the north can be characterized as a kind of "push resistant nationalism" which emerges in reaction to a concrete step taken by the United States that would affect Canada.[32] While few Canadians ever go to their northland, most Canadians become upset at the prospect of the Americans being there.

The United States has not been engaged since the acrimonious Yukon-Alaska boundary dispute was settled in favor of the United States in 1903 in any major dispute about ownership of or sovereignty over land Canada considers its own, including the islands of the Canadian Arctic Archipelago.[33] The United States has proceeded in its defense arrangements with Canada on that basis; its challenges to Canadian sovereignty on land have been entirely inadvertent.[34] (At sea, as will be discussed below, the situation is markedly different.)

But unhappily, inadvertent U.S. challenges to Canadian sovereignty in the north have marked the Canada-U.S. defense relationship. In fact, the U.S. presence in the Canadian north during both the Second World War and the postwar years has had a permanent impact on Canadian attitudes towards military cooperation with the United States. It has often appeared that Canada had lost or was on the verge of losing control there to Americans.

During the Second World War, the U.S. military presence in Northwest Canada grew "to what Canadians came to refer to—neither jocularly nor without justification—as a United States occupation."[35] By 1943 U.S. military and civilian personnel substantially outnumbered the Canadians in Northwest Canada. The official U.S. Army history of Canada-U.S. wartime relations describes how Canadians chafed at the very extent of the U.S. intrusion on Canadian soil in an area remote from the combat theaters and peopled by Canadians engaged in reasonably normal pursuits. The substantial U.S. garrison operated in Canada independently of Canadian control and legal jurisdiction to an extent considered unwarranted by many Canadians. This garrison constructed, maintained, and operated bases and facilities as if they were on U.S. soil. Command organizations with their independent signal communications systems were established over segments of Canadian territory. Strenuous U.S. efforts were made to have Canadian forces placed under U.S. command on Canadian soil. All these arrangements presented to Canadians serious questions of domestic policy, which were aggravated by sundry accompanying complications. . . . Too often it seemed to Canadians that U.S. requests for arrangements that resulted in these intrusions into Canada, as well as U.S. motivations in other dealings, were based exclusively on military requirements, without adequate consideration of the political factors involved."[36]

Before the war was even over, the Canadian government was pursuing negotiations with Washington to ensure that the Americans did not overstay their welcome on Canadian soil. Agreements were reached in 1943 and 1944 whereby the United States would turn over all its facilities in Canada to the Canadian federal and provincial governments.

At the war's end, Canadian officials calculated that while "the development of air power has diminished the physical isolation of the North American continent by opening up the northern approaches," no concrete threat to the security of the continent would materialize for several years.[37] Ottawa resolved to undertake all the measures necessary on Canadian soil for the protection of North America. That meant cooperating with the Americans, but keeping their military forces out of Canada, or at least limiting them to small contingents. On the basis of their wartime experiences with the Americans, though, Canadian bureaucrats warned their political masters that not only could the United States "be expected to take an active interest in Canadian defence preparations in the future," but "that interest may be expressed with an absence of the tact and restraint customarily employed by the United Kingdom in putting forward defence proposals."[38]

This prediction seemed to be borne out in 1946, when a group of zealous American and Canadian airmen proposed a grandiose plan for northern air defenses. Prime Minister William Lyon Mackenzie King, after being briefed on the plan, wrote despondently in his diary that "Canada could simply not do what was necessary to protect itself. Our country would be a mere pawn in world conflict."[39] The plan, which never really had Pentagon backing, faded away and Ottawa resolutely secured a 1947 defense agreement with the United States stressing that "as an underlying principle all cooperative arrangements will be without impairment of the control of either country over all activities in its territory."[40]

With the Soviet Union's development of an intercontinental bomber by 1947, and its explosion of an atomic bomb in 1949, Canada and the United States began to be exposed to real risk. Both deployed air defenses, beginning in 1948. Ottawa ran short of the money and the trained personnel to operate a complete radar network at home. Radars on Canadian soil were essential, though, for both countries' air defenses. The United States needed early warning; Canada needed both warning and ground control intercept capabilities to direct fighter aircraft to their targets.

So the Americans would have to be let back in. Canadian diplomats wrung their hands and told the Cabinet in 1951 that "Since Canada is geographically an air corridor between the United States and the whole Eurasian air mass we could scarcely refuse the United States the use of facilities in Canada or overflight of Canadian territory, in the event of a major war and possibly could not avoid commitments in advance of a major war." This raised "the extremely delicate problem of maintaining our autonomy: which involves a series of intractable problems," including "the status of U.S. defence installations and personnel in Canada."[41]

The two countries agreed in 1951 to build in southern Canada what was called the Pinetree radar system. Two-thirds of the system's costs were to be paid by the United States and many of the stations were to be manned by American service personnel. Ottawa did what it could to limit the impact, negotiating an agreement whereby all of the stations were to be constructed under Canadian supervision (except the ones in Newfoundland where the United States enjoyed special rights dating back to the war when Newfoundland was still a British colony and had not yet joined Canada). Titles for the stations would be vested in the Crown in right of Canada, and Canada would retain the right to take over their manning.[42] Most telling, the details of the agreement were kept secret for a number of years. As the U.S. Embassy in Ottawa reported back to the State Department, the Canadian government wanted to avoid the implication of "another cession of territory by Canada to the United States, the advent of additional U.S. troops on Canadian soil, and all that."[43]

The impact of the Pinetree system was soon overshadowed by the 1955 agreement to allow the United States to pay for, build and man the DEW Line in the high Arctic. To the south, Canada would build, operate and pay for a less-expensive Mid-Canada Line, which would provide confirmatory details of an attack first detected by the DEW Line. Once again, the Canadian government tried to limit the impact of the American presence. The 1955 DEW agreement specified that the exact location of the radars would be determined jointly by the United States and Canada. Title for all DEW Line sites also would be vested in the Crown. Canadian criminal and civil law was to be respected. Special provisions were to be observed for the protection of Canadian Inuit, air carriers, telecommunications policy, and geological, topological, hydrographic and geophysical data, as well as Canadian archaeological and historical sites. Canadian customs and immigration regulations were to be respected as were the hunting and fishing regulations of the Yukon and the Northwest Territories.[44] Despite all this, and despite generally scrupulous observance of the agreement by the U.S. Air Force, stories abounded about U.S. security regulations prevailing, U.S. military and civilian officials dominating, and U.S. flags flying preeminently or in place of either the Canadian red ensign or the blue flag of the Royal Canadian Air Force. These tales "all gave rise to a vague but uneasy conception that for all the rules and regulations drawn up in the international agreement of 1955, de facto control of the Canadian north had passed into American hands."[45]

Throughout the next twenty years the Canadian government took advantage of opportunities, when they presented themselves, to reduce slowly the impact of the American military presence in Canada. In 1959 a small detachment of Royal Canadian Air Force officers was dispatched to the DEW Line to exercise at least nominal sovereignty over the civilians operating the line under contract to the U.S. Department of Defense. In 1961 Canada took over from the United States operation of all the Pinetree stations, (except those in Newfoundland).[46]

The Trudeau government placed a major emphasis on sovereignty protection, making it at least nominally the first of its defense priorities. Its 1971 white paper, *Defence in the 70s* announced that "The Government has decided that in normal peacetime circumstances the guiding principle should continue to be that, to the greatest extent possible, defence activities in and on Canadian territory will be carried out by members of the Canadian Armed Forces."[47] As a result, the radars in Newfoundland remaining in American hands were turned over to Canada and the Canadian air force at least nominally assumed peacetime responsibility for air defense operations in all of eastern Canada. Canadian aircraft also assumed increased peacetime responsibility for interception roles over the Prairie provinces which had previously been undertaken mostly by U.S. aircraft flying into Canadian airspace from bases across the border. Air defense regions were later reconfigured to allow Canadian commanders to control all of Canadian airspace. "Although," explained *Defence in the 70s,* "from a strictly air defence point of view it may make little difference whether the aircraft is Canadian or U.S., from a national point of view the Government believes that normal peacetime identification should be performed by Canadian aircraft."[48]

Under the Mulroney government, what was left of the U.S. military presence on Canadian soil continued to decline. In particular, the North Warning System which is replacing the DEW Line in the Canadian Arctic—the very last vestige of an American "army of occupation"—

is to be Canadian-operated. The Progressive Conservatives, in announcing the 1985 North American Air Defense Modernization Agreement, sought both to allay fears that the modernization program could mean letting the Americans back into the Canadian north and to take full credit for helping them move further out. Thus the Minister of National Defence, Erik Nielsen, told the House of Commons that he wanted

> to emphasize the importance of fully exercising sovereignty in our north. The DEW Line has served Canada well, but Canadians do not control it. The DEW Line is operated by the U.S. Air Force. Canadian involvement has been limited to small detachments. . . . The North Warning System will be a Canadian-controlled system—operated, maintained and manned by Canadians. Canadian sovereignty in our north will be strengthened and assured for the future. . . .
>
> Let there be no misunderstanding. By this agreement, Canadian sovereignty has been enhanced, including sovereignty over Canadian territory, sovereignty over Canadian defences, sovereignty over Canada's North and sovereignty over our own airspace.[49]

This did not stop the official opposition in the Commons from giving the politically powerful charge of northern sovereignty sellout at least a good try. "Why" asked Jean Chrétien, at the time spokesman on foreign affairs for the Liberal Party, referring to the FOLs provided for in the agreement, "will there be a series of airstrips built everywhere in the North while under the DEW Line system we did not need these airstrips? Is it for skidoo races? Is it for fishing trips?" A day later he offered an explanation. The Mulroney government, he charged, had decided to "give Canadian territory to the Americans for operational purposes," namely "a sophisticated series of military bases in the Canadian north."[50] The government responded in exasperation that the airstrips were to be just that, not bases; and would be used primarily by Canadian CF-18 aircraft.

Once the North Warning System is complete, a physical presence by the U.S. military on Canadian soil will be all but nonexistent. There are no longer any functioning U.S. bases or nuclear weapons on Canadian soil. Soon there will be no U.S.-operated radar stations. While under various arrangements, especially the NORAD agreement, U.S. military aircraft can and do fly into Canadian airspace and use Canadian airbases, none is permanently deployed there. The U.S. Air Force maintains a detachment of about fifteen personnel at Goose Bay, Labrador, to support military airlift operations between Europe and the United States; U.S. Air Force personnel serve in smaller numbers at Canadian air defense installations. A significant exception to the reduction in the U.S. presence is the U.S. Navy detachment of about 100 personnel at Argentia, Newfoundland, which is responsible for the operation of part of the U.S. SOSUS submarine detection system and about which little public information is available.[51]

While from the perspective of Canadian sovereignty protection the situation on land has improved, at sea the open dispute between the two countries over the legal status of the waters of the Northwest passage has come to the fore. This dispute has at times been far more corrosive for Canadian-U.S. relations than the inadvertent challenges on land, for here the U.S. challenge to Canadian legal sovereignty is direct. Its importance has been magnified by the role of Arctic waters in submarine operations.

The Northwest "passage" is the convenient term used to describe several water routes between Baffin Bay and the Atlantic on the east, and the Beaufort Sea and the Arctic on the west through the islands of the Canadian Arctic Archipelago. Canada maintains that all the waters between the islands of the archipelago, including those constituting the Northwest Passage, are Canadian internal waters, falling within full Canadian sovereignty, and constituting an integral part of Canadian territory. Canada, in its own view, therefore has the legal right to grant or deny transit through the passage to foreign civilian and naval vessels.

The United States, on the other hand, insists that the passage is a strait used for international navigation, linking one part of the high seas with another. As such, in the official American view, the waters of the passage are high seas and at certain narrower points what international law calls "territorial seas" and thus not waters internal to Canada. Territorial seas are subject to "the regime of transit passage" (a recent innovation in the international law of the sea) which cannot be suspended by the coastal state. Thus navigation and overflight require neither Canadian permission nor prior notification, according to the United States.[52]

The dispute over the Northwest Passage is rooted deeply, probably intractably, in the national interests of the two countries. The United States is a global maritime power with nothing short of an essential interest in keeping a wide variety of straits around the globe open to its fleet. The United States government could, in all probability, happily accept the notion that the Northwest Passage is under the sovereignty of its partner, friend and ally, Canada—except for the legal precedent it would establish. Such a precedent would weaken the United States' position elsewhere in the world where coastal states claim maritime sovereignty. Canada, on the other hand, is a coastal state with a tiny navy. And then there is the identity question.

Canadians argue that acceptance of the Northwest Passage need not constitute for the United States an unfortunate precedent, for the Passage has a number of distinguishing characteristics, in particular the fact that it is covered with ice for most of the year, making it unique. To U.S. government maritime lawyers and many of their colleagues in private practice or academic positions, this is yet another case of "creeping uniqueness." They identify other instances of uniqueness that have made their way into international law (the unique coastline of Norway, Indonesia's unique archipelagoes, the unique dependence of Iceland on its fisheries) and point to other straits whose characteristics are equally unique, and whose openness to international navigation the United States needs to defend. Canadian officials, for their part, counter that the passage is sailed with extreme infrequency. To the United States, that is irrelevant: what counts is that the passage is potentially a useful one.[53]

The dispute has grated on Canadians. As a leading Canadian expert on the Arctic, Franklyn Griffiths, has put it, "It is an irony that the challenge to Canada's control over its Arctic waters comes from the government and the people with whom Canadians have the most in common."[54] The irony goes still deeper. To a good extent *because* Canadians have much in common with Americans, so much in fact that the national identity is thereby weakened, they get so upset when the United States threatens what many Canadians see as one of the sources of their national, boreal distinctiveness.

Further exacerbating Canada-U.S. relations in the Arctic is the dispute over the boundary between each country's 200-mile offshore economic zone in the Beaufort Sea. Canada argues that the Alaska-Yukon land boundary along the 141st meridian should be extended seaward. The United States claims that the sea frontier veers offshore to the east at a 90-degree angle to the lie of the coast. At stake is a wedge-shaped section of 6,000 nautical square miles containing extensive oil and gas reserves.[55]

Two voyages over the past two decades through the passage by American vessels have each lead to a major ruckus in Canada-U.S. relations and have caused each time a hardening of Canada's legal position. The discovery of oil in Prudhoe Bay, Alaska (off the Beaufort Sea) in 1968 opened the possibility of oil tankers traveling through the Northwest Passage to refineries and markets on the United States's east coast. Humble Oil, a Standard Oil of New Jersey (Esso) subsidiary, announced late that year that it would outfit a tanker, the S.S. *Manhattan* and sail it through the passage in 1969 in order to test its suitability as a delivery route. Ottawa had no objection on environmental grounds to the voyage itself. Moreover Humble had always sought the cooperation of Canadian authorities, which Ottawa took as tacit recognition of Canadian jurisdiction. Difficulties arose only when the U.S. Coast Guard volunteered to assist the *Manhattan* in the voyage by sending a ship to accompany it. In keeping with the United States's view that the passage was an international strait, Washington refused to ask Ottawa's permission for the Coast Guard vessel's transit.

It soon became painfully obvious that whereas Canada considered the passage Canadian, "jurisdictional claims were not nailed down."[56] While the *Manhattan* proceeded east and west through the passage in 1969, accompanied by U.S. and Canadian coast guard vessels, Ottawa tried to nail its claims partially down. Parliament adopted legislation in 1970 extending the Canadian territorial sea from three to twelve miles creating legal "gateways" in the passage where straits were under twenty-four miles across. At the same time legislation was adopted establishing a 100-mile offshore pollution prevention zone and a new fishery zone, and removing jurisdiction over matters related to these two zones from the International Court of Justice.[57]

No American surface vessel sailed through the Northwest Passage again until the summer of 1985 when the U.S. Coast Guard dispatched its icebreaker, *Polar Sea,* from Greenland to Alaska. The voyage of the *Polar Sea* was bound to produce an even greater uproar than that of the *Manhattan,* for several reasons. First, since 1973 Canadian officials quietly had taken to describing the waters of the passage as historically internal to Canada.[58] Second, the voyage came at a time when the modernization of the North American air defense system, announced earlier that year, had focussed Canadian attention once again on the strategic significance of the Canadian Arctic, and the U.S. Strategic Defense Initiative (SDI) program had lead to vague but often intense worries about American intentions there. Third, Prime Minister Mulroney and President Reagan had taken to stressing their personal friendship and intent to pursue good relations between their two countries. The dispatch of the *Polar Sea* by the U.S. government was often interpreted in Canada as revealing the hollowness of those claims of friendship and goodwill on the part of the American president.

"For the United States," one shrill commentator later claimed, the voyage "was more than a prod at the Canadian flank; it was yet another in a series of carefully calculated moves to show the flag and reassert the U.S. view that the right of innocent passage must be guaranteed through international waters."[59] In fact, however, it was nothing of the kind. The voyage originated in purely operational concerns. Early in the summer the *Polar Sea* was assisting in surface resupply of U.S. military activities in Thule, Greenland, and was needed in Alaska to prepare for late summer operations. With little thought for the political consequences, the U.S. Coast Guard scheduled the voyage through the Northwest Passage in order to save the twenty extra days and additional fuel costs a trip through the Panama Canal would require. It can scarcely be denied that the savings in fuel and time were hardly worth the subsequent damage the *Polar Sea* caused Canada-United States relations. The U.S. government swiftly concluded though, once the voyage was scheduled and came to the attention almost simultaneously of the

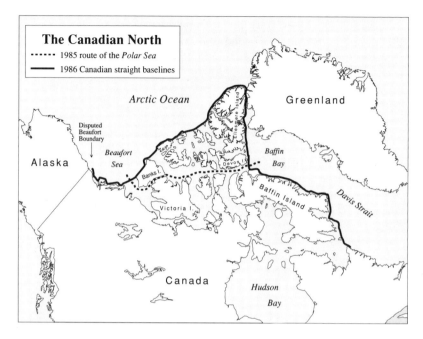

The Canadian North

...... 1985 route of the *Polar Sea*

—— 1986 Canadian straight baselines

Arctic Ocean

Greenland

Alaska

Disputed
Beaufort
Boundary

Beaufort
Sea

Banks I.

Victoria I

Baffin
Bay

Baffin Island

Davis Strait

Canada

Hudson
Bay

State Department, the Canadian government, and the Canadian public, that it could not be canceled, for that would entail recognition of Canadian claims to full sovereignty over the passage.

The Mulroney government and the Reagan administration tried to make the best out of an unfortunate situation. Washington and Ottawa set aside their legal differences, agreeing that "the transit, and the preparations for it, in no way prejudice the juridical position of either side regarding the Northwest Passage." For its part Ottawa notified Washington that "in the exercise of Canadian sovereignty over the Northwest Passage" it was "pleased to consent to the proposed transit" and prepared to render appropriate assistance to the U.S. vessel.[60] Two Canadian Coast Guard icebreaker captains as well as an official of the Canadian Department of Indian and Northern Affairs were on board the *Polar Sea* during its transit of the passage, and both the Canadian Coast Guard and Department of the Environment provided the ship with routing advice, communications and ice reconnaissance services. Washington, while welcoming Canadian assistance, reiterated that Canadian permission had neither been requested by the United States nor was legally necessary. The transit was, after all, according to the United States, through an international strait.

This cooperative approach to damage limitation was by no means enough to prevent a political flap and an emotional outburst of the highest order that summer in Canada. The Americans had violated Canadian Arctic sovereignty and the Canadian government had let them do it! Franklyn Griffiths wrote that the Mulroney government had responded "pathetically" to the situation,[61] while journalists left and right called the cooperative arrangements "a major flop by a spineless government"[62] and a "servile, wimpy response . . . enough to enrage even a lukewarm Canadian nationalist."[63] The leader of the official opposition, John Turner of the Liberal Party, called the voyage "intolerable" and an "affront to Canada."[64] If the voyage itself was not sensation enough, the Council of Canadians, a nationalist group, sent an airplane to drop a Canadian flag on the *Polar Sea* while it was underway in the Northwest Passage, gathering for itself headlines as it issued verbal blasts against the American and the Canadian governments, and for its pilot a criminal charge of endangering navigation.

It is hard to see what the Mulroney government could have done otherwise. The United States was not prepared to cancel the voyage, for fear of weakening its legal position and it was unthinkable that Canada would have tried to threaten force to stop it. Nonetheless, the voyage had underlined how sparse the Canadian presence in the Arctic, especially Arctic waters, really was. The contradictions in Canada's sentimental and not very palpable attachment to the Arctic were being laid bare. And the Mulroney government was on the verge of being convicted publicly of the unpardonable, not to mention electorally fatal, sin of handing the Arctic over to the Yanks.

Before the summer of 1985 was out, the secretary of state for external affairs, Joe Clark, stood in the Commons to make a statement on northern sovereignty. "The Arctic," he told the House, "is not only a part of Canada, it is a part of Canadian greatness." The government was determined "to preserve that Canadian greatness undiminished."[65] Several legal steps had or soon would be taken. Most importantly for Canada's legal case, an order-in-council had at long last been issued establishing straightbaselines around the outer perimeter of the Canadian Arctic Archipelago in order to define precise limits to the waters Canada had been claiming since 1973 to be internal. Legislation would be introduced fully extending Canadian civil and criminal law to offshore zones in the Arctic. Confident that international law had evolved to the point where it would support the 1970 legislation establishing new fishing and pollution control zones, Ottawa also removed the reservation to the jurisdiction of the International Court of Justice.

The secretary of state for external affairs also announced an increase in Arctic surveillance flights by Aurora patrol aircraft, and that planning was underway for "naval activity in Eastern Arctic waters." Canadian naval vessels were still unable to sail into ice-infested waters of the archipelago itself. To establish a surface presence in those waters,

Clark also announced, the government would construct and equip the Canadian Coast Guard with a "Polar class-8" icebreaker, capable of year-round Arctic operation.[66] It was to have been the world's largest icebreaker. Wags soon said it would be "the world's most expensive floating flagpole."

Among the other steps Clark announced were talks with the United States "on co-operation in Arctic waters on the basis of full respect for Canadian sovereignty." The United States government welcomed the proposed discussions, so much so that at the urging of the United States Embassy in Ottawa, it refrained from formally protesting the proclamation of straight baselines, which it saw (and still sees) as unjustified under international law.[67]

Canadian expectations for the talks with Washington apparently were unrealistic, as Clark's formula of "on the basis of full respect for Canadian sovereignty" seemed to reveal. The United States simply could not and still will not recognize the Northwest Passage as internal Canadian waters. An agreement, albeit a modest one, did emerge from the talks and was signed by Clark and U.S. Secretary of State George Schultz in January 1988. It left the sovereignty issue unresolved, with both sides still holding to their respective positions. The United States did "pledge that all navigation by United States's icebreakers within waters claimed by Canada to be internal will be undertaken with the consent of Canada."[68] While the agreement does nothing to resolve the legal status of any future surface traffic by U.S. commercial vessels, no such traffic is expected for years, if ever.

And, in the wake of the 1988 agreement, there will thus be no more *Polar Sea*-type incidents. Indeed, the agreement was invoked for the first time without controversy when the United States asked Canadian permission in the fall of 1988 for a voyage through the passage of the USCGC *Polar Star,* sister ship of the *Polar Sea.* With such American intrusions under control, the Mulroney government announced in 1990 the cancellation of the Polar class-8 icebreaker construction program. Here was a classic instance of Canadian "push-resistant" nationalism in the north. Canada still will have no equivalent icebreaking capabilities of its own in the high north. But with the American icebreaking "push" eliminated or at least moderated, the motivations based on Canadian resistance disappeared.

The dispute over sovereignty in Arctic waters might have faded away again, as it had in 1970, were it not for the issue of submarine transits in the Canadian Arctic. The issue emerged in May 1986 into the super-heated political atmosphere left behind by the *Polar Sea* when three U.S. nuclear powered attack submarines (SSNs) of the *Sturgeon* class surfaced at the geographic North Pole in what was apparently intended as a dramatic display of Arctic operational capability. U.S. officials and the Canadian Secretary of State for External Affairs refused either to confirm or deny that the boats had passed through Canadian waters on their way to the pole. Other public statements by Canadian officials did little to clarify publicly the full extent to which the U.S. Navy informs Canadian officials of the presence of U.S. submarines in Canadian waters much less whether Canadian military and political authorities had been told about the three subs on their way to a public rendezvous at the North Pole.

Two facts did become painfully clear to the public. First, Canada has no under-ice detection capabilities, much less operational capabilities in Arctic waters: the three obsolete Canadian Oberon-class submarines could not venture into the ice-infested and ice-covered archipelagic waters. The sonobuoys which the Aurora patrol aircraft could toss into open water to detect the presence of submarines were not ice-penetrating. There are no fixed underwater detection systems in the archipelago, of the kind that the United States in cooperation with allies (including Canada) operates in other ocean areas. That means Canada is dependent on the United States for information about both Soviet and U.S. submarine activity in the region. Second, Canadian defense officials believed that such activity could be on the increase, especially as the Soviets equipped attack submarines with nuclear-armed cruise missiles capable of striking at targets in Canada and the northern United States from Arctic waters.

Ottawa faced and today continues to face an unhappy dilemma. The Soviet Union recognizes Canadian sovereignty in the Arctic, but its submarines would constitute there a distinct threat to Canadian and U.S. security. The United States is apparently undertaking greater efforts in the Arctic in response to that Soviet threat. But to leave those efforts entirely in the hands of the United States is an unattractive prospect. Experience has taught that it could be difficult enough being overwhelmed by the American military on land in a region which the United States fully recognized as Canadian. To do so in Canadian internal waters which the United States government insists are an international strait would be still worse.

In short, recent events put the Canadian government under new pressures to deploy forces, especially maritime forces, in the north to protect Canadian sovereignty. But at the same time, pressures to keep some Canadian forces committed to Europe have been compelling.

THE CANADIAN COMMITMENT TO EUROPE

Canada is the "other" member of an alliance often seen as a partnership between Europe and the United States. In fact, it is a founding member of NATO. Canadian diplomats played a prominent role in the discussions leading up to the signing of the North Atlantic Treaty in

1949. Their successors will continue to want to play a role in the European security discussions of the 1990s.

Until very recently, Canadian interest in European security has stemmed, in the first instance, from the fact that a third world war could begin on the Central Front. Even if Canada were not tied to Europe, as long as the United States is, the danger remains that a breakdown in deterrence in Europe could escalate to the level of a nuclear exchange between the United States and the Soviet Union in which Canada would suffer.

Canada first committed armed forces to the defense of NATO Europe in 1951, as part of a general rearmament precipitated by the outbreak of the Korean War. Eleven air squadrons and an army brigade group of almost 6000 men were dispatched to join NATO forces on the Central Front; two more reinforcement brigades in Canada were earmarked to be sent in the event of an emergency. These were significant military contributions at a time when Western Europe had not yet recovered from the Second World War, and the Federal Republic of Germany was not yet a NATO partner.

Yet almost immediately, Ottawa felt the painful problem of attempting to deploy forces on both sides of the Atlantic despite, at the time, fairly high levels of Canadian defense spending. The Canadian Secretary of State for External Affairs, Lester B. Pearson, told U.S. Secretary of State John Foster Dulles in December 1954, when the United States had begun operating air defense installations on Canadian soil and at the same time was urging the Canadian government to increase its force levels in Europe, that "Canada was anxious to play a full part in these northern defence developments, especially in respect to those which were on Canadian territory. This might result eventually in reducing somewhat our air defence contributions in Europe. . . . the problem for us existed, and was becoming more difficult as our resources would not permit an increase of our defence activities in Canada and a maintenance of those activities in Europe on the present scale."[69]

As its resources available for defense declined, Canada let the size of its contributions to the land and air defense of the NATO Central Front also decline. As compensation, the Canadians accepted in the 1960s reinforcement commitments to the NATO Northern Flank. While committing winter-warfare-trained Canadians to Norway made in theory excellent military sense, many of the preparations for the Canadian commitments there were often no more than desultory, made by a government seeking cheap alternatives to increasingly untenable, more expensive commitments on the Central Front. For the Canadian Armed Forces, already spread across two continents, the addition of a second area of operations in Europe posed troubling problems.[70]

With the arming of West Germany, followed by its admission to NATO, and with the economic recovery of Western Europe, Canada's declining efforts obviously had become, as Pierre Trudeau explicitly put it in 1969, "marginal . . . in strict military terms."[71] And so they have remained.

Canadian governments have twice sought tentatively to escape from Canada's defense dilemma by terminating altogether the standing Canadian military presence in Germany. Both attempts met fierce allied resistance, and were abandoned as Ottawa feared that a pullback would cost Canada influence within the Alliance and could damage its ties with Western Europe.

The Trudeau government, upon the entreaties and blandishments of the NATO allies, backed away from notions of withdrawal in 1969, deciding instead upon the compromise measures of halving personnel strength of Canadian Forces Europe (CFE), (to about 5000 personnel) terminating nuclear roles, cutting the air element from six to three squadrons, cramming the air and land elements into two inadequate bases in southern Germany, and planning to strip the army brigade group of its heavy armor.

Members of the Trudeau government were certainly not about to claim at the time that the small, ill-equipped, and demoralized forces to be left in Germany could make a significant contribution to the defense of NATO Europe. Rather, as the government openly admitted, in *Defence in the 70s*, those forces were to constitute "a tangible expression of Canadian support for the principle of collective security in the North Atlantic area." They would also "reinforce" Canada's "political role in the important negotiations in progress, or in prospect, designed to lead to a resolution of some of the tension-producing issues which persist from the Second World War."[72] In 1975, under allied pressure, Ottawa reversed the decision to lighten the brigade group, buying it Leopard tanks. "No tanks, no trade," West German Chancellor Helmut Schmidt is alleged to have told Prime Minister Trudeau, then pursuing an economic "contractual link" with the European Community.

In March 1985, the Mulroney government, seeking to distance itself from its Liberal predecessor's poor defense record, announced that the stationed strength of the Canadian forces in Europe would be increased by 1200 personnel, bringing them closer to war establishment. The decision was followed by Canadian insistence that a March 1985 declaration on security, issued by President Reagan and Prime Minister Mulroney at their 1985 "Shamrock" summit in Quebec City include the statement, "We attach great importance to our continuing commitment to station Canadian and United States forces in Europe."[73]

It thus came as something of a shock to the decision-makers of several NATO countries, notably the United States, Germany and the U.K., when in late 1985 they were quietly approached by Erik Nielsen, then deputy prime minister and minister of national defence in the Mulroney government, and asked about their reactions to a possible Canadian withdrawal from Germany in favor of an enlargement of Canada's contribution to North American air defense and an enhanced Canadian reinforcement role in the defense of Norway.

Militarily, the Alliance might have profited from strong Canadian commitments to an area of increasing concern. The NATO allies, especially the United States were in fact mindful of the value of a timely and effective Canadian contribution to the northern flank and aware of the problems Canada faced deploying forces on two continents. U.S. Secretary of Defense Caspar Weinberger reportedly reacted positively after the initial approach by Nielsen. Subsequent reactions by the German and British defense ministers were, however, extremely negative. Other U.S. officials soon joined in the opposition. Canada was proposing what some U.S. officials called a "shell game": withdrawing forces from Germany to Canada whence they might or might not be sent to the northern flank. Better, the allies felt, a physical Canadian presence on West German soil. The Germans worried as well that a Canadian pullout would send the wrong signals; first to the smaller alliance partners, Belgium and the Netherlands, which also have contingents of troops on German soil and might be tempted to follow suit; secondly to the United States Congress which might be similarly tempted to follow the Canadian example; and finally to the German public which had become calm once again after a lengthy period of agitation over defense issues. In the face of these vehement rejections, and once again fearful that Canada's influence in the alliance could be damaged, Ottawa dropped the idea.

Although Canada plays no major military role in Europe, Canadian attachment to NATO membership remains, nonetheless, deep. NATO membership has always been Canada's ticket to the big league discussions of East-West security issues. If it can not have a decisive voice in East-West matters it might, in the company of other smaller NATO states, find ways to influence the bigger members, above all, the United States. Therefore, preservation of "the seat at the table" in NATO and NATO-related discussions has been and remains an absolute imperative for any Canadian government. Canadian governments have generally taken great care with the quality of the diplomatic representation it sends to NATO headquarters in Brussels.

Canada is also tied economically, culturally and even psychologically to Europe. These ties have been important in offsetting the overwhelming links to the United States. Thus Canada has often seen its participation in NATO as part and parcel of its pursuit of its broader relations with Europe. It is no coincidence that the Canadian government insisted upon the inclusion of what came to be called the "Canadian article" in the North Atlantic Treaty, pledging the member states to economic collaboration. In short, as the diplomat and scholar John Holmes once put it, "Canadians also saw NATO as a counterweight . . . it would give Canada a multilateral forum in which, by combining with other lesser powers, it could make its weight be felt and so be relieved, at least psychically, of the inhibitions of life with one gigantic neighbour."[74]

So participation in NATO is popular in Canada, even as Canada has become psychologically disengaged from the defense of Europe and its forces there have fallen to token levels. Public opinion poll after poll has shown that the Canadian public firmly supports NATO membership and fully expects Canadian leaders to play an active diplomatic role in the Alliance, even though the Canadian public certainly does not clamor for the kind of defense spending that would allow the Canadian Armed Forces to make significant military contributions to it and does not punish governments for failing to do so. As long as the seat at the table is safe, Canadians are content.

These Canadian motivations remain all but unchanged in the 1990s. As Joe Clark put it in 1990, "Nothing should be taken for granted; we must strengthen our ties in order to consolidate our position in the Europe of tomorrow."[75] But the Canadian dilemma of stitching together and maintaining a credible, trans-Atlantic defense posture on an extremely low budget has thus far also remained unchanged.

NOTES

1. Canada has also participated in a wide range of international peacekeeping operations, including every U.N.-sponsored operation. These operations require far lower commitment of resources than North American- and Europe-based operations. Today, well over a thousand personnel of the Canadian Armed Forces are on duty with various longstanding peacekeeping operations in Cyprus and the Middle East. The most recent assignments have been in 1988 to the United Nation's efforts along the Iran-Iraq border, and in 1989 to the sometimes tumultuous U.N. effort in Namibia, as well as the U.N.'s contingent in Central America.
2. Canada, Department of National Defence, *Challenge and Commitment: A Defence Policy for Canada* (Ottawa: Minister of Supply and Services, 1987), 43.
3. General A.J.G.D. de Chastelain, " 'The Art of Prudent Walking:' Coming to Grips with Detente—An Update from a Canadian Military Perspective," *Canadian Defence Quarterly* 19, no. 6 (June 1990): 13.
4. *Challenge and Commitment*, 10.
5. North Atlantic Assembly, Civil Affairs Committee, *Interim Report of the Sub-Committee on Public Information on Defence and Security: The Netherlands, Turkey, and Canada,* Brussels (September 1987): 38.
6. R. J. Sutherland, "Canada's Long Term Strategic Situation," *International Journal* 17, no. 3 (Summer 1962): 199.
7. See James Eayrs, *In Defence of Canada: Peacemaking and Deterrence* (Toronto: University of Toronto Press, 1972), chap. 5; and C. P. Stacey, *Arms, Men and Governments: The War Policies of Canada, 1939–1945,* part 8 (Ottawa: 1970).

8. James Eayrs, "Military Policy and Middle-power: The Canadian Experience," in *Canada's Role as a Middle Power,* ed. J. King Gordon (Toronto: Canadian Institute of International Affairs, 1965), 84.

9. *Challenge and Commitment,* 89

10. Geoffrey Pearson, "On Fireproof Houses: Canada's Security," *Points of View,* no. 4 (Ottawa: Canadian Institute for International Peace and Security, December 1988): 4.

11. Transcript of radio interview, August 1984; text courtesy of Progressive Conservative Party of Canada.

12. *Western Report* 1, no. 59 (5 January 1987): cover.

13. Unclassified telex, National Defence Headquarters, Ottawa/Chief of the Defence Staff to Canadian Forces, 27 April 1989.

14. "The 1989 Federal Budget: The Death of Defence?" *Strategic Datalink,* no. 12 (Toronto: Canadian Institute of Strategic Studies, May 1989). Canadian officials have pointed out that U.S. defense spending under the Bush Administration is also set at zero real growth for fiscal 1990 and is expected to grow at only 1 percent and 2 percent in the following two years. Of course, comparisons in growth are irrelevant in the face of the enormous disparities between the two countries in GPD shares devoted to defense.

15. Charles F. Doran, *Forgotten Partnership: U.S.-Canada Relations Today* (Baltimore and London: Johns Hopkins University Press, 1984), 67.

16. See David G. Haglund, ed., *Canada's Defence Industrial Base: The Political Economy of Preparedness and Procurement* (Kingston: Ronald P. Frye, 1988), especially the chapter by Robert Van Steenburg, "An Analysis of Canadian-American Defence Economic Cooperation: The History and Current Issues;" and Canada, Department of National Defence, *The Environment for Expanding the North American Industrial Base,* June 1987. For critical assessments of the impact of DD/DPSA, see Ernie Regehr, *Arms Canada: The Deadly Business of Military Exports* (Toronto: James Lorimer and Company, 1987); and Roger Hill, "Unified Canada-U.S. Defence Production: A Hazardous Road,' *Peace and Security* (Summer 1989): 4.

17. For a discussion of the possibility of singling out Canada for its spending deficiencies, see chapter 4 and the foreword by John G. H. Halstead in Joseph T. Jockel and Joel J. Sokolsky, *Canada and Collective Security: Odd Man Out* (The Washington Papers; New York: Praeger, 1986).

18. Canada, Secretary of State for External Affairs, *Foreign Policy for Canadians* 1 (Ottawa: 1971): 21.

19. J. Bartlett Brebner, *Canada: A Modern History* (Ann Arbor: University of Michigan Press, 1960), i.

20. For example, Bill McKnight, minister of national defense, defended the April 1989 cuts as being critical to Canada's "economic sovereignty." Speaking notes, the Hon. Bill McKnight, Minister of National Defence to ARMX Dinner, Ottawa, 24 May 1989; text courtesy Department of National Defence.

21. Frank Underhill, "False Hair on the Chest," *Saturday Night* (3 October 1936), cited in *Colombo's Canadian Quotations,* ed. John Robert Colombo (Edmonton: Hurtig, 1974), 607.

22. For a useful introduction to the Canadian Arctic, in comparison to the far more developed Soviet Arctic, see James R. Gibson, "The Geographic

Context: Canadian-Soviet Comparison," in *Strategy and the Arctic,* Polaris Paper no. 4, ed. R. B. Byers and Michael Slack (Toronto: Canadian Institute of Strategic Studies, 1986), 14. The economy of the Canadian north is surveyed by Jack C. Stabler in his "Development Planning North of 60: Requirements and Prospects," *The North,* Studies of the Royal Commission on the Economic Union and Development Prospects for Canada, ed. Michael S. Whittington (Toronto: University of Toronto Press, 1985).

23. This page is largely based on W. Harriet Critchely, "Defence and Policing in Arctic Canada," in *Politics of the Northwest Passage,* ed. Franklyn Griffiths (Kingston and Montreal: McGill-Queen's University Press, 1987), 200.

24. Ibid., 203.

25. Claude T. Bissell, *The Strength of the University* (Toronto: University of Toronto Press, 1968), 190.

26. Robert Page, *Northern Development: The Canadian Dilemma* (Toronto: McClelland and Stewart, 1986), 314.

27. Franklin Griffiths, "Beyond the Arctic Sublime," in *Politics of the Northwest Passage,* 243.

28. Thomas G. Barnes, " 'Canada, True North': A 'Here There' or a Boreal Myth," *The American Review of Canadian Studies* 19, no. 4 (Winter 1989): 370.

29. Northrup Frye, *Divisions on a Ground: Essays on Canadian Culture* (Toronto: Anansi, 1982), 59.

30. Canadian national attention has, in recent years, also been compellingly drawn to the north by the rise, after "two centuries of social and cultural erosion" of "a powerful internal movement in the native communities" (p. 59). Canada's native peoples have been arguing throughout the country for recognition of aboriginal rights to land, and extension of self-governing authority. The Inuit and Dene (Indians) of the Northwest Territories have proposed creating out of the territories two provinces. In one, the Inuit would be in the overwhelming majority. In the other, where the Dene and white populations would be about equal, Dene rights would be specially protected. See Michael S. Whittington, "Political and Constitutional Development in the N.W.T. and Yukon: The Issues and the Interests," and Gordon Robertson, "Northern Political Development within Canadian Federalism," both in *The North,* Studies of the Royal Commission on the Economic Union and Development Prospects for Canada, ed. Michael S. Whittington (Toronto: University of Toronto Press, 1985).

31. E. J. Dosman, "The Northern Sovereignty Crisis 1968–70," in *The Arctic in Question,* ed. E. J. Dosman (Toronto: Oxford University Press, 1976), 34.

32. The term was apparently coined by H. Basil Robinson in his *Diefenbaker's World: A Populist in Foreign Affairs* (Toronto: University of Toronto Press, 1989), 309.

33. The ninety-nine year U.S.-U.K. agreement of September 1940, providing the United States with special rights in Newfoundland, is still in legal force although the United States has closed the bases it once operated in the province.

34. One very small exception: sovereignty over the tiny Machais Seal Island on the Main-New Brunswick border is currently in dispute.

35. James Eayrs, *In Defence of Canada: Peacemaking and Deterrence* (Toronto: University of Toronto Press, 1972), 349. See the recently released study

by Shelagh D. Grant, *Sovereignty or Security? Government Policy in the Canadian North 1936–1950* (Vancouver: University of British Columbia Press, 1988), especially chap. 5, "The Army of Occupation."

36. Col. Stanley W. Dzuiban, *Military Relations between the United States and Canada, 1939–1945* (Washington: Office of the Chief of Military History, Department of the Army, 1959), 340.

37. Report of the Advisory Committee on Post-Hostilities Problems, "Post-War Canadian Defence Relationship with the United States: General Considerations," 23 January 1945, Privy Council Office Records, Public Archives of Canada.

38. Ibid.

39. J. W. Pickersgill, ed., *The Mackenzie King Record, 1945–1946,* vol. 3 (Toronto: University of Toronto Press, 1968), 266.

40. "Joint Statement by the Governments of Canada and the United States Regarding Defence Co-operation between the Two Countries," *Canada Treaty Series,* no. 43 (1947).

41. Department of External Affairs, "A Survey of Relations between the United States and Canada" (20 June 1951). Brooke Claxton Paper, vol. 96, Public Archives of Canada, Ottawa.

42. Exchange of notes, 1 August 1951, 5 *United States Treaties,* 1721.

43. Dan C. Bliss, U.S. Embassy to Officer in Charge of Dominion Affairs, State Department, *Foreign Relations of the United States, 1951* 2 (USGPO, 1979): 888.

44. Exchange of notes, 5 May 1955, 5 *United States Treaties,* 763.

45. James Eayrs, *Canada in World Affairs, October 1955 through June 1957* (Toronto: Oxford University Press, 1959), 151.

46. The Canadian motivation was not solely related to sovereignty. Relieving the United States of the costs of the stations was part of a transaction whereby the United States transferred fighter aircraft to the Royal Canadian Air Force.

47. Canada, Minister of National Defence, *White Paper on Defence: Defence in the 70s* (Ottawa, 1971), 31.

48. Ibid., 20.

49. Canada, House of Commons, *Debates* (13 March 1985), 2976–77.

50. Ibid. (19 March 1985), 3164; (20 March 1985), 3200–1.

51. The SOSUS operation at Argentia briefly became the subject of national attention in Canada in March 1988. A Newfoundland court convicted a Canadian citizen, who had been apprehended in a joint U.S.-Canadian operation, of spying on the installation for the Soviet Union.

52. The standard work on this subject undoubtedly will become Donat Pharand, *Canada's Arctic Waters in International Law* (Cambridge: Cambridge University Press, 1988), especially part 4, "The Waters of the Canadian Arctic Archipelago and the Northwest Passage."

53. See Aldo E. Chircop and Susan J. Rolston, eds., *Canadian Arctic Sovereignty: Are Canadian and U.S. Interests Contradictory or Complementary, Proceedings of the 1986 Ronald St. John Macdonald Symposium* (Halifax: International Insights Society, Law School, Dalhousie University, 1987), especially 11–12.

54. Griffiths, "Beyond the Arctic Sublime," 241.
55. See Donat Pharand, "Sovereignty and the Canadian North," in *The North,* Studies of the Royal Commission on the Economic Union and Development Prospects for Canada, ed. Michael S. Whittington (Toronto: University of Toronto Press, 1985). There are, in fact, two other maritime boundary disputes between Canada and the United States, both outside the Arctic: the boundary seaward between British Columbia and Washington off the Strait of Juan de Fuca, and the Dixon Entrance between Alaska and British Columbia.
56. Dosman, 35.
57. Washington protested the pollution control and fishery zones, and retaliated by cutting Canadian oil import quotas. While U.S. officials were unhappy as well about the new twelve-mile territorial sea, they were not deeply troubled about its impact on the status of the passage. Passage rights exist through territorial seas. Had the government declared them then and there, Canadian internal waters, that would have been another matter. The dispute faded from the Canada-U.S. bilateral agenda as the multinational oil companies abandoned, for the time being, the notion of shipping Alaska hydrocarbons by tankers in favor of relying on pipelines.
58. On this point, see Donat Pharand's comments in *Canadian Arctic Sovereignty,* 4–5.
59. John Honderich, *Arctic Imperative: Is Canada Losing the North?* (Toronto: University of Toronto Press, 1987), 41.
60. Department of State to Canadian Embassy, Diplomatic note 222, 24 June 1985; Canadian Embassy to Department of State, Diplomatic note 433, 31 July 1985.
61. Franklyn Griffiths, "Use Arctic or Lose It," *Toronto Globe and Mail,* 30 July 1985, 4.
62. Christopher Young, "We've Flopped on Polar Sea," *Montreal Gazette,* 6 August 1985, B1.
63. Don Braid, "Polar Sea a Turning Point for Mulroney," *Montreal Gazette,* 14 August 1985, B3.
64. "Ship Protest Could Bring Legal Action," *Toronto Globe and Mail* 10 August 1985, 1.
65. For the text, see Canada, House of Commons, *Debates* 10 September 1985, 6462.
66. See Kim Richard Nossal, "Polar Icebreaker: The Politics of Inertia," in *Politics of the Northwest Passage,* ed. Franklyn Griffiths (Kingston and Montreal: McGill-Queen's University Press, 1987), 11. The voyage had other long-term impacts, as well. According to John Merritt, executive director of the Canadian Arctic Resources Committee, "One effect of the *Polar Sea* episode was to reveal the existence of a large and increasingly restless expert and informed Canadian community of Northern affairs personnel—academics, consultants, interest groups—who are now beginning to put together their own agenda. . . . This is in part a reaction to the perceived caution of Canada's foreign service, in part a sense that the North as a whole has been too long understated by Canada's national government." "Factors Influencing Canadian Interest in Greater Non-military Co-operation in the Arctic," in *The*

Arctic Challenge: Nordic and Canadian Approaches to Security and Cooperation in an Emerging International Region, ed. Kari Motolla (Boulder and London: Westview Press, 1988), 288–89.

67. Prof. Pharand, on the other hand, argues that "Canada has validly drawn straight baselines around the Canadian Arctic Archipelago, with the result that the enclosed waters, including those of the Northwest Passage, have the status of international waters." *Canada's Arctic Waters in International Law*, 252.

68. Agreement between the Government of Canada and the Government of the United States of America on Arctic Cooperation, 11 January 1988.

69. L. B. Pearson, *Mike: The Memoirs of the Right Honourable Lester B. Pearson*, vol. 2 (Toronto: Signet, 1975), 91–92.

70. See Joseph T. Jockel, *Canada and NATO's Northern Flank* (Toronto: York University Centre for International and Strategic Studies, 1986).

71. "Excerpts from an address by Prime Minister Trudeau to a Dinner of the Alberta Liberal Association, Calgary, 12 April 1969; Canada, Department of External Affairs, *Statements and Speeches* no. 69/8.

72. *White Paper on Defence: Defence in the 70s*, 35.

73. "Declaration by the Prime Minister of Canada and the President of the United States of America Regarding International Security," Quebec, 18 March 1985.

74. John W. Holmes, *Canada: A Middle-Aged Power* (Toronto: McClelland and Stewart, 1976), 128.

75. "Canada's Stake in Europe," notes for a Speech by the Secretary of State for External Affairs, the Rt. Hon. Joe Clark, at a luncheon sponsored by the Conseil des Relations Internationales de Montréal, 20 June 1990; Department of External Affairs, 90/38.

III

The Deepening Commitment-
Capability Gap—and
Retrenchment to North America

The task here is to outline the deepening commitment-capability gap confronting the air, land, and sea elements of the Canadian Armed Forces in the wake of the 1987 defense White Paper, *Challenge and Commitment,* and the April 1989 budget statement. Even before the dramatic changes in Europe occurred, a Canadian retrenchment to North America had become highly probable, if not inevitable. The changes underway in Europe now afford Canada the opportunity to pull back with the acquiescence of its allies.

THE 1987 WHITE PAPER AND THE 1989 BUDGET

As seen in the last chapter, in 1985 the Mulroney government abandoned a quiet effort to end the Canadian military presence in Germany. Meanwhile, the United States has posed a new challenge to Canadian sovereignty in Arctic waters. The essential starting point of the 1987 White Paper inevitably became, therefore, that "Canada will continue to participate in collective deterrence and defence in North America, in Western Europe and at sea."[1]

Much more than a simple declaration of policy would be needed. To undertake roles on two continents and at sea, the Canadian Armed Forces would have to be rescued from a disastrous lack of personnel and modern equipment, resulting from years of underfunding. The White Paper summarized the state of the Canadian Armed Forces with admirable directness:

> Even if the Canadian forces were fully manned and had modern, state of the art equipment, to fulfill existing defence commitments would be a daunting challenge. The truth, however, is that much of the equipment of most elements of the Canadian Forces is in an advanced state of obsolescence or is already obsolete. The maritime forces have too few operational vessels, very limited capacity to operate in the Arctic and no capability to keep Canadian waterways and harbours clear of mines. The land forces have severe equipment shortages and too few combat-ready

soldiers, and the Militia is too small, ill-equipped, and insufficiently trained to make up the difference. The air forces suffer from a serious shortage of air transport to move troops and equipment to Europe in times of tension to sustain them during hostilities. They have too few maritime patrol aircraft. They lack sufficient numbers of modern weapons for the CF-18s and have no replacements for CF-18s lost in peacetime.[2]

An immediate solution was not at hand. No Canadian political party—once in power—could promise dramatic increases in defense spending that would buy an end to the travails of the Canadian Armed Forces. Rather, the Mulroney government more modestly promised to overcome "the results of decades of neglect" with what it called "a long-term solution: a steady, predictable and honest funding program based on consistent political leadership."[3]

The White Paper thus outlined a fifteen year program to provide the armed forces with the necessary equipment and personnel to fulfill commitments in Canada and in Europe. To pay for this program, the government promised that it would increase defense spending by at least 2 percent annually, in real terms. Further increases, it admitted, would "be necessary in some years as major projects forecast in this White Paper are introduced."[4] David Cox of Queen's University in Ontario and the Canadian Institute for International Peace and Security estimated that "Conservatively . . . the acquisition programme described in the paper would require 4 per cent real growth."[5]

Those major projects were to be undertaken within the context of the White Paper's two principal defense policy thrusts:

- a geographic *consolidation* of Canada's air and land efforts in defense of NATO Europe, focussing on Germany at the expense of Norway, without reducing the number of Canadian military roles on that continent;
- an *expansion* of Canadian sovereignty protection efforts to include for the first time, in the form of nuclear-powered attack submarines (SSNs), a Canadian naval presence under the ice in Arctic waters. These submarines were also to constitute an enhancement of Canada's contributions to NATO and Canada-U.S. antisubmarine warfare efforts.

The "long-term," we know, lasted until April 1989. The April cuts constituted more than just a case of mere belt tightening, for they included not only an immediate, five-year limitation on defense spending, but also the out and out abandonment of many of the reequipment and personnel plans that were central to the fifteen-year program outlined in *Challenge and Commitment.*[6]

In 1987 the government starkly warned that if underfunding "were allowed to continue unaltered, it would soon lead to 'rust out,' the unplanned and pervasive deterioration in the military capabilities of the Canadian Forces."[7] The Canadian Armed Forces now again face that condition. Worse, the commitments made in the White Paper—to many of which the Canadian government has nominally remained wedded, without the accompanying funding—have further aggravated the dilemma. Emerging from the confusion is the necessity for retrenchment.

To be sure, the minister of national defence, Bill McKnight, insisted for months after the release of the April budget statement that "The White Paper is not dead. Its basic parameters still remain the defence policy of the Canadian government."[8] But in early 1990 the government began to admit that Canadian defense policy would require rethinking: the 1989 cuts, it conceded, would "have far-reaching implications for defence policy and will be felt across the full range of defence activities. . . . There is no longer any internal flexibility to absorb any further major reductions against the . . . current range of commitments."[9] The new Chief of the Defence Staff, General John de Chastelain, put the reality in still starker terms.

> . . . Canadians have to ask themselves at a certain point: "Do we want a defence force." If so, what are they prepared to pay for it? If you go much beyond the level we have now, we won't have a defence force.[10]

A general review by the Mulroney government of Canadian defense policy is now underway. That review is expected to be released in 1991.

The state of each of the three Canadian combat elements will now be considered in turn. In 1967 the three armed services were unified into the single-service Canadian Armed Forces under a single Chief of the Defense Staff. After years of reshuffling, three major commands emerged that in reality are the air force, navy and army, and are informally referred to as such. Formally, they are titled Air Command (AIRCOM), Maritime Command (MARCOM) and Mobile Command (FMC, after its French name).

THE AIR FORCE[11]

Challenge and Commitment affected AIRCOM the least among the armed forces. But the 1989 budget cuts will affect it substantially.

The air force is temporarily in the best shape of the three armed forces, as a result of its recent acquisition, authorized by the Trudeau government, of 138 CF-18 fighter aircraft, a version of the F/A-18 *Hornet*. The last of these was acquired in September 1988.

Nonetheless, the inventory is stretched extremely thin (see Table 3.1). The fighters are now organized into eight squadrons, three based in Germany and five in Canada. The squadrons in Germany, originally planned to total fifty-four aircraft, constitute 1 Canadian Air Group

TABLE 3.1
PEACETIME DEPLOYMENT OF CF-18 AIRCRAFT
IN CANADA AND GERMANY EARLY 1989

Squadron	Location	Aircraft (1989)
410 (Op Training)	Cold Lake	23
441	Cold Lake/Comox	12
425	Bagotville/Goose	12
416	Cold Lake*	12
433	Bagotville*	12
Aerospace Engineering Test Establishment	Cold Lake	2+
War reserve/attrition assests		6+
SUBTOTAL	**CANADA**	**79**
409	Baden-Soellingen	16
421	Baden-Soellingen	16
439	Baden-Soellingen	16
SUBTOTAL	**GERMANY**	**54**
TOTAL		133

*Rapid reinforcement squadrons committed to Germany

NOTE: This chart reflects official deployment figures as of early 1989. Figures reflecting more current deployment of the inventory of 127 (August 1990) are not available.

Sources: Department of National Defence; Martin Shadwick, York University (with thanks)

(1CAG) and operate at two Canadian Forces Bases, Baden-Soellingen and Lahr, both located in southwestern Germany at the edge of the Back Forest, just a few miles from the French border. In wartime they would undertake conventional air-to-ground and air defense roles as part of the 4th Allied Tactical Air Force.

Base conditions for the Canadian forces in Germany are not good, inasmuch as the air squadrons share the two crowded facilities with units of the Canadian army. In wartime, Lahr would be the principal airbase; in peacetime it is the heart of army operations. "There is no doubt," recently observed General Manson, "that we face a serious problem in trying to bring our infrastructure in Europe to the level where it can provide us with adequate facilities for the units in theatre, and for the assigned formations and units which will be deployed in a crisis."[12] Accordingly, the 1987 defense White Paper included the pledge to reduce what it called "the mutual interference of colocated land and air forces" in Europe.[13]

Yet the White Paper also complicated the mutual interference problem. The five Canada-based CF-18 squadrons are based at Cold Lake, Alberta and Bagotville, Québec (with small detachments of aircraft at Goose Bay, Labrador, and Comox, British Columbia). Two of these squadrons were dedicated to the rapid reinforcement of Norway. Arguing that these squadrons constitute "a small force which would be much more effectively employed as part of a concentrated air commitment in those locations where we have already made large investments in survivable support facilities tailored to the unique requirements of the CF-18," the White Paper announced a switching of destinations for the aircraft from Norway to the Canadian bases in southern Germany where, in a crisis, they would join the three squadrons located there to form a Canadian air division.[14] Still further complicating mutual interference was the accompanying announcement that the army's reinforcement efforts would also be switched from Norway to Germany.

Of the three remaining Canada-based squadrons, one is for operational training; the other two are committed to NORAD roles. These North American roles will be discussed in chapter VI. However, it should be noted here that the thinness of the fighter aircraft inventory in Canada devoted to North American air defense is not covered by reserve or auxiliary squadrons, the way the Air National Guard squadrons back up the U.S. Air Force for air defense in the United States. There simply are no extra aircraft.

The 1989 budget cuts dealt two heavy blows to the air force. First, as General Manson conveyed the unhappy news to the Canadian Armed Forces, all "major items of equipment and infrastructure for our land and air forces in Europe . . . have been put on hold."[15]

Far more significantly, though, the Mulroney government shocked the air force with the announcement that replacements would not be purchased for CF-18 aircraft lost through normal peacetime attrition. This was to be the case despite the explicit pledge in *Challenge and Commitment* that "We will maintain the strength of our fleet of CF-18 aircraft and arm them effectively."[16]

Eleven CF-18 aircraft have already been lost. Several can be expected to be lost every year, at a rate highly dependent on the number of flying hours the air force now exacts from its increasingly scarce inventory. As that inventory wears thinner and thinner, AIRCOM could be obliged within the next several years to curtail the number of squadrons and abandon commitments.[17]

THE ARMY

For several years, the Canadian army has faced three major problems: a geographic fragmentation of combat responsibilities resulting from commitments in Germany, Norway, and Canada; inadequate equipment;

and insufficient personnel. *Challenge and Commitment* outlined policies to help remedy all three.

The army's combat forces are organized into four brigade-sized units of over 4000 personnel each (see Table 3.2). One of them, 4 Canadian Mechanized Brigade Group (4CMBG), is located at the Lahr and Baden-Soellingen bases. 4CMBG is committed to the NATO Central Army Group Commander's tactical reserve. In wartime, it would move forward, to the east, thereby largely freeing Lahr for air force operations.

TABLE 3.2
PEACETIME DEPLOYMENT OF THE CANADIAN ARMY'S COMBAT UNITS IN CANADA AND GERMANY, EARLY 1989

CANADA

1 Canadian Brigade Group (1CBG)
Western Canada

4300 personnel
1 light armored regiment, 3 mechanized infantry brigades, 1 artillery regiment, 1 engineer regiment, support units

Principal wartime tasks: provision of one battalion group for AMF-L on NATO northern flank, provision of reinforcement personnel

Special Service Force (SSF)
Ontario

4100 personnel
1 light armored regiment, 1 infantry batallion, 1 airborne regiment, 1 artillery regiment, 1 engineer regiment, 1 support unit

Principal wartime tasks: home defense

5ième Groupe-brigade du Canada (5GBC)
Quebec (small component in Maritimes)

4300 personnel
1 light armored regiment (Cougar and Lynx armored vehicles), 3 mechanized infantry batallions, 1 artillery regiment, 1 air defense battery, 1 engineer regiment, support units

Principal wartime task: deployment to Germany

GERMANY

4 Canadian Mechanized Brigade Group (4CMBG)
Lahr and Baden-Soellingen

4400 personnel
1 armored regiment (77 Leopards), 2 mechanized infantry batallions, 1 artillery regiment, 1 engineer regiment, support units; one helicopter squadron

Principal wartime task: committed to SACEUR strategic reserve

Sources: *Challenge and Commitment;* IISS, *Military Balance,* 1989

The other three brigades are in Canada: one in the western provinces, one in Ontario, and one in Québec and the Maritime provinces. The Special Service Force (SSF), in Ontario, is light and air-transportable. It includes the army's only airborne regiment, which is committed to defense operations within Canada, including those against low-level incursions such as commando raids in the north.[18] The westernmost, 1 Canadian Brigade Group (1CBG) would have the task of providing, in an emergency, personnel to bring 4CMBG up to wartime strength.

1CBG also has the task of providing a battalion-group of about 1200 troops to the NATO Northern Flank as part of the Allied Mobile Force-Land, which is NATO's "fire brigade: a relatively light, multinational, brigade-sized, quick reaction unit. AMF-L deployment on the Northern Flank would be intended as a signal to the Soviet Union of allied solidarity and determination to defend the alliance's northern region. While relatively small in numbers, the Canadian commitment is in good shape. Most of the battalion-group's troops, their equipment (including vehicles), and support units can arrive in Norway in AIRCOM transport planes in a matter of days. This commitment was left in place by the White Paper and not immediately affected by budget cuts.

It is the brigade in Québec (with a small component in the Maritime), the 5ième Groupe-brigade du Canada (5GBC) that has been, and remains problematic. It, too, was committed to reinforce Norway. In theory, it could have made a significant contribution there. As a senior official of the U.S. Department of Defense assessed its quality:

> [It] is of the size, training, and equipment needed to have a major impact upon the battle and is also experienced in the Arctic conditions of northern Norway. It is equipped to survive and fight effectively in that kind of weather and terrain, having a large component of over-snow vehicles. It has significant fire support, anti-armor potential and, unlike most other potential NATO reinforcements, also has some organic air defense.[19]

But Canada lacks sufficient air transport to carry 5GBC's equipment across the Atlantic. Some equipment for its use was stocked in North Norway and is now being left in Norway for use by the Canadian AMF-L battalion-group. But most equipment would have been carried in Norwegian merchant shipping, requiring a transit time of at least two weeks. The military utility of the commitment was predicated on its arrival in Norway *before* the outbreak of hostilities, for two reasons. First, the stocked equipment was placed not in a hardened facility, but above ground. Second, given the ferocious struggle which would break out in the Atlantic Ocean and in particular, the Norwegian Sea, it would be all but impossible for the brigade's Norwegian merchant shipping to arrive in North Norway before the beginning of hostilities. It was hard, although not impossible, to construct a scenario which would have afforded the kind of warning time necessary to get the equipment across to Norway.

Moreover, Canada lacked the necessary infrastructure on the ground in Norway to provide the logistic and medical support for the brigade. A 1986 test exercise of the commitment demonstrated that this lack would have lead to catastrophic consequences for the brigade's troops if they were ever committed to battle in Norway.[20] Canadian soldiers have taken to calling the brigade commitment to Norway "Hong Kong in the snow," an allusion to the bitter memory of the devastation that befell an ill-prepared Canadian army unit at the fall of that British Crown Colony in 1941.

Thus, the Mulroney government, as it had with the two rapid reinforcement air squadrons, switched 5GBC's destination from Norway to Germany, where it would join 4CMBG thereby "enabling the Canadian army to field a division-sized force in a crisis. The resulting combat power will be enhanced and made more effective than what could have been achieved by two separately deployed brigades."[21] Over time, equipment for 5GBC would be prepositioned in Germany, additional airlift capability would be acquired, and logistic and medical resources enhanced. A division headquarters is to be established for the "two-brigade posture."

To fight in Germany, the Canadian army would need a host of new equipment, including new tactical command, control and communications systems. At the top of the list of necessary equipment, though, is armor. The army's 114 Leopard tanks are aging. Moreover, only 4CMBG has a full complement of 77 Leopards; the other 37 being located in Canada for training purposes. Accordingly, the White Paper promised the acquisition of new main battle tanks for the two brigades, along with the other necessary equipment.

If Canadian reinforcements were indeed sent off in wartime to Norway and Germany, the Canadian army would face a severe personnel shortage. It would be left with very few regular soldiers in Canada to help civilian authorities maintain order, it would lack sufficient numbers of support personnel for combat forces, and it would find it extraordinarily difficult to sustain combat force levels in Europe in the face of battle casualties.[22] In theory, the army's ranks would be filled by members of the Militia (army reserve). But their numbers are very small. Canada, in fact, is the only NATO country where regular forces outnumber reservists.[23] Moreover, as a senior army official recently observed, "the Militia is simply not able to produce the necessary reinforcement and sustainment forces, regardless of their earnest desire to do so. This is attributable to the simple reality that over a long period of time Militia training support, equipment, and facilities have been inadequate for their needs."[24]

Challenge and Commitment promised to remedy this with a modernization program for the reserves. While all three services would be involved, the army would be the largest beneficiary. Not only was the army reserve to be expanded and reequipped, but the army itself was to be reorganized according to a hybrid model that it called the "Total Force Concept," whereby reservists and reserve units could be rapidly incorporated into wartime forces.[25]

The 1989 cuts have been nothing short of devastating for the army. The increase in the size of the reserves will be cut back, although the government has not yet released the details. Funds for training and re-equipping the reserves are also to be cut. As the Canadian Institute of Strategic Studies assessed the impact of the cuts on the reserves, "The punch-drunk Canadian militia was just beginning to recover from decades of neglect—just in time for a knockout blow. The coming tight fiscal policies may well nickel and dime many units to death."[26]

But it has been the out and out termination of the plans to reequip 5GBC that has truly shocked the army. New tanks are *not* to be purchased for it, the government announced in 1989. Moreover, authority to buy tanks for 4CMBG has been put "on hold."[27]

Having canceled the purchases necessary for 5GBC, the only responsible course of action for the government would have been the cancellation, as well, of its commitment to Germany as a reinforcement unit. Without tanks and other necessary equipment the brigade-group cannot fight on the central front. And indeed, the day after the budget announcement, the Chief of the Defence Staff informed the Canadian Armed Forces that "we will not proceed with the establishment of a land division for the central region."[28]

Yet, remarkably, General de Chastelain, then Vice Chief of the Defence Staff was dispatched two weeks later to appear before a Senate committee, where he made the public announcement that 5GBC would remain committed to Germany—despite its lack of armor and equipment, and the earlier statement by the Chief of the Defence Staff. As the Vice Chief told the committee,

> I should mention here that the original, and by the same token, the current plan to field the combined force . . . without new equipment *entails some risk*. However, it was considered that in the present circumstances of negotiations towards Force reductions in Europe, *this risk was acceptable in the short term*. Studies are now being conducted within the Department to examine the consequences of all the budgetary options. These consequences will be discussed, initially among ministers and subsequently with NATO through the usual consultation process. (emphasis added)[29]

The "cancellation of the cancellation" as it is being called in Ottawa, seems to have been precipitated by the Mulroney government's unwillingness to admit to a reduction in the Canadian commitment to Germany on the eve of a NATO heads of government meeting which the prime minister attended. Moreover, as the Vice Chief's statement indicated, the government hopes to keep the paper reinforcement brigade commitment on the books long enough to be able to offer it up as a Canadian contribution to conventional force reductions in Europe.

The Canadian army, for its part, still reeling from the loss of reequipment authority for 5GBC, from the postponement of the reequipment of 4CMBG, and from the limitations being placed on the implementation of the "Total Force Concept" has begun to consider a future in which its NATO responsibilities will be, at the very least, drastically reduced.

THE NAVY

Antisubmarine warfare is MARCOM's focus. The navy's rescue was a centerpiece of *Challenge and Commitment,* prompting the MARCOM commander to write, upon the release of the White Paper, that his service was "poised and ready to embark on one of the brightest eras in its 78-year history."[30] In the wake of the 1989 cuts, that bright era, it is now clear, will not be materializing.

Thirty years ago what was then called the Royal Canadian Navy could put to sea a formidable fleet of forty-five major combat vessels, including an aircraft carrier, HMCS *Bonaventure.* Ties with the U.S. Navy were close, Canadian responsibilities under NATO and Canada-U.S. naval arrangements were fairly extensive, and the reputation of Canadian sailors was impressive.

But years of financial neglect have left MARCOM in bad shape (see Table 3.3). Its ships are surprisingly few in number and "obsolete, dangerous to men at any time and out of their league in a modern wartime scenario at sea."[31] Of MARCOM's twenty destroyers and frigates, all but four helicopter-carrying DDH 280 *Iroquois* or *Tribal* class destroyers are completely antiquated. Many of the sixteen aged vessels are being kept in service largely by dubious "destroyer life-extension" (DELEX) measures, although several have been simply left tied up in port. The *Tribals* are themselves fifteen years old and at least a generation behind in their capability. MARCOM's three conventionally powered *Oberon*-class submarines (SSKs), deployed on the Atlantic coast, are aged, being based on World War II and 1950s technologies and having entered service in the mid-1960s. Their chief role has been that of training the crews of aircraft and surface ships in the detection of submarines, a task they will continue to perform for several more years thanks to a Submarine Operational Update Program (SOUP).

The situation for naval aviation has not been as bad. In the mid-1970s MARCOM's air arm acquired a new long-range patrol aircraft (LRPA), dubbed the CP-140 Aurora, a version of the USN's P-3 Orion. While the Aurora is certainly a capable ASW platform, the eighteen Canadian aircraft are too few, especially since they must be divided among

TABLE 3.3
EAST AND WEST COAST DEPLOYMENT OF
CANADIAN PRINCIPAL NAVAL FORCES 1989

	East Coast	West Coast
DDH-280 *Tribal*-class destroyers	3	1
Other destroyers/frigates*	9	7
Reserve destroyers/frigates*	1	2
Oberon-class submarines*	3	0
Aurora long-range patrol aircraft	14	4
Tracker medium-range patrol aircraft#	15	3
Sea King ASW helicopters**	31	4

*Vessels obsolete or approaching obsolescence
#Ordered out of service, April 1989
**Approaching obsolescence; replacement in project definition stage

ON ORDER:

12 *City*-class patrol frigates
12 minesweeping-patrol vessels
3 Arcturus long-range patrol aircraft

CANCELLED:

10–12 nuclear-powered attack submarines
6 additional Aurora long-range patrol aircraft

Sources: *Challenge and Commitment*, 1989 budget documents.

operations in the Atlantic, Pacific and Arctic regions. The Auroras were complemented by eighteen aged but still serviceable Tracker medium-range patrol aircraft. The Trackers were useful for ASW, especially inasmuch as they were the only maritime aircraft MARCOM had with air to surface offensive capability, in the form of rockets, and were a mainstay of maritime operations to enforce sovereignty, especially pollution and fishing regulations.

The low point for Canada's naval forces may very well have been reached in 1983. That year a former MARCOM commander told the Canadian Senate's Subcommittee on National Defence that he simply would not, if he were still in command, authorize the sixteen decrepit vessels to go "to sea in a modern war, and I have even doubts about the four Iroquois 280 class."[32] The subcommittee itself concluded that MARCOM "cannot meet its commitments to the protection of Canadian sovereignty, to the defence of North America—much less to NATO." Its equipment, the Committee went on, was "barely adequate in peacetime" and "by any measure, wholly inadequate in wartime."[33]

But a turn-around, albeit a modest one, in the Canadian fleet's fortunes began in 1983. Faced with the prospect of a four-ship navy, the

Liberal government announced a construction program for six modern helicopter-carrying *City* class ASW patrol frigates, with the possibility of fourteen more being built in "batches" of six and eight each, if subsequently authorized. The first ship of the first "batch," HMCS *Halifax,* is behind schedule and is now expected for 1991.

The government also authorized a thorough overhaul of the four DDH 280 *Tribal* class destroyers, dubbed the Tribal Class Update and Modernization Program (TRUMP), scheduled to be completed in 1992. A host of improvements is involved. Among them, the propulsion and machinery control systems are being replaced and the hull improved. Significantly, each overhauled *Tribal* will also be able to provide area air defense and serve as a command ship for newly-formed Canadian ASW task groups. Since HMCS *Bonaventure* left service in 1970, Canadian helicopter-carrying destroyers in the Atlantic had been tasked out individually on a piecemeal basis for Canadian, Canada-U.S. or NATO exercises. This created operational inefficiencies, as well as logistic headaches for MARCOM. Each new task group to be formed around a "TRUMPed" *Tribal* will eventually include several modern patrol frigates, as they become available. The frigates and the destroyers will be equipped with new ASW helicopters to replace the thirty-five aging "Sea King" helicopters now in service.

As the Canadian navy made do, and awaited the arrival of better equipment, the geographic demands made of it increased. MARCOM's emphasis has long been on NATO-related ASW tasks in the North Atlantic, where the bulk of its vessels, including all three submarines, all four *Tribals,* all its other ships capable of carrying ASW helicopters, as well as all but four of its Aurora long-ranged patrol aircraft were deployed. Cynics had taken to calling MARCOM's western subordinate, Maritime Command Pacific (MARPAC), headquartered at Esquimalt, on Vancouver Island in British Columbia, the "West Coast Sailing Club."[34]

MARCOM has just modestly "rebalanced" its fleet between the Atlantic and Pacific. One *Tribal,* HMCS *Huron,* has now been relocated to Esquimalt, while an antiquated destroyer has been moved from the west coast to Halifax. This has had the immediate effect of providing MARPAC with maritime ASW helicopter capability. Eventually one "TRUMPed" vessel will form the heart of a Pacific ASW task force. Two other task forces are to be formed in the Atlantic, with a fourth *Tribal,* also to be deployed out of Halifax, available to serve as relief flagship for the three task forces or with NATO's multinational Standing Naval Force Atlantic, to which Canada always contributes a vessel.

The "rebalancing" of the fleet was prompted by a combination of strategic, sovereignty, and domestic political concerns. Soviet SSN activity in the northeast Pacific has increased, drawn by the presence of the USN base for *Trident* SSBNs on Puget Sound at Bangor, Washington.

Tridents leaving or returning to Bangor pass through the Straits of Juan de Fuca, through which the Canada-U.S. border runs. Soviet SSNs attempt to pick up and trail the U.S. SSBNs in nearby Pacific waters. Soviet SSNs carrying short-range SLCMs and Soviet SSBNs have also been present in peacetime off North America's Pacific coast. This has led to the familiar problem for Canada of either undertaking itself at least some of the surveillance of the Soviet boats necessary in and near Canadian waters, or leaving the job entirely to the Americans. Sovereignty and security concerns together militated in favor of the increased Canadian presence, especially since without substantial naval assets in the Pacific, MARPAC has not been provided with the same access to U.S. ASW data Canadian forces in the Atlantic have long enjoyed.

Canada's "Eurocentric" defense emphasis has sometimes irritated Western Canadians. Observed two British Columbia scholars: "Governments in Ottawa have usually centred Canada's military efforts and attention on Western Europe and the north Atlantic links to it . . . Disgruntled western Canadians have frequently complained that Ontarians and Québécois act as if Canada ended at the Rocky Mountains rather than the Pacific shore."[35] The small increase in MARPAC's forces probably also represents a political response by Ottawa to these complaints.

The final step in the rescue of MARCOM from oblivion was to have been the replacement of the three *Oberon*-class SSKs with newer boats, also conventionally powered. A Canadian Submarine Acquisition Program (CASAP) office was opened in the Department of National Defence, and began to consider eight European designs. While the Senate Subcommittee and many defense analysts concluded that a minimum of ten submarines would be necessary to provide enough boats for operational roles in both the Atlantic and Pacific, as opposed to mainly training roles in the Atlantic performed by the aged "O-boats," the CASAP program operated on the assumption that funds could initially be found only for four new SSKs. Canada would still have been without a naval presence in the Arctic. Ice cover there prevents SSKs from coming to the surface for the air needed by their batteries and inhibits operations by surface naval vessels.

This timidity was swept away by the Progressive Conservative government's bold step, announced in *Challenge and Commitment,* of canceling the CASAP program in favor of the acquisition of ten to twelve SSNs, at a projected "sail-away" cost for the boats themselves of C$5 billion, with projected acquisition costs for shore and other support facilities on the order of C$2–3 billion, all spread over twenty years, in constant 1987 dollars. It also announced that a fixed, under-ice submarine detection system would be constructed in the Canadian Arctic. To help meet these costs, the proposed third batch of eight patrol frigates was canceled. On the other hand, the government did give its approval to the construction of the second batch of six vessels as well as minesweepers to be operated by the naval reserves. All twelve patrol frigates are expected to be in service in the late 1990s. Six additional LRPAs were also to be purchased, to relieve that strain on the eighteen aircraft in service, and to permit enhanced operations in the Arctic.

The roughly C$800 million cost per boat of the most advanced U.S. SSNs put them out of Canada's price range. Instead, the Canadian government considered a French and a British design for boats that were to be built, in increasingly large portions, in Canada. At the outset, Canadian naval officials clearly preferred a British design, the *Trafalgar* class, "a deep-water attack boat designed to operate in Arctic conditions" which also had "the supreme advantage of being one of the world's quietest nuclear attack boats."[36] The French entry, the *Amethyste* update of the *Rubis* class, a smaller, somewhat slower boat than the British design, was not only reputed to be noisier, but the original design could not operate in Arctic waters or accommodate the U.S. torpedo MARCOM wanted to use. The French promised the necessary modifications. Cost considerations favored the French: Canadian officials estimated the cost of building in Canada *Rubis/Amethyste* boats at C$350 million as opposed to C$500 million for the *Trafalgar* (constant 1987 dollars). Moreover, to sell the *Trafalgar* design to Canada, the British would have needed the permission of the United States, including the U.S. Congress, because its reactor technology is U.S. in origin.

Challenge and Commitment emphasized that Canadian SSNs would provide MARCOM with a balanced fleet of surface vessels, aircraft and submarines affording it greater Pacific and Atlantic ASW capability. In the Pacific, diesel submarines could in fact perform equally well as SSNs MARPAC's close to shore ASW roles. However, as the Canadian Institute of Strategic Studies argued, "Nuclear powered subs are clearly superior for Canada's Atlantic fleet. . . . The requirement to be able to move long distances quickly, to manoeuvre extensively fully submerged for long periods of time while remaining concealed, and to carry the more complex combat systems required for ASW operations in the Atlantic makes the diesel much less capable than the nuclear sub."[37]

And for Arctic operations, only SSNs would do. The attraction of what the white paper called a "three ocean navy" clinched the SSN decision. Working in conjunction with the fixed-under ice detection system, Canadian SSNs would have undertaken peacetime patrols in the Canadian Arctic region, presumably in cooperation with the USN, to detect and trail Soviet submarines.[38]

Canadian officials made it clear that in peacetime Canadian SSNs would not be authorized to attack any Soviet submarine that had violated Canadian sovereignty by entering the waters Canada considers to be internal. Instead, they were to "log the location, the time and the character of the submarine," information to be used in subsequent diplomatic and legal proceedings.[39] Encountering a Soviet submarine, Canadian SSNs may also have been instructed "to communicate to him the fact that he has been identified, that his geographic position is such and such and that he is in Canadian waters and that he should leave or surface."[40] However, they might alternatively have been instructed not to reveal their own position in the region.

Not surprisingly, the Canadian SSN program was also intended to strengthen Canadian Arctic sovereignty in the face of U.S. submarine operations in the region. After all, it is the United States, not the Soviet Union, which denies that the waters of the Northwest Passage are internal to Canada. Not for a moment did the Canadian government ever even hint at the possibility of attempting to use SSNs to close the disputed passage to U.S. submarines; it is unthinkable that it would. Nor did the Mulroney government assert that the very presence of Canadian SSNs in the region would have nailed down Canada's sovereignty claims.

Rather, as seen in the last chapter, it is the oldest goal of post-World War II Canadian sovereignty protection that, to the extent possible, defense activities undertaken in Canada not be left entirely to U.S. forces, especially in the north. As Perrin Beatty put it in the case of the SSNs, "If we claim these are our sovereign waters, one of the things we should be doing is developing the capacity to patrol it. If we contract out the defence of these waters to somebody else, it certainly weakens our case in terms of sovereignty."[41] Moreover, Canada, once its boats were operating and the fixed, under-ice detection system installed, would have been able to monitor the movements of U.S. submarines in the Canadian Arctic. Indeed, acquiring the independent capability to verify U.S. movements "appears to be one of MARCOM's key objectives in acquiring a fleet of SSNs."[42] This would have obliged the United States to come to some kind of *modus vivendi* with MARCOM for operating in Canadian Arctic waters.

The April 1989 cuts dealt MARCOM three heavy blows: the SSN acquisition program was terminated, the acquisition of the six new Auroras was also terminated, and the Trackers were ordered out of service. On the other hand, the navy is still to be equipped with the twelve patrol frigates, and minesweepers. The government has also promised to build the fixed, under-ice system in the Arctic and to provide MARCOM with several conventional submarines.

The Canadian SSN program never found a constituency outside the navy and the defense contractors who would have been involved in building the boats. In Canada, opponents raised several objections.

First, there was widespread skepticism about the government's estimates of the costs of the submarines. Canada's small shipbuilding industry has never built a modern submarine, much less a nuclear-powered one. But, as a Canadian academic commentator observed, "the practical reality is that the cost of servicing, refueling, and training on nuclear submarines is entirely outside previous Canadian naval experience."[43] If costs eventually got out of hand, the SSNs could have become "the centerpiece not simply of the Canadian Navy, but of the Canadian Armed Forces as well."[44]

Second, opponents argued that Canadian acquisition of SSNs would have damaged the international regime of nuclear nonproliferation and thereby "tarnish Canada's long-standing image as a leading proponent of nonproliferation and . . . diminish its highly respected status and influence in the United Nations."[45] Canada committed itself under the Nuclear Nonproliferation Treaty of 1968 not to acquire nuclear weapons and to observe the safeguards of the International Atomic Energy Agency on the transfer of nuclear materials that might be used to make such weapons. To fuel SSNs, Canada would have needed to import enriched uranium, which is also capable of being used for nuclear weapons. As the aegis of the IAEA currently extends only to civilian projects, the fuel would have been withdrawn from its safeguards. No one feared that Canada actually would have used the fuel to build weapons. Rather, critics charged that the withdrawal would set a bad precedent for other non-nuclear weapon states contemplating the acquisition of SSNs (with Brazil at the head of the list) that might take advantage of the opportunity.[46]

Third, opposition political parties, while recognizing the sacrosanct necessity of protecting Canadian Arctic sovereignty, insisted that SSNs were unnecessary for the task. Instead, the fixed, under-ice detection system, they insisted, should provide sufficient information concerning the presence of submarines in Canadian waters to allow for diplomatic protests. The opposition parties also argued that the boats would contribute to the militarization of the Arctic, and associate Canada with the U.S. Navy's efforts to destroy Soviet nuclear missile-carrying submarines, thereby contributing to international instability.

By far most important, though, was the vague, but still often intensely-held feelings that Canada just had no business with any weapon system that was labeled "nuclear-powered" and "attack." Canada would thereby abandon, as the Liberal Party leader, John Turner, put it, "the traditional deterrent roles of our armed forces."[47] Largely as a result of these feelings, opinion polls continually showed weak public support for the SSN program, despite the government's efforts to sell it.[48]

Washington was no more enthusiastic than the domestic opponents. Pentagon officials shared the doubts about Ottawa's cost estimates and, for reasons to be outlined in chapter VIII, the U.S. Navy was upset about the potential impact on its own under-ice operations of Canadian SSNs.[49]

The Progressive Conservative government originally expected kudos from Washington for the contributions to collective security Canadian SSNs could make and accolades from Canadian nationalists for the role the boats would play in protecting Canada's Arctic sovereignty. Instead, the government discovered that the submarine acquisition program, far from being welcomed either by the U.S. government or Canadian nationalists, had become a domestic and international political liability. And so it was canceled.

MARCOM has been given to understand that the Mulroney government will equip it with a very small fleet of replacement submarines, probably numbering four, all to be based on the East Coast. This is not only far fewer than the ten to twelve SSNs, but the government is not prepared to restore the "third batch" of patrol frigates that was sacrificed for the SSN program. The fleet is thus to consist in the late 1990s of the four Tribals, twelve patrol frigates and, in all probability, four conventionally-powered submarines (SSKs).

A small, balanced fleet in the Pacific appears now out of the question. On the East Coast, MARCOM is confronted with a difficult choice. With its three *Oberon*-class boats facing complete obsolescence the temptation will be strong to recommend the swift purchase of SSKs from an allied country either "off the shelf" or involving some construction in Canada. This would entail the abandonment, at least in the short run, of hopes of submarine operations in Arctic waters. There is, however, substantial interest among the Canadian naval community in the development and acquisition of hybrid submarine technology that would permit Arctic operations. This technology, which also will be discussed in chapter VIII, is still under development.

In the meantime, the Canadian navy will not be entirely without new equipment for Arctic operations. In June 1989, McKnight announced that to partially replace the canceled six additional Aurora LRPA's, three P-3 airframes would be bought from Lockheed Corp. for the Canadian navy's Maritime Air Group at a cost of $265 million. Each is to become a new Arctic patrol aircraft, to be called the Arcturus. The acquisition, said the minister in his public statement, "is a cost-effective measure to address the need to effectively patrol Canada's coastline and enforce our sovereignty." The Arcturus will be able to do little more than fly the Canadian flag in the high north. The aircraft will be equipped only with standard navigation and weather radar facilities. No ASW equipment, no special equipment for pollution detection and no fisheries surveillance equipment is to be carried. Faced with reporters incredulous at the announcement, McKnight's assistant could only respond that "The minister knows exactly what he is buying."[50] Nonetheless, Arcturus flights will replace those currently being undertaken in the Arctic by the more-capable Aurora LRPA, usefully freeing them for ASW duties.

THE LOOMING RETRENCHMENT TO NORTH AMERICA

"We are still resolved," McKnight insisted in 1989, "to narrow and eventually close the gap between our military commitments and our defence capabilities."[51] It is hard to escape the conclusion that the only way for this to occur will be through a reduction of Canadian commitments in Europe in favor of those in North America. The only open question is whether Ottawa will retain *any* military presence in Germany. Canadians are debating whether this was in fact the government's intent behind the cuts it selected.[52] Whatever the intent, though, the cancellation of critical components of the fifteen-year program will soon force choices between military roles at home and those abroad.

Roles at home will all but inevitably be favored. It remains the case that no Canadian government can ignore with impunity the demands of territorial sovereignty. Having fretted throughout much of the Second World War and then again in the 1950s and into the 1960s over the implications of the U.S. military presence in Canada; and then having seen, with satisfaction, that presence dwindle and all but disappear in the 1970s and 1980s, Canadians will be reluctant to turn defense operations in Canada back over to the U.S. forces. As a study released by the Canadian Institute for International Peace and Security put it, "A Canadian government which rejected its nominal responsibilities for asserting a Canadian military and government presence in the Canadian Arctic is likely to find itself in serious electoral difficulty. . . . Indeed, without Canadian participation, it is scarcely farfetched to envisage a future in which a wide band of the Canadian Arctic became, de facto, the exclusive area of military operation of the U.S."[53]

At the same time, the growing economic integration of Canada and the United States, culminating in the North American Free Trade Agreement of 1987, will probably exacerbate Canadian anxieties about national distinctiveness. The extraordinarily bitter 1988 general election in which a majority of Canadians voted for parties opposed to free trade brought these worries again to the fore.[54] Canadian anxieties could very well create strong incentives for Canadian governments, over the next decade or so as the Free Trade Agreement is implemented, to emphasize other areas of national distinctiveness, such as the northern or Arctic aspects of the Canadian heritage. The possibility of foreign, i.e., U.S., military operations on Canadian soil, especially in northern regions, could consequently become even more undesirable.

These feelings could further intensify if Québec leaves Canada (a possibility which will be discussed in chapter IX). In such a case the Canadian government, or both the Canadian and Québec governments might place an extra premium on the defense of national sovereignty.

The cancellation of the Canadian SSN program and the ensuing curtailment of the planned role for the Canadian navy under the Arctic ice can obscure the direction the April 1989 cuts point to. But, as explained above, the Mulroney government ended the program because of the immediate political liabilities it entailed at home and abroad, certainly not because of any lack of interest in Canadian Arctic sovereignty. The retention of the fixed under-ice system and the scramble to announce the last-minute acquisition of the toothless, flag-flying Arcturus aircraft attest to this.

The political imperatives are clearest and strongest in the case of the Canadian air force. North American air defense relies on relatively visible operations undertaken in Canadian airspace and from Canadian territory. These cannot be turned over to U.S. forces. For that reason the Canadianization of the old DEW Line into the North Warning System is proceeding apace, unaffected by the cuts. As AIRCOM loses aircraft through attrition, it might itself argue in favor of curtailing or abandoning its roles in Germany.

The army is in trouble. The handwriting is on the wall for 5GBC. Authority to purchase tanks and other necessary equipment for 4CMBG will probably never be taken off "hold."

In the present tight fiscal climate the army's need for new tanks and equipment competes with the navy's needs for new ships and submarines. The navy will have the upper hand, for naval forces in Canada—unlike tanks and other heavy army equipment in either Germany or Canada—can be devoted to both the protection of Canadian sovereignty and the fulfillment of NATO responsibilities.

The incentives for a Canadian pullback to North America will become all the greater if the United States decides that an expansion of North American aerospace or naval defenses, involving Canadian territory, airspace or waters, is necessary. This possibility will be explored in subsequent chapters.

As was discussed earlier, Canada's allies have in the past resisted Canadian retrenchment from the defense of Europe. However, the situation is now dramatically different. With the United States beginning its own reduction of forces in Europe, there is ample political room for such a Canadian step. The decision of the Mulroney government, announced in September 1990, to reduce the Canadian presence in Germany by 1400 personnel, is in all probability a harbinger.

Still, some minor Canadian contribution to the defense of Europe— even smaller than the present token force—would remain welcome. Despite the impending reduction of forces in Europe both East and West, including those from the United States, a continued U.S. conventional presence on the ground in Europe will clearly be desirable over the next decade in order to provide a sign of linkage to North American mobilization capability and U.S. strategic nuclear weaponry. There is thus very good reason to believe that very small *Canadian* ground or air contributions to the alliance will be valued by the European members as an additional symbol of North American commitment.

Indeed, U.S. forces in Europe, as they decrease in numbers, will come to resemble more than ever those of Canada in the roles they play as tokens of trans-Atlantic solidarity and of North American mobilization capability. Moreover, and just as important, the premium the NATO partners will be placing on demonstrating the full incorporation of German military efforts in a broader allied effort will probably also lead the allies to value a Canadian military presence on the ground in Germany.

This could consist of a small, light, army formation. In late 1989 the NATO Defense Planning Committee moved towards the creation of a multinational division for the Northern Army Group, to consist of British, German, Belgian and Dutch ground forces under an integrated headquarters. NATO will probably be considering the option of establishing a similar division in the Central Army Group, consisting of German, United States, Canadian and possibly even French forces. NATO's "London Declaration," issued by its heads of government in July 1990 confirmed that the alliance would be increasingly relying on such multinational units. Participation could be especially attractive for Canada, because a Canadian contribution to an integrated force would be cheap to equip and maintain.[55]

Alternatively, Canada may end its presence on the ground in Germany and limit itself to the reinforcement of either Germany or Norway from Canada-based units. This would fit smoothly into the new alliance force structure which is emerging whereby North America (chiefly the United States, of course) shifts towards mobilization capability as its contribution to European stability. Opting for just the reinforcement of Norway would also meet a real strategic need: the withdrawal of Soviet forces from Eastern Europe, now underway, back to the Soviet homeland enhances Soviet ability to threaten Norway with little warning, a development that has made the Oslo government decidedly nervous.

In short, if Ottawa wants to reduce dramatically its military commitments and expenses but still wants to remain directly involved in the defense of NATO Europe, in some very minor fashion, there are several options available to it. Given the Canadian financial crunch, and given the situation in Europe, it will be very surprising indeed if the Canadian government does not take such a step in the early 1990s.[56]

The possibility cannot be excluded that the Canadian government might even decide to play no active role at all in the defense of Europe. Ottawa could remind its allies, as a recent academic study has suggested, "that the Alliance is not an arrangement for North American defence of Western Europe but an agreement of all to defend the areas covered by the Atlantic Treaty; that North America, including its Pacific shores, is as much a part of the treaty area as is Western Europe; and that in view of the greater need to take part in the defence of North America, Canada was redeploying its effort within the treaty area."[57] However, the traditional desire to preserve Canada's seat at the European table will militate against this, especially if such a seat can be safeguarded at extremely low cost. In any event, the focus of Canadian defense policy in the 1990s will be, more than ever, on North America.

CANADIAN FORCES FOR A "NEW WORLD ORDER"?

Canada committed forces in January 1991 to the war against Iraq. The very small Canadian contingent in the Gulf, consisting of three ships (two destroyers and a supply vessel), one squadron of 24 CF-18 aircraft flown over from Germany and a field hospital unit, all with about 2000 personnel, constituted tangible support for the allied war effort and created a Canadian right to be consulted, especially by the U.S. The versatility of the CF-18 aircraft was demonstrated, as was, in the absence of the new patrol frigates, the rag-tag condition of the Canadian navy: weapons from museums were procured for the naval force in the Gulf.

Was the success of the U.S.-led multinational coalition in the Persian Gulf a unique event? Or was it the harbinger of what President Bush calls a "new world order," to which Canada might want to be able to contribute armed forces again? Since naval forces are by their nature highly mobile, this may be a new incentive for Canada to continue with the construction of the new patrol frigates.

However, there were some considerable misgivings in 1991 about Canadian involvement. "Many Canadians," observed the editor of *The Globe and Mail* with disapproval, "simply do not believe that we should be an actor in world events of this kind; we are, in essence neutral when the gauntlets go down; it is against our 'tradition' to join the battle when conflict occurs. . . ."[58]

NOTES

1. Canada, Department of National Defence, *Challenge and Commitment: A Defence Policy for Canada* (Ottawa: Minister of Supply and Services, 1987), 49.
2. Ibid., 43.
3. Ibid., 47.
4. Ibid., 67.
5. David Cox, short essay in the collection, "*Challenge and Commitment:* Comments on the Defence White Paper," *Behind the Headlines* 45, no. 1 (September 1987): 4.
6. The best (critical) summary of the 1989 cuts is "The 1989 Federal Budget: The Death of Defence?" Canadian Studies Institute of Strategic Studies, *Strategic Datalink,* May 1989, 12.

7. *Challenge and Commitment,* 45.
8. Speaking notes to ARMX dinner, Ottawa, 24 May 1989; text courtesy Department of National Defence.
9. Canada, Department of External Affairs, public guidance statement, "The 1990 Federal Budget," 19 February 1990.
10. *Legion,* May 1990, 6ff.
11. AIRCOM's combat air forces consist of fighter aircraft, tactical aircraft, and maritime aircraft. This section is limited to fighter aircraft, as tactical aircraft fall under the operational control of the army and maritime aircraft under the operational control of the navy.
12. General Paul Manson, "Consolidation in Europe: Implementing the White Paper," *Canadian Defence Quarterly,* 17, special number (1 February 1988): 30.
13. *Challenge and Commitment,* 64.
14. Ibid., 60.
15. Unclassified telex, National Defence Headquarters, Ottawa, Chief of the Defence Staff to Canadian Forces, 27 April 1989.
16. *Challenge and Commitment,* 56.
17. Because of the political sensitivity of the issue, the air force declines to estimate the rate at which it might have to curtail squadron numbers.
18. Canada-U.S. arrangements also exist to deal with this remote possibility. See Canada, House of Commons, Standing Committee on External Affairs and National Defence, *Minutes of Proceedings,* 3 October 1985, 33:20–21.
19. Jon L. Lellenberg, "The Military Balance," in *Deterrence and Defense in the North,* ed. Johan Jorgen Holst (Oslo: Norwegian University Press, 1985): 61.
20. For a report on the 1986 exercise, dubbed BRAVE LION, see Lieutenant-Colonel G. D. Hunt, "Reinforcing the NATO North Flank: The Canadian Experience," *Canadian Defence Quarterly* 16, no. 4 (Spring 1987): 31.
21. *Challenge and Commitment,* 62.
22. To meet its wartime commitments, the army estimates it would need 88,000 personnel, whereas it has only about 41,000. Brigadier-General Gordon J. O'Connor (Project Director, Army Structure Implementation, National Defence Headquarters), "Effective Reserves: The Challenge of the Total Force Army," *Canadian Defence Quarterly* 18, no. 5 (April 1989): 19.
23. In 1987 the army's regular force personnel strength was 22,500; while the primary militia strength was 15,500.
24. Ibid., 19.
25. Ibid. See also Colonel Brian S. MacDonald, "The White Paper, the Army Reserve and Army Reform, 1987–2002," *Canadian Defence Quarterly* 17, no. 4 (1988): 9.
26. "The 1989 Federal Budget: The Death of Defence?"
27. Unclassified telex, National Defence Headquarters, Ottawa, Chief of the Defence Staff to Canadian Forces, 17 April 1989.
28. Ibid.
29. Notes for VCDS Presentation to the Special Committee of the Senate, 16 May 1989; text courtesy Department of National Defence.
30. Vice-Admiral Charles M. Thomas, "A Message from the Commander of Maritime Command," *Canada's Navy Annual* (Calgary: Corvus Publishing Group, 1988), 8.

31. "Fleets of the Future," *Canada's Navy Annual* (Calgary: Corvus Publishing Group, 1986), 86.
32. Canada, Senate, Standing Committee on Foreign Affairs, Subcommittee on National Defence, *Proceedings*, 8 February 1983, 38:25.
33. Canada, Senate, Standing Committee on Foreign Affairs, Subcommittee on National Defence, *Canada's Maritime Defence*, May 1983, 2, 35.
34. As quoted in P. J. Taggart, "Canada's Blind Spot," U.S. Naval Institute *Proceedings* 113/3/1009 (March 1987): 145.
35. Frank Langdon and Douglas Ross, "Towards a Canadian Maritime Strategy in the North Pacific Region," *International Journal* 42, no. 4 (Autumn 1987): 860.
36. James Bagnall, "British Boat Must Navigate Past Obstacles," and "Cost Key Factor for Adjustments to French Sub," *Financial Post*, 8 February 1988, 42.
37. Brian S. MacDonald, "A Nuclear Navy for Canada," *Strategic Datalink*, Canadian Institute of Strategic Studies, 1987.
38. The fixed, under-ice detection system is still in the planning stages. A discussion of where its elements might be located and how it might be operated is to be found in Rear-Admiral F. W. Crickard, "An Anti-Submarine Warfare Capability in the Arctic: A National Requirement," *Canadian Defence Quarterly* 16, no. 4 (Spring 1987): 24.
39. Canada, House of Commons, *Debates* 9 June 1987, 6891.
40. Canada, House of Commons, Standing Committee on National Defence, *Minutes of Proceedings and Evidence*, 3 July 1988, 29:27.
41. Canada, House of Commons, Standing Committee on National Defence, *Minutes of Proceedings and Evidence* 7 March 1988, 29:36.
42. Joel J. Sokolsky, "Striking a Balance: Seapower, Security, Sovereignty and Canada," conference paper, Workshop on Canadian Oceans Policy, University of British Columbia, March 1988, 30.
43. David Cox, "Canada's Defense Debate," *Washington Quarterly* 10, no. 4 (Autumn 1987): 105.
44. Ibid.
45. William Epstein, "New Stance Tarnishes Canada's Reputation," *Bulletin of the Atomic Scientists* 3, no. 8 (October 1987): 11.
46. See David G. Haglund, "The Canadian SSN Program and the Nonproliferation Question," Centre for International Relations, Queen's University, Occasional Paper no. 29, Kingston, 1988, 16; and John Lamb and Tariq Rauf, "When Choosing Nuclear Submarines Take Arms Control Seriously," in Canadian Centre for Arms Control and Disarmament, *Arms Control Communiqué*, no. 49 (16 May 1988).
47. John Turner, Leader of the Liberal Party, quoted in the Toronto *Sun*, 8 February 1988, 4.
48. In May 1988 Environics Research Group Ltd., in a national poll conducted for the Canadian Centre for Arms Control and Disarmament, asked the following question: "The federal government plans to buy a fleet of 10 to 12 nuclear-propelled submarines at a total cost of at least $8 billion. Do you strongly approve (etc.)." The results were: strongly approve 9%, somewhat approve 23%, somewhat disapprove 24%, strongly disapprove 35%, don't

know/no answer 8%. Canadian Centre for Arms Control and Disarmament, *Arms Control Communiqué,* no. 50 (25 May 1988): 1.

49. For a thorough analysis of the Canadian SSN program from an American point of view, see Ronald O'Rourke, "Canadian Nuclear-powered Submarine Program: Issues for Congress," Congressional Research Service, *Issue Brief,* no. IB88083 (15 July 1988).

50. *Globe and Mail* (Toronto), 1 July 1989, A2.

51. Minister's speaking notes. (See footnote 8, above.)

52. As the Canadian Institute of Strategic Studies has put it, "The reality of the budget cuts is that new priorities have been established. However, the question of intent is most debatable." "Moving to Fortress North America?" *Strategic Datalink,* no. 14 (May 1989).

53. David Cox, *Trends in Continental Defence: A Canadian Perspective,* Ottawa, Canadian Institute for International Peace and Security, Occasional Paper 2, 1986, 42.

54. Canada has a "first past the post" electoral system based on parliamentary districts. While the Progressive Conservatives only took 43 percent of the nation-wide vote in the 1988 election, this translated into a comfortable majority in the House of Commons of 169 seats out of 295, permitting the Mulroney government to implement the Free Trade Agreement. The two other parties opposed the deal. The Liberal Party took 32 percent and won 83 seats; the New Democratic Party took 20 percent and 43 seats.

55. For a complete discussion, see LTC Dierck Meyer, "Enhancement of NATO's Military Integration: Multinational Formations for Central Europe," *The Martello Papers* (Kingston: Queen's University Centre for International Relations, 1990).

56. For a discussion see Andrew Latham and Michael Slack, "Security Policy at the Crossroads: What Direction for Canada in Europe?" *Canadian Defence Quarterly* 19, no. 6 (June 1990): 23.

57. Franklyn Griffiths, "Beyond the Arctic Sublime," *The Politics of the Northwest Passage,* 256.

58. William Thorsell, "The Canadian character: it's time to give Peter Pan the hook," *The Globe and Mail* (Toronto) 19 January 1991, p. D6.

IV

The United States, Canada, and Strategic Nuclear Deterrence

If the prediction made in the last chapter is correct, Canada's defense efforts will be focused more than ever on North America. At home on this continent, Canada copes with "the perplexing paradox facing a lesser power neighbour to a superpower:"[1] if it were to deploy no or very few armed forces of its own, its territorial sovereignty would be jeopardized as the United States by necessity put its own forces on Canadian soil. Yet the forces Canada does deploy at home are directly linked to the U.S. strategic posture, over which Canada has minimal influence and of which it may not approve.

At issue is the Canadian relationship with U.S. strategic nuclear weapons. Protection of the U.S. strategic nuclear deterrent is the preeminent military purpose of Canada's contributions in NORAD to continental air defense and one of the main purposes of its antisubmarine warfare efforts.

Most Canadians, like most Americans, accept the necessity of nuclear deterrence. "Unfortunately, deterrence means different things to different people (though all agree it should be 'enhanced')," once observed an official of the Canadian Centre for Arms Control and Disarmament.[2] Canadians tend to see the role of strategic nuclear weapons differently than Americans. In fact, as will be explored in the next four chapters, which deal with the functional areas of North American defense, differences over nuclear deterrence have sometimes posed dilemmas for the Canadian government as it structures and justifies Canadian defense cooperation with the United States.

This chapter deals with the origins of those differences, which are deeply rooted in the different roles the United States and Canada play in world affairs. A consensus on deterrence does not exist in the United States, where two approaches to nuclear strategy contend. The first part of this chapter summarizes the strategic debate in the United States and the evolution of U.S. declaratory nuclear strategy. Both have led in the past not only to controversy but also to a great deal of confusion in

Canada, which continues to this day. It then briefly touches on where U.S. strategy may be heading in the 1990s. The second part deals with what can be called the Canadian consensus on nuclear deterrence, how it differs from the predominant U.S. approach, and finally how a greater Canadian focus on North American defense could contribute to an aggravation of those differences.

It must be stressed that these differences between Canadians and Americans may very well pose few or no problems for Canada-U.S. defense relations in the 1990s. With the rapid improvement in East-West relations, fear of nuclear war and concern over nuclear armaments have decreased in Canada, as elsewhere. But Canadians may become in the 1990s more optimistic, or less cautious than Americans in their assessments of the East-West security relationship and of the Soviet Union. Should this occur, the deeper, and now longstanding differences over U.S. nuclear strategy may come to the fore.

THE UNITED STATES AND
THE BURDENS OF DETERRENCE

The first approach to nuclear strategy in the United States has been called "apocalyptic"[3] and rests on a model of finite, stable deterrence. As the American analyst Philip Bobbitt has summarized, it "stresses the sufficiency of the countervalue deterrent and the benefits of such sufficiency so that we can know when we have 'enough' weapons for deterrence; it stresses the risks of threatening the enemy's capacity for retaliation and the value of stability; and it assumes the inevitability of the annihilation of the developed world if nuclear weapons should ever come to be used.[4] ("Countervalue" strikes are against cities and industrial areas.)

The contending, or "flexible" approach "focuses on the *relative* outcome of a nuclear war, implicitly assuming that something short of complete destruction is possible both for one's own country and for one's adversary; it focuses on preparing to achieve significant strategic objectives should deterrence fail (and by such preparation, ensuring deterrence); and it aims to deny the enemy the achievement of his objectives by destroying his capability to wage war and limiting the damage he can inflict."[5] It "relies on counterforce strikes and technologies for defense."[6] (Counterforce refers to attacks on military targets, including but not limited to nuclear weapons.)

The United States has always sought to achieve two goals through the deployment of nuclear weapons. (These two goals are not to be confused with the two approaches to strategy.) The first is deterring an attack on the American homeland. This has variously been called "basic" or "simple" or "central" deterrence. The credibility of central deterrence postures has generally been believed to be high: the United

States can with high credibility threaten to retaliate with nuclear weapons if the Soviet Union attacks the United States. A necessary precondition is the retention of a secure "second strike" capability consisting of nuclear weapons and launchers capable of being used despite a Soviet attempt at a disarming first strike. The same, of course, is true for the Soviet Union: with its second strike capability it also can with relatively high credibility threaten to retaliate in the event of an American attack. Viewed solely within the context of central deterrence, the retention by both the Soviet Union and the United States of second strike capabilities is stabilizing.

Yet, the implications of that Soviet nuclear capability have been ominous for the second U.S. goal, extended deterrence, which is the ability of the United States to contribute its nuclear deterrent to the protection of its allies, especially the European members of the North Atlantic Alliance.[7] Extended deterrence is a proverbial cornerstone of U.S. and NATO policy, the "existential concept from which all U.S. postwar strategy has been derived."[8] The United States has sought to deter nuclear attacks on its allies. It also has sought to engage its strategic arsenal in bolstering NATO's deterrent capability against conventional attack. In the Cold War, the sufficiency of NATO's conventional forces themselves to repulse an attack by the Warsaw Pact was long the subject of debate. But even had they been sufficient, the great fear of the Western Europeans has been that their countries would be decimated by a conventional or nuclear war fought to a "victorious" finish on their territories. The United States, by coupling its strategic nuclear forces to local conventional and nuclear forces, has attempted to assuage those fears. "The Soviets," summarized the President's Commission on Strategic Forces (the Scowcroft Commission) in 1983, "must continue to believe what has been NATO's doctrine for three decades: that if we or our allies should be attacked—by massive conventional means or otherwise—the United States has the will and the means to defend with the full range of American power . . . effective deterrence requires that early in any Soviet consideration of attack, or threat of attack with conventional forces or chemical or biological weapons, Soviet leaders must understand that they risk an American nuclear response."[9]

Unhappily, "the mutual achievement of a secure, second-strike capability by the superpowers, considered by many to be crucial to the stability of central deterrence, may have eroded the credibility of the American nuclear guarantee to NATO since it casts doubt on the effectiveness of a nuclear first strike against the Soviet Union."[10] Coping with this dilemma has driven debate in the United States over nuclear strategy and has precipitated recent modifications in U.S. strategic policy, to the dismay of many Canadians.

Some advocates of the finite, stable deterrent approach either concede that coupling the U.S. strategic arsenal to Europe for extended deterrence is no longer possible in the face of Soviet strategic nuclear capabilities, or may be possible only to deter nuclear threats. "Nuclear weapons serve no military purpose whatsoever. They are totally useless—except only to deter one's opponent from using them."[11] Others argue that because Western Europe is so clearly an area of critically vital interest to the United States, the capability of the United States to devastate the Soviet Union credibly serves the purposes of extended deterrence. Thus, McGeorge Bundy has argued that extended deterrence rests on "two great facts: the visible deployment of American military forces in Europe, and the very evident risk that any large-scale engagement between Soviet and American forces would rapidly and uncontrollably become general, nuclear, and disastrous."[12]

Proponents of flexible nuclear responses emphasize above all that if deterrence were to fail, the United States must be able to respond with less than an annihilating blow, in hopes of controlling the extent of the catastrophe. They also argue that if the United States were to structure its forces only so that it could respond to a Soviet attack on itself or its allies with a devastating counterattack on Soviet society, extended deterrence could be extinguished; in a crisis the United States could be "self-deterred" from responding on behalf of its allies knowing that an attack designed to destroy Soviet cities would be met with one in kind. Limited nuclear strike options must therefore be prepared.

Such steps are condemned by the stable, finite deterrent model on related grounds. First, nuclear war cannot be controlled. Even limited strikes could entail such a high level of violence and destructiveness that escalation to the level of mutual devastation would inevitably follow. Second, the enemy might perceive immediately even limited strikes as an attempt at a disarming first strike and thus immediately respond with a massive countervalue attack.

Among those who argue for a flexible approach, two principal schools have contended. First, "countervailing" strategists seek to reconcile, through the preparation of limited nuclear options, extended nuclear deterrence with continued U.S. vulnerability to Soviet countervalue strikes. Because of that ultimate vulnerability, the United States cannot hope to "win" a nuclear war or militarily "defeat" the Soviets through the destruction of its armed forces, including its nuclear forces, making further pursuit of war by the Soviets impossible. Rather, according to countervailing strategists, the United States must demonstrate to the Soviets that the costs of aggression at any level would outweigh the gains. Thus, the United States "must have a doctrine and plans for the use of our forces (if they are needed) that make clear to the Soviets the hard reality that, by any course leading to nuclear war and in any course a nuclear war might take, they could never gain anything amounting to victory on any plausible definition of victory or gain an advantage that would outweigh the unacceptable price they would have to pay."[13] The second—and far less influential school—adheres to concepts of nuclear "war fighting" or "prevailing."[14]

The official, or declaratory, nuclear policy of the U.S. government has long embodied elements of both the apocalyptic and flexible approaches, all but exclusively of the countervailing variety. It continues to do so. In part, a certain tension or ambiguity has been intentional. The credibility of threatening nuclear war for purposes of extended deterrence may be enhanced through stressing capabilities to execute less-than-apocalyptic, limited nuclear strikes; while at the same time an emphasis on the unpredictability of nuclear war and on the utter mutual destructiveness that a full-scale nuclear exchange could well bring, serves both to underscore the ultimate cost which might have to be paid for aggression, and to reassure that the United States recognizes that it must not lightly turn to the use of nuclear weapons. As a group of Harvard University scholars put it, "the existence of a capability for mutual destruction deters, but the doomsday machine must be linked to events in a credible way."[15]

Yet the flexible approach to nuclear strategy has for decades been more influential over U.S. policy than the apocalyptic, in that the United States has been unwilling to limit itself to the ability to destroy Soviet cities and has periodically sought to maintain limited options in the face of evolving Soviet and U.S. nuclear capabilities. The historical continuity of flexibility in U.S. strategy has been obscured, including in Canada, by misinterpretations of the doctrine of "assured destruction," first publicly articulated by Secretary of Defense Robert McNamara in 1965. "Assured destruction" consisted of three elements. It was, first, a metric for U.S. second strike capability. The United States, McNamara argued, should base its strategic weapons acquisition policy on retaining the capability, even after being struck in a Soviet attack, to destroy the Soviet Union as a major power for many years or, as he later put it "as a viable 20th Century nation." This would entail killing about one-quarter to one-third of the Soviet Union's population and eliminating two-thirds of its industrial capability. McNamara's motivation was partially budgetary. The nuclear forces the United States already was acquiring were expected to provide such a level of destructiveness. McNamara sought to stave off pressures for expensive increases in U.S. offensive capabilities.

Second, "assured destruction" was also a targeting option, that is, the United States put in place the plans and weapons that would allow it to execute strikes on the Soviet Union with the level of ruin McNamara described. But it was not the sole option, much less a policy of "mindless, orgastic [sic] countervalue retaliation that is the usual misunderstanding of assured destruction."[16] For, third, "assured destruction" was a flexible strategy, the strategic nuclear component of the broader NATO policy of "flexible response," officially adopted in 1967 at the urging of the United States.' Flexible response emphasized NATO's ability to respond appropriately to Soviet attacks across the full spectrum of violence, from low level conventional to full-scale conventional war, (for which NATO's conventional forces were enhanced) through "theater" nuclear exchanges in Europe, to the strategic nuclear level where the United States single integrated operations plan (SIOP) provided a variety of targeting options culminating in *but not necessarily leading to* the destruction of the Soviet Union. Implicit to flexible response were notions of escalation control, intra-war deterrence and bargaining: during a conflict the United States would seek to deter attacks on American cities by reserving its "assured destruction" forces while demonstrating to the Soviet Union that it would gain nothing by proceeding to the next higher level of violence, leaving for the Soviets termination of the conflict as the sole attractive option.

The acquisition of a secure second strike capability by the Soviets in the 1960s created a condition of "mutual assured destruction" or MAD. By the mid-1960s McNamara came to the conclusion that due to limitations in the technologies of the day for ballistic missile defense (BMD) or antiballistic missile (ABM) defense as it was then more commonly called, there was no immediate escape to be had from mutual vulnerability to nuclear destruction. Attempts to erect defenses would be met by an increase in the number of offensive weapons in order to overwhelm the defenses, resulting in an arms race, and no increase in security. In the late 1960s, McNamara sought to stave off, as well, pressure to erect a "thick" ABM system by agreeing to endorse a "thin" system. The Johnson administration also set in motion efforts to reach agreements with the Soviets on limiting offensive and defensive systems, which culminated in 1972 under the auspices of the Nixon administration, in the US-USSR Anti-Ballistic Missile (ABM) Treaty and the Strategic Arms Limitation (SALT I) accord. The ABM Treaty accorded both sides the right to maintain ABM defenses around its capital and one other site. In 1976 the United States shut down the limited system it had erected to protect its missile fields. No system was ever deployed to protect Washington.

While the ABM Treaty in effect recognized, indeed, legally protected, mutual assured destruction as a condition of the strategic environment, it by no means committed the United States to the destruction of the Soviet Union as its sole nuclear option. To be so restrained, United States decision-makers have always felt, could extinguish extended deterrence. Thus, according to Thomas Schelling, "Since 1964 the correct name of the strategy is not 'assured mutual destruction' but assured *capability* for mutual destruction."[17] The Nixon administration and its successors have retained the policy of flexible response and introduced modifications at the nuclear level intended to maintain its viability.

It is understandable that a perception exists in the United States (and, as shall be discussed below, in Canada) that MAD was United States doctrine, in the sense that mutual annihilation was the sole strategic option. "In their anxiety to build a constituency for arms control, President Johnson and Secretary McNamara made the American position appear more absurd than it in fact was, sometimes depicting the American strategy as a kind of suicide pact, with only one devastating option available to fend off a Russian attack."[18] President Nixon engaged in similar rhetoric, although intended to ridicule the nonexistent policy of his predecessor. Several times he asked "Should a president in the event of a nuclear attack be left with the single option of ordering the mass destruction of enemy civilians, in the face of the certainty that it would be followed by the mass slaughter of Americans?" knowing full well that American plans already gave him several options. Other senior U.S. officials have occasionally indulged in similar statements.[19]

The rise to strategic nuclear parity by the Soviets at the beginning of the 1970s, while stabilizing in the exclusively bilateral context, was feared to have a negative impact on extended deterrence. "Parity is a fine state of affairs for a strictly one-on-one military balance. Equal forces imply equal deterrence. But this works only to deter attacks on each other."[20] Later in the decade the Soviets deployed intercontinental ballistic missiles (ICBMs) capable of destroying on the ground the accurate U.S. ICBMs which the United States would rely upon to execute selective strikes on the Soviet Union, potentially leaving the United States only with the forces with which it could undertake a massive countervalue strike, from which it could be deterred by the remaining Soviet nuclear forces. The Nixon administration sought, through the introduction and public articulation of what it called "limited nuclear options," to reassure America's allies that the United States was still prepared to engage its strategic arsenal on their behalf. These limited options were embodied in National Security Decision Memorandum 242, signed by the president in early 1974, and entailed preparations for strikes on individual missile silos and military bases, as well as military industries, on a smaller scale than had previously been provided for in the SIOP. By further limiting the violence of the initial nuclear strikes with which the United States would respond to Soviet aggression, it was hoped, the credibility of the U.S. pledge to resort to strategic nuclear weaponry would be enhanced. As NSDM 242's principle architect, Secretary of Defense James Schlesinger explained the motivation, "To the extent that we have changed our targeting doctrine, we have recoupled

U.S. strategic forces to the security of Western Europe and as long as we have that coupling action, I think we have strengthened deterrence—reduced the risk of war."[21] As he later elaborated on the overall approach,

> If, for whatever reason, deterrence should fail, we want to have the planning flexibility to be able to respond selectively to the attack in such a way as to (1) limit the chances of uncontrolled escalation, and (2) hit meaningful targets with a sufficient accuracy-yield combination to destroy only the intended target and to avoid widespread collateral damage. If a nuclear clash should occur—and we fervently believe that it will not—in order to protect American cities and the cities of our allies, we shall rely into the wartime period upon reserving our 'assured destruction' force and persuading, through intrawar deterrence, any potential foe not to attack cities. It is through these means that we hope to prevent massive destruction even in the cataclysmic circumstances of nuclear war.[22]

The Carter administration took two steps intended to solidify extended nuclear deterrence. Largely at the behest of European governments, in particular the West German government of Chancellor Helmut Schmidt, it agreed in 1979 to deploy in Europe new intermediate range nuclear forces (INF), namely 108 Pershing II missiles and 464 ground-launched cruise missiles and at the same time attempt to engage the Soviets in negotiations leading to a mutual reduction of such forces. The deployments were intended to respond to Soviet SS-20 missiles targeted on western Europe and to demonstrate the alliance's continuing ability to respond flexibly across the spectrum of violence, with the U.S. strategic nuclear deterrent "coupled" to European security.[23]

Second, it modified U.S. strategic nuclear policy under the rubric of what it called the "countervailing strategy," or the "countervailing doctrine" which was formally incorporated in Presidential Directive 59, signed in 1980. PD 59 set out the requirement for the United States to be able to engage in protracted nuclear conflict, initially based on limited strikes, especially against Soviet political and military command and control facilities, as well as military forces, in particular those that would be engaged in a war in Europe. It was not a strategy to "win" a nuclear war. Again, the motivations were to provide options should deterrence fail, and to enhance the credibility of U.S. nuclear resolve. These were to be achieved by de-emphasizing attacks on Soviet cities which could elicit a response in kind, and emphasizing political and military targets. Similarly, a capability for protracted conflict was intended to underline that the United States would not respond with indiscriminate nuclear strikes but rather, at each stage of the war, would assess Soviet actions, including strikes on the United States and respond with the appropriately controlled level of violence. "It is our policy," Secretary of Defense Harold Brown explained, "to ensure that the Soviet leadership knows that if they chose some intermediate level of aggression, we could by selective, large (but still less than maximum) nuclear attacks, exact an unacceptably high price in the things the Soviet leaders appear to value most—political and military control, military force both nuclear and conventional, and the industrial capability to sustain a war." The United States would as a matter of course, he added, retain the capability, "to attack the full range of targets, including the Soviet economic base, if that is the appropriate response to a Soviet strike."[24]

While innovative in its emphasis on strikes against political and military command and control facilities and in its requirement for the capability to engage in a protracted conflict, the "countervailing doctrine" was in essence no more than an evolution in the policy of flexible response the United States had been pursuing for years. Brown himself emphasized this point.

> This doctrine . . . is *not* a new departure. The United States has never had a doctrine based simply and solely on reflexive, massive attacks on Soviet cities. Instead, we have always planned both more selectively (options limiting urban-industrial damage) and more comprehensively (a range of military targets). Previous administrations, going back into the 1960s, recognized the inadequacy of a strategic doctrine that would give us too narrow a range of options. The fundamental premises of our countervailing strategy are a natural evolution of the conceptual foundations built over the course of generations, by, for example, Secretaries McNamara and Schlesinger, to name only two of my predecessors who have been most identified with development of our nuclear doctrine.[25]

To engage in protracted nuclear conflict, the U.S. command, control, communications, and intelligence (C^3I) system for strategic forces would have to be "hardened" to withstand Soviet nuclear strikes. PD-59 was accompanied by a directive intended to set such a process underway. The Carter administration was voted out of office in 1980, though, before it had the opportunity to implement it. The incoming Reagan administration adopted not only the principal elements of the countervailing strategy, incorporating it in a decision of its own, National Security Decision Directive 13, but included an overhaul of the C^3I system as a top priority in its modernization program for strategic forces, announced in 1981.

The Reagan administration had come to power with the intent to reverse what it saw as a serious decline in United States military power relative to that of the Soviet Union, as well as with a hostility to the SALT II agreement negotiated by the Carter administration (and being held in abeyance in the wake of the Soviet invasion of Afghanistan) which it saw as an instrument freezing the United States in a disadvantageous position. Statements made by senior officials, including the president, about U.S. nuclear policy touched off waves of concern at home and abroad, including Canada, that the Reaganites were blind to the dangers of nuclear war. In retrospect, though, almost all of these observations were hardly major departures from the policies of previous administrations.[26] Perhaps the most quoted remark was President Reagan's response in 1981 to the question whether he believed that a limited nuclear war between the United States and the Soviet Union was possible: "I could see where you could have the exchange of tactical weapons against troops in the field without it bringing either one of the major powers to pushing the button."[27] Secretary of Defense Caspar Weinberger's first Defense Guidance statement was leaked to the press and revealed to contain the directive "Should deterrence fail and strategic nuclear war with the USSR occur, the United States must prevail and be able to force the Soviet Union to seek earliest termination of hostilities on terms favorable to the United States."[28] The term "prevail" was undoubtedly unfortunate, for it evoked images of the "nuclear war-fighting" school and its emphasis on escaping the consequences of mutual vulnerability. But the concept of attempting to compel the Soviet Union, in the event deterrence failed, to seek termination of hostilities on terms favorable to the United States was no more an innovation than the notion, expressed by the president, that a nuclear war might be kept limited. Denying that possibility would have undercut an essential element of "flexible response." While Weinberger defended the use of the word "prevailing" ("You show me a Secretary of Defense who's planning not to prevail and I'll show you a Secretary of Defense who ought to be impeached"[29]), the term was dropped from subsequent versions of the document.

Both the secretary of defense and the president thereafter sought to take a more reassuring tone at home and abroad. "We, for our part," Weinberger told a U.S. Senate committee in December 1982, "are under no illusions about the consequences of a nuclear war: we believe there would be no winners in such a war." He went on to defend the pursuit of flexible nuclear options as the cornerstone of U.S. strategy for deterrence, and should deterrence fail: "we must plan for flexibility in our forces and in our response options so that there is a possibility of reestablishing deterrence at the lowest possible level of violence, and avoiding further escalation."[30] The implication was that while there could be no "winners" there were various degrees of losing. President Reagan, the following year, told the Japanese Diet that "A nuclear war can never be won and must never be fought." He would return to that formulation frequently during his presidency.[31]

The reopening of strategic arms limitations talks with the Soviets, and the thawing of East-West relations in the Gorbachev era have calmed public fears of nuclear war. Nonetheless the debate in the early and mid 1980s led many to realize that U.S. nuclear strategy was not what they thought it had been. This has especially been the case in Canada, where many have seen the recent trends in U.S. strategy as not only lamentable, but a sharp break from the past.

While it is too early to say precisely what U.S. nuclear strategy will be in the 1990s, it is nonetheless clear that it will all but certainly be a variant of the flexible approach. There are two reasons for this. First, it still remains the case that no U.S. president could tolerate being left, should deterrence fail, with the sole option of ordering the general destruction of the Soviet Union.

Second, the need for extended deterrence based on U.S. nuclear weapons will not disappear. This will be the case if only because there is no viable alternative. Neither the British nor French nuclear deterrents could, for the foreseeable future, serve as substitutes. Nor is a Western European nuclear force anywhere in sight. But here, as well, it is too early to say how difficult it will be to secure extended deterrence. On the one hand, the dramatic reduction of the Soviet conventional threat will make the task easier. Thus the NATO heads of government, in their June 1990 "London Declaration" called, at the behest of President Bush, for the eventual adoption of "a new NATO strategy making nuclear forces truly weapons of last resort." Yet that same declaration, in somewhat contradictory fashion, emphasized as well that nuclear weapons "will continue to fulfill an essential role in the overall strategy of the Alliance to prevent war by ensuring that there are no circumstances in which nuclear retaliation in response to military action might be discounted."[32] The impending removal of ground-based nuclear systems from German soil (not to mention the potential denuclearization of Germany) could result in an even greater emphasis being placed on the role of not only air-launched and sea-based systems in the European region, but on U.S. strategic systems. "Linkage" questions could again arise.

Finally, it can at least be tentatively concluded that the United States in the 1990s will continue to seek to preserve flexibility not only through flexible targeting, but through counterforce options and the survivability of its strategic forces. As William W. Kaufmann of the Brookings Institution puts it in a recent study of the future of U.S. defense policy, "given a history of nearly thirty years during which successive presidents have chosen to maintain options in addition to countercity attacks, and given that retargeting does not seem to be a reliable mechanism while an attack is underway, the target list is likely to remain fairly long and the number of weapons dedicated to these targets fairly large, with control exercised by means of withholding certain weapons rather than retargeting a smaller number." He later adds, "That in turn means that most forces should be survivable over a matter of days or even weeks so that there would be no incentive 'to use them or lose them.'"[33]

THE CANADIAN "APOCALYPTIC" CONSENSUS

There has been little debate in Canada about what the appropriate nuclear strategy is for the United States. Canadians and their governments have tended to focus on central deterrence and the need to preserve stability in the central nuclear relationship. A consensus in Canada so firmly, so automatically supports the "apocalyptic" or finite deterrence approach that Canadians have often been bewildered and shocked by the attempts of the U.S. government to preserve the credibility of extended deterrence. Meanwhile, their governments have ducked the issue.

The Canadian "apocalyptic" consensus can be attributed to three factors: first, longstanding fear of the consequences of being dragged into a strategic nuclear war without any say in the matter; second, the irrelevance of extended deterrence for the protection of Canada; and finally a strong desire to see a special, distinctive, military and political role for Canada in the world, one that strengthens stable, mutual deterrence.

Canada would suffer in a strategic exchange as no other ally. Canadian governments, including the Mulroney government, have long calculated that "Soviet strategic planners must regard Canada and the United States as a single set of military targets no matter what political posture we might assume."[34] Soviet targeters, planning preliminary missile strikes on the North American air defense system intended to facilitate follow-on strikes by bombers and cruise missiles, would have to include for destruction installations in Canada. Soviet plans for the destruction of American society and the American economy might include the elimination of the large and small Canadian cities located close to the border which engage in extensive commerce with the United States and from which, if unscathed, some measure of assistance and recovery could be undertaken for the devastated nation to the south. Yet "even in the unlikely event that the United States alone were attacked, geographic proximity and common interest would ensure that the effect on Canada would be devastating."[35] The Windsor-Quebec City axis in southern Canada, which includes the country's two largest cities, Toronto and Montreal, and contains half the country's population, could be devastated by fallout plumes created to the west by the destruction of ICBM fields, and the portion of the U.S. industrial heartland located on the southern side of the Great Lakes. Montreal is less than sixty miles from a Strategic Air Command Base at Plattsburg, New York while Vancouver, the country's third largest city is close to both Seattle and the U.S. Navy's Trident submarine base in Bangor, Washington.[36]

Canadians have no control over the use of the U.S. nuclear arsenal, which remains in the hands of the president of the United States. "Incineration without representation," is a fairly well-known expression in Canada to describe one prospect.[37] The combination of being potentially exposed to the horrendous effects of strategic thermonuclear war without control over the decision-making has long made Canadians (not unlike other allies) worry about the conduct of American foreign and defense policy in general and U.S. nuclear weapons policy in particular. It has also made them search for ways in which they might influence American decision making. Lending impetus to the search are Canadian doubts dating back to the very beginnings of the Cold War, about the cool-headedness of their American friends and allies. "Canadians," Melvin Conant, an astute American Canada-watcher, once concluded, "often think that their neighbor to the south exhibits wild swings of emotional attachments in its relations with other countries; that it is impatient, is prone to making sweeping judgments, and generally lacks sophistication and subtlety in its approach to the Soviet bloc and the cold war."[38]

American officials have from time to time chafed at the cautious approach, and the sometimes chiding tone of "unctuous righteousness"[39] Canadians have taken with them in discussions over strategic policy. What the German journalist Joseph Joffre once grumpily observed of his fellow Europeans could easily be applied to the Canadians: "Nations that depend for their security on others want the best of all possible worlds . . . full protection but minimal risks; they will the end; which is the credibility of American power, but not necessarily the means, which entail the re-assertion of American power."[40]

Canada's plight, however, is clear and longstanding. Canada has always been a country in alliance with a great power, first France, then Britain, and now the United States. Twice in this century those ties have lead it to war. "Thousands of Canadians fought and died in two world wars that Canada had no hand in starting," Prime Minister Pierre Trudeau once said in an address to the House of Commons.[41] So, of course, did thousands of Americans. But the United States has substantial influence in what will occur in world affairs. In the nuclear age, Canada's fate is tightly bound to decisions reached in its latest imperial capital. It had become an "inescapable fact," wrote the Canadian secretary of state for external affairs, Lester B. Pearson, at the height of the Cold War, "that no country in the world has less chance of isolating itself from the effect of American policies and decisions than Canada."[42]

Fear of the consequences of U.S. nuclear policies has been a persistent theme of Canadian-American postwar history. Even before North America was itself in much danger of a Soviet assault, Ottawa was alert to the possibility that the U.S. finger might rest too heavily on the nuclear trigger. An offhand remark by President Harry S Truman at a November 1950 news conference to the effect that the United States had not entirely excluded the use of nuclear weapons in Korea made Canadian officials "shudder."[43] These worries, once laid to rest, were overtaken by more persistent ones precipitated by the 1954 "massive retaliation" speech of the U.S. Secretary of State, John Foster Dulles after the Eisenhower administration's "new look" at defense policy. "From that time on," the Canadian ambassador to Washington later recalled, "Ottawa was almost continuously anxious about the course of U.S. foreign policy."[44]

The "new look" was designed to take advantage of the overwhelming U.S. nuclear superiority of the day for extended deterrence. "Local defenses," Dulles said, "must be reinforced by the further deterrent of massive retaliatory power." The decision had been reached by the administration to depend primarily upon "our great capacity to retaliate instantly by means and at places of our own choosing."[45]

Ottawa was irritated at not having been informed in advance, much less consulted, about the new U.S. policy and shocked at its content. A staff paper prepared for the Canadian Chiefs of Staff Committee warned that "the U.S. have relaxed the former restriction on the use of 'A' weapons and are now planning their use in any type of military action. Therefore, because of our close association with the U.S. in the military field we may find ourselves involved in an atomic war without much consultation."[46] Diplomatic consultations were launched to elicit clarification of exactly how the Americans intended the new policy to work. Pearson took the unusual step of delivering a speech of his own on American soil commenting on U.S. policy, entitled "A Look at the New Look" before the National Press Club in Washington. Calling for further explanation of what Dulles had meant by "instantly," "means" and "our," he told his American audience that Canadians had grown anxious that Canada's "destiny may be decided not by ourselves, but across the border by means and at places not of our choosing."[47]

When the Kennedy administration sought to replace the Eisenhower administration's reliance on nuclear firepower with "flexible response" the European members of the alliance had to be sold on the concept, fearing that it might imply both an unacceptable devaluation of the U.S. nuclear guarantee and an unbearable conventional defense burden. First enunciated by McNamara in 1961, because of these European doubts it was not formally adopted by NATO until 1967. Ottawa, on the other hand, did not have to be sold at all, and joined Washington in urging the adoption of the strategy upon the Europeans, calling it "a reaction against the doctrine of massive retaliation. It is based upon the proposition that the Western Alliance should not be placed in a position of excessive reliance upon nuclear weapons or, more generally, of being compelled to employ force in a manner incompatible with Western objectives."[48]

Thus Ottawa was motivated in embracing the new approach not so much out of concern for the maintenance of extended deterrence as by worries over undue American reliance on strategic nuclear weaponry. Extended deterrence is largely irrelevant to the direct defense of Canada. Geography dictates that Canada is protected by central deterrence. An attack on air defense installations in Canada would be an attack on critical elements of the U.S. strategic nuclear infrastructure. Any nuclear attack, in fact, on Canada would be seen by the United States as the crossing by the Soviet Union of a critical geographic threshold. To be sure, there are those who insist that "there are many possibilities in which one can separate, in a purely military sense, Canadian from American targets."[49] The Soviets, according to this view, might want to launch several nuclear "demonstration" shots at targets in Canada, especially in the north, far from populated areas, thereby showing the United States at the same time Soviet resolve and restraint. This scenario is based on the assumption that the Soviets might believe in a crisis that the United States would be able to perceive the explosion of nuclear weapons not far from its borders as containing, because of their location in Canada, an unambiguous indication of restraint. At the very least, those who hold that central deterrence does not include Canada would probably find it hard to challenge the proposition that extended deterrence protects Canada as it does no other ally.

The irrelevance of extended deterrence has two consequences. First, it removes any incentives Canadians have to support, for their own direct protection, United States efforts to shore it up. If it can be said that Europeans often worry that the United States might not be willing enough to use its strategic arsenal on their behalf, thereby allowing conventional and "tactical" nuclear war to be fought out on their territory, then the equivalent Canadian worry is that the United States might be *too* willing to unleash strategic nuclear weapons, thereby bringing war to *Canadian* territory.

Paradoxically, Canada does have an interest that deterrence holds in Europe. But this interest has not extended to either the provision of substantial numbers of Canadian conventional forces in Europe so that the nuclear "threshold" could have been held high, or to the endorsement of U.S. flexible nuclear options intended to shore up the credibility of extended deterrence.

Second, the irrelevance of extended deterrence also removes the necessity of nuclear weapons being based in Canada. Strategic nuclear weapons have never been based on Canadian soil. Canadians, not unlike the citizens of other smaller countries, have come to see the absence of nuclear weaponry in their country as a contribution to arms limitation and a reflection of national virtue. Thus Canada, it has been said, also is affected by a form of the "nuclear allergy."[50]

The Canadian nuclear allergy has been evident over the past several decades. In 1963,the Canadian government agreed to equip Canadian air defense forces in Canada and Canadian forces in Europe with the capability to use American owned and controlled nuclear weapons. The air defense weapons, which were to be located on Canadian soil, had no offensive capability: they were capable of being used only against Soviet bombers in North American airspace. Nonetheless, the 1963 decision was reached only after one of the greatest imbroglios in Canadian political history, involving continued pressure by the United States, several years of hesitation by the Progressive Conservative government of the day, persistent obfuscation on the part of senior Canadian officials, above all by Prime Minister Diefenbaker, concerning the nature and extent of the Canadian nuclear commitments, and growing rancor with Washington made worse by the poor personal relations between the prime minister and Pres. John F. Kennedy. The decision also came after a bitter national debate that pulled the Progressive Conservative cabinet apart upon the resignation in protest of the minister of national defence, lead to the government's defeat on the floor of the House of Commons, and was a prime cause of its loss of a mandate in the general election of 1963. The Liberal government that took power under Lester B. Pearson accepted the nuclear weapons with unhappiness, more to fulfill a commitment to the United States and the Alliance than out of conviction that it was necessary or proper for Canadians to be able to use them.[51]

After a decent interval had passed, the government announced in 1971 the termination of the nuclear roles in Europe. Obsolescence eventually put an end to the nuclear-tipped air defense weapons in Canada. The last such warhead, designed for use with an air-to-air missile, was shipped back across the border into the United States, with absolutely no Canadian regrets, in 1984.

Today there are no nuclear weapons of any kind in Canada, and as the Mulroney government has repeatedly emphasized, there are no standing arrangements granting the United States permission to move nuclear weapons into the country. Yet it would be a mistake to see Canada as a sort of North American New Zealand. Visits to Canadian ports by nuclear-capable U.S. Navy ships are routine. It is public knowledge as well that for over thirty years arrangements have existed to move, in an emergency, U.S. nuclear weapons or nuclear weapons carriers, especially SAC bombers, into Canada or through Canadian airspace *if at that time* the Canadian government were to agree to a United States request.[52] Members of parliament from the opposition, especially the New Democratic Party (NDP) repeatedly have called for "a commitment from the Government now that nuclear weapons will never be stationed on Canadian soil."[53] This, successive Canadian governments have refused to do. The NDP has pledged to take such a step if it ever comes to power. The Liberal Party has also included in its program a pledge to make Canada an official nuclear-free zone. But Liberal Party governments have never felt tightly obliged to implement the party program. Few Canadians expect that a Liberal government would ever attempt to move in such a direction.

For its part, the United States government has repeatedly denied in recent years sensational and widely reported allegations that, unbeknownst to Ottawa, it has plans to deploy nuclear weapons in a crisis on Canadian soil without Canadian permission. In the wake of one such sensation President Reagan emphasized this point in an interview with the Canadian newsmagazine, *Maclean's*. "Over the years," he said, "NATO has worked out various plans designed to strengthen deterrence. But under these plans any deployments would be carried out only—let me repeat only—with the prior agreement of the states involved."[54] Not everyone was convinced.[55]

Canada is associated in myriad other ways with the support of U.S. nuclear operations. The most important, and the most visible, is its North American air defense efforts in protection of the U.S. strategic nuclear arsenal. That relationship has always been a matter of concern. When the 1958 diplomatic agreement confirming NORAD's creation was submitted for approval by the Canadian House of Commons, Pearson, then leader of the opposition, pointed out that there was a "pretty close link" between the U.S. Strategic Air Command (SAC) and NORAD. While SAC was "completely outside our control it gives us, perhaps a feeling of increased gravity and seriousness when we realize that an agency inside our control could in certain circumstances, because of its responsibility to the Canadian and United States governments, determine the action to be taken" by SAC.[56] Canadian air defense forces had been, in the unhappy expression of James Eayrs, reduced to serve "indentured labour as continental chore-boy for the Strategic Air Command."[57] Other Canadians worried that the tight ties, especially in NORAD, would so taint Canada as junior partner to the U.S. nuclear behemoth that its credibility in the eyes of the world would be irreparably diminished.[58]

The Canadian government welcomed the ABM Treaty and the public statements of Secretary of Defense McNamara and President Johnson in the late 1960s emphasizing mutual vulnerability to nuclear destruction and implying at times that the United States had one devastating nuclear option, in other words, emphasizing central strategic stability and de-emphasizing the role of nuclear weapons for extended deterrence. This approach was incorporated in the Trudeau government's 1971 white paper, *Defence in the 70s*, which took a decidedly "apocalyptic" approach to strategic nuclear weaponry. "One of the most important changes in international affairs in recent years," said that document, "has been the increase in stability in nuclear deterrence, and the emergence of what is, in effect, nuclear parity between the United States and the Soviet Union. Each side now has sufficient nuclear strength to assure devastating retaliation in the event of a surprise attack by the other, and thus neither could rationally consider launching a deliberate attack."[59]

Defence in the 70s can be taken as the expression of a public consensus that had crystallized in Canada as to the most appropriate role for U.S. strategic nuclear weapons. But more importantly, it also expressed a consensus as to the way Canadians preferred to view *their closest involvement* with such weapons. The attractions to Canada of, in essence, finite, stable deterrence at the expense of flexible nuclear responses went beyond just an emphasis on the central stability that could keep the horrors of a central thermonuclear exchange from Canada. It corresponded to deep desires as to the role Canadians preferred their armed forces, and ultimately their country itself, to play in world affairs.

Of his dealings with Canadians, Henry Kissinger once observed that their "instinct in favor of the common defense" had often been in conflict "with the temptation to stay above the battle as a kind of international arbiter."[60] An emphasis on nuclear stability, and Canada's role in helping to preserve it, would, at least psychologically, help to ease those burdens. As *Defence in the 70s* put it,

> A catastrophic war between the super powers constitutes the only major military threat to Canada. . . .
> Canada's overriding defence objective must therefore be the prevention of nuclear war by promoting political reconciliation to ease the underlying causes of tension, by working for arms control and disarmament agreements, and by contributing to the system of stable mutual deterrence.[61]

Thus the Canadian air defense effort and Canadian foreign policy, especially efforts encouraging arms control, could be joined. So could self interest and international service. Geography placed Canada in a precarious position. But it also conferred upon it, and upon its air defense forces, the role of helping to prevent war, by contributing to stable *mutual* deterrence through the protection of the U.S. nuclear deterrent. So conceived, Canada's role in NORAD was not to serve SAC but to help protect global stability.

Moreover, mutual deterrence, in turn, could be seen as freeing Canada to pursue other international duties and interests. As John Holmes put it, "In the SALT age . . . it may seem increasingly as if we were protected not by the U.S. deterrent but by the system of deterrence itself, which enables not only Canada but all lesser powers to pursue their contribution to world politics relatively free of the threat of oblivion."[62]

This notion of Canada's serving mutual deterrence can be pushed to an extreme. It is striking how regularly the idea crops up that Canadian surveillance systems need not point just "northward," that is, be designed to detect only Soviet bombers and cruise missiles. Suggestions are frequently made by academics, journalists and "peace" group activists to give "the information instantaneously to both superpowers as a means of increasing information and reducing tension and concern about first-strike dangers. . . . It could reduce somewhat the tensions in a hair-trigger atmosphere of nuclear confrontation."[63] As a Canadian women's "peace" convention recently concluded, "Canada is in a perfect geographic position to keep the two superpowers apart just as a mother would two warring children."[64]

No Canadian government, it should be stressed, has ever taken such proposals seriously. That they are frequently made, though, is still another reflection of a deep wish felt by many Canadians to be able to rise above the country's ancillary role to a nuclear superpower and make a distinctive contribution to international peace and security.

So Pierre Trudeau's 1983–1984 Canadian "peace initiative" found fairly widespread support in Canada. Trudeau had grown uneasy over the deteriorating relationship between the superpowers, arguing that they "must find some way to stop shouting at each other, when the world is teetering on the brink of disaster and atomic war."[65] His initiative was intended to encourage a relaxation in international tension and progress in arms control by creating a "third rail" (his term) infused with new "political energy." It took him to consultations with United States, Soviet, British, Chinese, east European and Commonwealth leaders. Canada's NATO allies were surprised at the suddenness of the peace initiative, puzzled as to what it meant, and often irritated that it came at a time when NATO was trying to close ranks around the impending INF deployment, although Ottawa continued to stress its support for the NATO "two-track" policy of deployment and willingness to negotiate reductions. Reagan administration officials treated Trudeau's efforts with studied politeness in public and scarcely concealed disdain off the record.[66]

DEALING WITH THE STRATEGIC DIFFERENCES

It has not gone unnoticed in Canada that the trend in United States declaratory strategy has been away from the "apocalyptic." In the 1980s, the public discovery in Canada that the United States has a declaratory policy of being able to strike at the Soviet Union with strategic nuclear weapons at levels below assured destruction often produced dismay. These reactions were often complicated by widespread confusion about what U.S. strategy had been in the past. Thus the debate in Canada often centered on what has variously been called "the doctrine of MAD" or "the strategy of MAD" or the "longstanding policy of MAD," usually understood to include two elements: preservation of the condition of mutual vulnerability as encompassed in the 1972 ABM Treaty, and mutual deterrence from the resort to nuclear weapons. "Since at least the late 1960s it has been assumed that MAD constitutes the core of the U.S. approach to strategic nuclear weapons and deterrence," observed the Standing Committee on External Affairs and National Defence of the House of Commons upon studying in 1985 the relationship between NORAD and U.S. strategy. "In the past several years, however, there have been suggestions that the strategy of the United States—in effect its nuclear doctrine—is changing, moving away from deterrence toward a war-fighting approach to nuclear weapons."[67]

Canadian "peace" groups multiplied in the 1980s, calling for a variety of measures to disassociate Canada from nuclear weaponry, and for the Canadian government to apply whatever pressure it could on the superpowers to reverse the arms race.[68] Peace activists saw strategic trends in the United States as particularly alarming. As Simon Rosenblum of Project Ploughshares, a disarmament political action group sponsored by the Canadian Council of Churches warned in a fairly widely read work, U.S. reliance on deterrence had become a "pretext," the United States having adopted "a new post-deterrence doctrine" based on protracted nuclear war.[69]

Traditional, mainstream supporters of Canadian participation in NATO and NORAD also became concerned. A typical formulation of the Canadian mainstream consensus, with an emphasis on the "apocalyptic" approach and a de-emphasis on flexibility was that of the Atlantic Council of Canada's group of "wise persons" in 1982.

> What is needed is to get back to the fundamental requirements of deterrence. In our view, the essential factor remains possession by the U.S. of a credible second-strike capability, that is, enough nuclear weapons remaining after absorbing a first strike to mount a counterattack that would be prohibitively costly to the other side. That would be sufficient to keep the Soviet Union mindful of the enormous risks it runs by initiating hostilities, however, much of an advantage it might enjoy in numbers of nuclear and conventional forces. The commitment of the U.S. to come to the defence of Europe is grounded much more firmly in a wide range of political, economic, and cultural ties binding the two than in hypothetical scenarios of finely graduated deterrence.[70]

Privately, Canadian officials and even cabinet ministers have sometimes expressed endorsement of U.S. countervailing strategy as being a necessary part of the overall NATO strategy of flexible response. In public though, Canadian officials and politicians have adopted a stance of either denying the direction of U.S. strategy, or avoiding the issue by shying away from explicit discussions of nuclear strategy, except broadly to endorse deterrence—and its "enhancement." What should be done if deterrence fails—and how best to prepare for that possibility—as well as the exact relationship between U.S. strategic nuclear weapons and the defense of Europe have been taboo subjects for Canadian politicians. Thus, "Canadian statements about the threat of nuclear war have tended to be abstract, clinical and devoid of substance except at the highest levels of generality."[71] As a result, the quality of defense discussions in Canada has suffered.

There is nothing new to this approach. *Defence in the 70s* considered nuclear weapons only within the context of the central deterrent relationship, which it pronounced as increasingly stable, without any reference at all to the importance of theater and strategic nuclear weaponry to extended deterrence in Europe. The Mulroney government has only been marginally more expansive. *Challenge and Commitment* blandly referred to "the survivability of U.S. strategic nuclear forces" as "the keystone of NATO's assured retaliatory capability" and defined the nuclear relationship between the United States and the Soviet Union in terms of *mutual* deterrence, without exploring the relationship between the two concepts:

> Each superpower now has the capacity to obliterate the other, even after having absorbed a nuclear strike. For that reason, the structure of mutual deterrence today is effective and stable. The Government believes that it must remain so.[72]

Today in Canada, as in other countries, fear of nuclear war has abated. There remains, though, as a result of the conception of Canada's armed forces as servants of mutual deterrence, and in the wake of the worries and the confusion of the early and mid-1980s, a standard for defense cooperation with the United States that any Canadian government can openly transgress only at its political peril: Canadian military efforts on this continent can be justified only as contributions either to Canadian sovereignty or to nuclear stability, *as understood according to the finite deterrence or Canadian "apocalyptic" perspective.* Any proposal for cooperation with the United States will be subjected to at least some scrutiny to determine whether it involves support for flexible nuclear options, or for the diminution of the mutual vulnerability of the United States and the Soviet Union to each other's second strike.

Yet, as suggested above, in the 1990s U.S. nuclear strategy will continue to include elements at variance with that perspective: flexible targeting, counterforce options, and survivable forces.

Still, Canadians may not care in the 1990s. The public in Canada has never paid any sustained attention to defense issues. If relations between the United States and the Soviet Union continue to improve during the 1990s, the Canadian government will be left alone as it sets defense policy—just so long as it does not try to spend much money. "Peace" group activists and academic specialists who warn about the perceived dangers of U.S. strategy could be ignored.

Nonetheless, if Canadians become substantially more sanguine than Americans about the amount of prudence needed in dealing with the Soviet Union, U.S. nuclear policy could again be subject to scrutiny. An early indication of such a possible trend already could be found in 1990. The Mulroney government that year, in its annual statement on the defense budget, explained that "the most serious threat to Canada is a Soviet attack on North America," for the "capability of the USSR strategic forces had not lessened." The statement was widely derided in the press and by academic commentators as 'Cold War' thinking.[73]

Moreover, if, in the next several years, Canadian defense efforts are limited to North America, as now seems possible, that scrutiny could become all the more intense. A geographic shrinking of Canada's security commitments could have a deep impact on the ways Canadians view North American defense cooperation with the United States. John Barrett, at the time deputy director of the Canadian Centre for Arms Control and Disarmament in Ottawa, outlined a possible evolution in Canadian thinking:

> In the future, political support for defence policy may well be tied to the way in which it addresses issues of Canadian sovereignty. This trend is part of the overall tendency to define Canada's security questions in terms of a rather narrow, self-regarding conception of Canadian defence interests whose objectives are territorial integrity, control of territorial and coastal waters, and protection of sovereignty. As a result, there is a risk that the defence of Canada will come to be conceived as ending, rather than starting, at the country's territorial boundaries.[74]

Withdrawal from Germany could further, if not entirely, reorient Canadian defense policy in the direction Barrett outlined, especially insofar as the Canadian public in concerned. This could create still another uncomfortable dilemma for the Canadian government: fully uncoupled from the air and land defense of Europe, and fixed on defense roles related to the protection of Canadian sovereignty, Canadians could become even less sympathetic than they currently are to United States attempts to structure strategic nuclear forces for purposes other than just deterring an attack on North America. Yet with Canadian defense efforts centered almost entirely on North American tasks, the focus would inevitably be on the relationship between those tasks and the U.S. strategic posture. It is thus not surprising that a recent Canadian study warned of "a myopic, introverted future inside the North American bunker."[75]

Finally, two events could occur in the 1990s which would precipitate a renewed Canadian debate about the relationship between Canada and U.S. nuclear forces. The first would be a decision by the United States to deploy a limited ballistic missile defense system. The second, and more likely to occur, would be a decision to further modernize the North

American air defense system. These two possibilities are the subjects of the next two chapters.

NOTES

1. Michael Tucker, *Canadian Foreign Policy: Contemporary Issues and Themes* (Toronto: McGraw Hill Ryerson, 1980), 150.
2. John Barrett, "Arms Control and Canada's Security Policy." *International Journal* 42, no. 4 (Autumn 1987): 731.
3. See chapter 2, "The Nuclear Debate: 'the Apocalyptics' versus 'the Conventionalists,' " in Charles-Philippe David, *Debating Counterforce: A Conventional Approach in a Nuclear Age* (Boulder and London: Westview Press, 1987).
4. Philip Bobbitt, *Democracy and Deterrence: The History and Future of Nuclear Strategy* (New York: St. Martin's Press, 1988), 3.
5. Ibid.
6. Ibid.
7. The pursuit of extended deterrence extends to other allies, such as the Japanese and can include "extensive purpose (to compel a political act, e.g., to commence peace negotiations in Korea)" (Bobbitt, 10). Discussion will be limited to NATO.
8. Michael Vlahos, *Strategic Defense and the American Ethos: Can the Nuclear World be Changed?* SAIS Papers, no. 13 (Boulder and London: Westview Press, 1986), 31.
9. *U.S. President, Commission on Strategic Forces, Report of the President's Commission on Strategic Forces* (April 1983), 5–6.
10. Bobbitt, 10.
11. Robert McNamara, "The Military Role of Nuclear Weapons," *Foreign Affairs* 62, no. 1 (Fall 1983): 79. McNamara's substantially different earlier views are discussed below.
12. McGeorge Bundy, "Strategic Deterrence Thirty Years Later: What has Changed?" *The Future of Strategic Deterrence, Papers from the 21st Annual Conference of the IISS,* Adelphi Paper no. 160 (London: International Institute for Strategic Studies, 1980): 11.
13. Walter Slocombe, "The Countervailing Strategy," *International Security* 5, no. 4 (Spring 1981): 18.
14. Colin Gray and Keith Payne argued in a now famous, controversial essay entitled "Victory is Possible" that "the U.S. should plan to defeat the Soviet state and to do so at a cost that would not prohibit U.S. recovery." This would require not only counterforce offensive targeting but also civil defense, a ballistic missile defense (BMD) system and robust air defenses which together "should hold U.S. casualties down to a level compatible with national survival and recovery." Colin S. Gray and Keith Payne, "Victory is Possible," *Foreign Policy*, 39 (Summer 1980): 14. Thus the "nuclear warfighting" or "prevailing" school seeks an escape from U.S. vulnerability to devastation by the Soviet Union, and in that escape a U.S. ability to impose its political will on the Soviets.
15. Graham T. Allison, Albert Carnesdale, and Joseph S. Nye, *Hawks, Doves*

and Owls: An Agenda for Avoiding Nuclear War (New York: W. W. Norton, 1985), 218.

16. Bobbitt, 72.
17. Thomas C. Schelling, "What Went Wrong with Arms Control," *Foreign Affairs* 64, no. 2 (Winter 1985/1986): 230.
18. Bobbitt, 111.
19. Richard M. Nixon, report to Congress, *U.S. Foreign Policy for the 1970s, A New Strategy for Peace* (February 1970): 122; Richard M. Nixon, *A Report to Congress, U.S. Foreign Policy for the 1970s, Building for Peace* (1971): 170–71.
20. Vlahos, 32.
21. Quoted in Bobbitt, 90.
22. Secretary of Defense James R. Schlesinger, *Annual Defense Department Report, FY 1976* 2 (February 1975): 4.
23. These weapons have been removed as a result of the 1987 INF accord between the U.S. and the Soviet Union.
24. Harold Brown, address at Newport, 20 August 1980. Quoted in Bobbitt, 93.
25. Ibid.
26. Some, however, were dumb. See Robert Scheer, *With Enough Shovels: Reagan, Bush and Nuclear War* (New York: Vintage Books, 1983).
27. *New York Times*, 18 October 1981, 1.
28. *New York Times*, 30 May 1982, 1.
29. *New York Times*, 12 August 1983, 8.
30. Prepared statement of Hon. Caspar M. Weinberger, in U.S. Congress, Senate, Committee on Foreign Relations, Hearing, *U.S. Strategic Doctrine*, 14 December 1982, 97th Cong., 2d sess., Washington, 1983, 18–19.
31. Address before the Japanese Diet in Tokyo, 11 November 1983, *Public Papers of the President of the United States: Ronald Reagan*, 1983, vol. 2 (Washington: USGPO, 1985), 1575.
32. Statement by the NATO heads of government, the "London Declaration," 7 July 1990.
33. William W. Kaufman, *Glasnost, Perestroika and U.S. Defense Spending* (Washington: The Brookings Institution, 1990), 11, 12.
34. Canada, Department of National Defence, *Challenge and Commitment: A Defence Policy for Canada*, Ottawa, June 1987, 10.
35. Ibid.
36. See Don G. Bates, et al., "What Would Happen to Canada in a Nuclear War," in *Canada and the Nuclear Arms Race*, ed. Ernie Regehr and Simon Rosenblum (Toronto: James Lorimer and Company, 1983), 7.
37. I have been unable to track down the origin of this phrase. Mr. Geoffrey Pearson has told me he believes it was coined by his father, Lester B. Pearson.
38. Melvin Conant, *The Long Polar Watch: Canada and the Defense of North America* (New York: Harper and Brothers, 1962), 67.
39. Desmond Morton, "Defending the Indefensible: Some Historical Perspectives on Canadian Defence 1967–1987," *International Journal* 42, no. 4 (Autumn 1987): 629.

40. Joseph Joffre, "Peace and Populism: Why the European Anti-nuclear Movement Failed," *International Security* 2, no. 4 (Spring 1987), 17–18.
41. "Prime Minister's Remarks in the House of Commons on Peace and Security," 9 February 1984. Text in Pierre Elliott Trudeau, *Lifting the Shadow of War* ed. C. David Crenna (Edmonton: Hurtig, 1987), 106.
42. Lester B. Pearson, "The Development of Canadian Foreign Policy," *Foreign Affairs*, October 1951, 25–26.
43. Lester B. Pearson, *Mike: The Memoirs of the Right Honourable Lester B. Pearson, II, 1948–1957* (Toronto: University of Toronto Press, 1973), 165.
44. Arnold D. Heeney, *The Things That Are Caesar's: The Memoirs of a Canadian Public Servant* (Toronto: University of Toronto Press, 1972), 115.
45. John Foster Dulles, "The Evolution of Foreign Policy," address, 12 January 1954, *Department of State Bulletin* 30, no. 761 (25 January 1954): 107.
46. Quoted in James Eayrs, *In Defence of Canada: Growing Up Allied* (Toronto: University of Toronto Press, 1980), 253–54.
47. "A Look at the New Look," Canada, Department of External Affairs, *Statements and Speeches*, 54/16, 15 March 1954.
48. Canada, Department of National Defence, *White Paper on Defence,* March 1964, 12.
49. Testimony of Prof. David Cox, Queen's University; Canada, House of Commons, Standing Committee on External Affairs and National Defence, *Minutes of Proceedings and Evidence,* no. 16, 23 October 1980, 20.
50. As the executive director of the Canadian Institute for International Peace and Security observed. See Geoffrey Pearson, "The Debate in Canada on Issues of Peace and Security," in *The True North Strong and Free? Proceedings of a Public Inquiry into Canadian Defence Policy and Nuclear Arms* (West Vancouver: Gordon Soules Book Publishers, Ltd., 1987), 33.
51. The best work on this subject remains Jon B. McLin, *Canada's Changing Defense Policy, 1957–1963* (Baltimore: Johns Hopkins Press, 1967).
52. These arrangements are briefly discussed in *Challenge and Commitment,* 18.
53. See, for instance, the exchange reported in Canada, House of Commons, *Debates,* 19 March 1985, 3187–88.
54. Interview with Ronald Reagan, *Maclean's* 98, no. 11 (18 March 1985): 14.
55. See, for example, the statement by the American anti-nuclear activist, William Arkin, in *The True North Strong and Free,* 87.
56. Canada, House of Commons, *Debates,* 10 June 1958, 6186.
57. James Eayrs, "The Road from Ogdensburg," *Canadian Forum*, February 1971, 364–66.
58. See, for example, Lewis Hertzman, et al., *Alliances and Illusions: Canada and the NATO-NORAD Question* (Edmonton: Hurtig, 1969).
59. Canada, Minister of National Defence, *White Paper on Defence: Defence in the 70s,* Ottawa, 1971, 4.
60. Henry A. Kissinger, *White House Years* (Boston: Little Brown, 1979), 383.
61. *Defence in the 70s,* 6.
62. John Holmes, *Canada: A Middle-Aged Power* (Toronto: McClelland and Stewart, 1976), 213.
63. Testimony of Prof. Stephen Clarkson of the University of Toronto, in Canada, House of Commons, Standing Committee on External Affairs and National

Defence, *Minutes of Proceedings and Evidence,* no. 46 (20 November 1985): 22.

64. Marion Kerans, "The Women's International Peace Conference," in *Roots of Peace; The Movement Against Militarism in Canada,* ed. Eric Shragge (Toronto: Between the Lines, 1986): 151.

65. Quoted in *Lifting the Shadow of War,* 63.

66. A short history and collection of documents related to Trudeau's "peace initiative" is to be found in *Lifting the Shadow of War.* For critical analyses of the initiative, see Michael Tucker, "Trudeau and the Politics of Peace," and Adam Bromke and Kim Richard Nossal, "Trudeau Rides the 'Third Rail,'" both in the May/June 1984 edition of *International Perspectives.* Michael Pearson, Gregor Mackinnon, and Christopher Sapardanis argue that the initiative can be termed a success in "'The World is Entitled to Ask Questions': The Trudeau Peace Initiative Reconsidered," *International Journal,* Winter 1985–86, 129. See also Richard and Sandra Gwyn, "The Politics of Peace," *Saturday Night,* May 1984, 19.

67. Canada, House of Commons, Standing Committee on External Affairs and National Defence, *NORAD 1986,* Ottawa, 1985, 35.

68. A scathing attack on the Canadian "peace" movement is to be found in Maurice Tugwell, *Peace with Freedom* (Toronto: Key Porter Books, 1988). A short account by a leading member of the movement is to be found in Robert Penner, "A Brief Overview and Analysis of the Canadian Peace Movement Since 1982," *The Name of the Chamber Was Peace* (Toronto: Samuel Stevens and Company, 1988), 45.

69. Simon Rosenblum, *Misguided Missiles: Canada, the Cruise and Star Wars* (Toronto: Lorimer, 1985), 10, 13–14. Just as the INF deployments became the focal point for European "peace" groups, and the nuclear "freeze" proposal that of the Americans, their Canadian counterparts focused on the proposed testing of unarmed air launched cruise missiles (ALCMs) by the U.S. Air Force in northern Canada where the terrain matched that of the Soviet Union. Many Canadians argued that "the cruise" was a destabilizing weapon designed to support the dangerous U.S. strategy. As the research director of Project Ploughshares put it, "The cruise missile is dedicated to the proposition that it is possible to fight and 'prevail' in a nuclear war. It seeks to present nuclear war as a viable alternative and it is this that makes it an immensely dangerous weapon." Ibid., 78.

70. R. B. Byers, et al., *Canada and Western Security* (Toronto: Atlantic Council of Canada, 1982), 24–25.

71. R. B. Byers, *Canadian Security and Defence: The Legacy and the Challenges,* Adelphi paper 214 (London: International Institute for Strategic Studies, Winter 1986), 17.

72. *Challenge and Commitment,* 17. Still, some Canadian analysts have attached importance to the fact that *Challenge and Commitment* identified the possibility of *Soviet* nuclear threat to North America as the prime threat to Canadian security, as opposed to the more even-handed "catastrophic war between the superpowers" that the Liberals had identified in *Defence in the 70s.*

73. *Defence Newsletter* (Toronto), no. 9, March 1990, 9-10. For a brief discussion of these reactions see Joel J. Sokolsky, "North American Defense and Security Collaboration: Sustaining a 'Limited' Partnership," forthcoming, The Institute for Foreign Policy Analysis, Inc.
74. Barrett, 731.
75. Tom Keating and Larry Pratt, *Canada, NATO and the Bomb* (Edmonton: Hurtig, 1988), vii.

V

Canada and Ballistic
Missile Defense

The Strategic Defense Initiative (SDI) was launched by President Reagan in 1983 to research and develop ballistic missile defense (BMD) technologies. The sweeping improvements in Soviet-American relations, doubts about BMD technology, questions about the strategic implications of BMD and the huge U.S. fiscal deficit have led many to conclude that there will never be BMD deployments. This may very well prove to be the case, especially since skepticism in Congress is deep.

Yet the SDI research program continues. So does the support for it of the Bush administration. The president emphasized in early 1990 that "In the 1990s, strategic defense makes sense more than ever before," although he made no commitment to actual deployment. The administration asked Congress for an appropriation of US$4.66 billion in FY 1991, an increase of 22 percent. *Aviation Week and Space Technology* concluded, "it appears that the Bush Administration's commitment to SDI research programs, while not as strong as the preceding administration's, is substantial. . . . Whatever the outcome of the debate on the changing nature of the Soviet threat, the Administration appears to want the program to move forward toward a decision on deploying a missile defense system in the mid-1990s."[1] In 1991 the program was politically boosted by the spectacle of Patriot missiles destroying Iraqi Scud missiles and by the successful test of a key BMD component, the ERIS missile. At this point, a presidential decision on deployment is scheduled for 1993.

SDI has been the most difficult defense development a Canadian government has had to deal with since the nuclear weapons imbroglio a quarter century ago. The debate in Canada has been quite different, though, from the one in the United States. Americans have been arguing with intensity since 1983 about the wisdom of spending billions of tax dollars on a BMD research program, about the characteristics and potential effectiveness of BMD technologies, and above all whether or not, as well as under what circumstances, it might make sense to put in place new strategic defenses. Canadians, for the most part, have been, since SDI was launched in 1983, utterly unenthusiastic about, if not hostile to the idea of such defenses. North of the border, the question is how to deal tactically (and tactfully) with the Americans and their unsettling new strategic defense schemes. The fact that the Mulroney government, early in its first term in office, endorsed the SDI research program, becoming thereby the first allied government to do so, tends to obscure widespread Canadian unease with the concept of BMD and deep concern about what it might mean for Canada.

These worries are shared by the Mulroney government. In fact, the possibility that the United States may proceed with the deployment of a BMD system again confronts Canadians with the paradox described at the beginning of the last chapter. Opting out of North American defense because it included a U.S. BMD system would come at a cost to Canadian sovereignty. Staying in could link Canadians to an effort of which they probably will not approve.

In one very real sense, the BMD issue is moot: today, there is no U.S. BMD system and, depending upon the fruits of SDI research and the decisions the U.S. government reaches over the next decade or so, there may never be one. So SDI debates consist of "discussion and analysis about something that does not exist, may or may not ever exist, and, if it does, may exist in ways and with capabilities that cannot be fully predicted. It is, in other words, impossible to pass final judgment on a system whose characteristics are unknown, although an unfortunate amount of analysis has attempted to do precisely that."[2]

But politically, the matter has been far from moot in Canada. It was not entirely jokingly that the great American scholar of Canada, John Sloan Dickey, once wrote that "Canadians are born knowing that 'the United States will get you if you don't watch out.' "[3] How to make sure *now* that any Canadian involvement in SDI remains minimal is a principal theme of Canadian defense debates and colors Canadian thinking defense cooperation with the United States, especially air defense.

This chapter describes the sources and nature of Canadian uneasiness over SDI, and how it is reflected in current policy. Then—with the warning cited above about the dangers of prediction in mind—it outlines the extent to which emerging BMD technologies may directly involve Canada. It offers no conclusion about whether the United States should ever deploy a BMD system, much less a prediction as to which decisions the president or the Congress will reach in the mid-1990s. Rather, the focus is on what a decision to deploy could mean for U.S.-Canadian defense cooperation.

CANADIAN ATTITUDES TOWARD BMD

From the very start, there was little chance that Canadians would embrace the SDI program. In fact, it would be hard to imagine a defense development in the United States more likely to elicit an unenthusiastic Canadian reaction. Canadian strategic thinking, political culture, and sovereignty worries all militate against its acceptance.

As discussed in the previous chapter, Canadian strategic thinking is all but universally of the "finite deterrence" or "apocalyptic" variant. Canadians, for the most part, have concluded that strategic stability and their national security are best to be found in the condition of superpower mutual vulnerability that currently prevails.

For adherents of this approach, strategic defenses are to be avoided. "If one's view of a proper nuclear strategy is based primarily upon attacks against urban-industrial targets, defenses—unless perfect—have little strategic value."[4] Finite deterrence adherents castigate limited defenses as destabilizing, in two senses: first, they would provoke an offense/defense competition, thereby accelerating the arms race. Second, they would decrease strategic stability in that it they would create a strong incentive to strike first, leaving the defenses the need to handle only the "ragged" remnants of the enemy's retaliatory forces.[5] Strategic arms control remains a prime goal for this approach. Preserving the 1972 ABM Treaty, which bans extensive missile defenses and limits the testing of BMD technology is consequently of paramount importance. The only circumstance in which most adherents might endorse a BMD deployment is in the context of a new Soviet-American arms control agreement, restricting numbers of offensive weapons and limiting BMD to the protection of those weapons, not urban populations.

The leadership of all three major Canadian political parties subscribe to this assessment of BMD. The Special Committee on National Defence of the Canadian Senate, dominated by members of the Liberal Party, gave voice to typical Canadian sentiment when it warned that if Canada were to support SDI

> it would be going against the grain of its own solidly-established policies on arms control and disarmament. For the world at large, the deployment of extensive ballistic missile defences would negate one of the key achievements of the post-war arms control process: the 1972 ABM Treaty. It would also run counter to the spirit of current arms control accords concerning outer space and might well destroy any hope of establishing new accords banning space weaponry. The result would be a world caught up in a massive new arms race when instead it desperately needs bold new moves to establish lasting peace and security.[6]

For its part, the New Democratic Party's official spokesman on defense issues described SDI as "the most destabilizing defence offensive system which has ever been devised by man to date."[7] Prime Minister Mulroney shares these concerns, although with an eye on good relations with the United States he has expressed them far more cautiously.

As he told the North Atlantic Assembly in 1987, if the United States were ever to proceed with the deployment of BMD,

> extreme care must be taken to ensure that defences are not integrated with existing forces in such a way as to create fears of a first strike. And second, we cannot allow strategic defences to undermine the arms control process and existing agreements: the transition should be mutually agreed upon. Without such mutuality, chaos would follow and stability could crumble.[8]

In keeping with this approach, Ottawa frequently urged the Reagan Administration through a wide variety of diplomatic channels in 1987 against the so-called "broad" interpretation of the ABM Treaty that would permit the fairly extensive testing of BMD technologies outside the laboratory.

As many have argued, the SDI program must be seen not only as a presidential vision or a strategic response to recent military trends, but also as the product of a uniquely American political and cultural ethos.[9] The Canadian reaction to the program has similarly been shaped by the legacy of Canadian traditions. Years ago James Eayrs put his finger on a key cultural difference between Canadians and Americans when he remarked on "that characteristically American belief that some swift and spectacular stroke may permanently solve problems that by their nature admit only of amelioration. The Canadian is struck by the American fondness for the 'one-shot solution,' for the 'crash program,' for 'doctrines.' "[10]

Outlining this fundamental difference between the two North American peoples is a traditional task for Canadian scholars and commentators, especially when dealing with an American audience. The acclaimed Canadian novelist Margaret Atwood once told such an audience that

> Americans think anything can be changed, torn down and re-built, re-written. Canadians tend to think nothing can. Both are wrong, of course. Americans get discouraged when they can't get instant results; they vacillate between romantic idealism and black humour, its opposite. Canadians on the other hand think any change will probably be for the worse. Consequently they are less easily stampeded, less extreme in their trends.[11]

There are several standard explanations for Americans having developed a strong "can do" strain in their culture ("unthinkingly and breezily aggressive" is Atwood's admittedly stereotypical summary) while the Canadian approach is often skeptical, if not timid ("peevishly and hesitantly defensive" is how she puts it). At the top of almost any list of explanations, including Eayrs', is the American revolutionary tradition and the Canadian lack thereof. Canada got underway in the eighteenth century as a collection of peoples who had consciously rejected the American revolution: Tories (Loyalists, as they are called in Canada) driven out of or fleeing the thirteen colonies as well as French Canadians in Québec seeking to preserve their language and values. All saw the British crown and British connection as protection against the threatening, unruly, exuberant rambunctiousness to the south. Many have argued that Canada's harsher climate and often more difficult geography have conditioned a stance of coping or surviving, as opposed to triumphant settlement. Finally, Canada's eternal linguistic and regional quarrels, as well as its status as a smaller power always in alliance with a greater, imperial power, and as an open economy subject to being buffeted by the trade and investment policies of other, larger economies, have always placed a premium on accommodation, negotiation, and putting aside that which for the moment cannot be resolved.

Whatever weight must be lent to whichever historical and geographic causes, great strokes and bold, confident schemes and gestures have not been encouraged in such a setting, although it is worth again observing that Canadians, without the exuberance and dynamism of their southern neighbors, still managed to create a second transcontinental country. It also bears underlining that Canadians are proud of not only that fact, but of the gentler, less violent, less aggressive nature of their society, in which the government continues to play a leading role.

Therefore, when Ronald Reagan announced in his 1983 SDI address that "tonight we're launching an effort which holds the promise of changing the course of human history,"[12] an automatic Canadian response was—"Here they [i.e., the Americans] go again." A great scheme was being launched, in typically American fashion designed to "solve" the nuclear weapons problem. The implications for Canada were uncertain and probably bad. A good deal of the negative reaction to SDI in Canada has been on this "peevishly and hesitantly defensive" level.

That Canadians would worry about the impact of any eventual BMD deployments on their territorial sovereignty is hardly surprising, given the history of sovereignty problems with the United States in the Second World War and in the bomber age. Just as the last major vestige of the American military presence on Canadian soil, the old Distant Early Warning (DEW) Line, is being turned into the Canadian-operated North Warning System, SDI has held out the prospect of threatening to reverse the process, now underway for years, of Canadianization of air defense activities in Canada. The sovereignty theme has played a very prominent role in discussions of the SDI issue, as Canadians imagine scores of BMD installations located across their northland, operated by Americans and put there with or without Canadian endorsement. "It is readily apparent," observed a sober study prepared at one of Canada's leading academic centers of strategic studies, "that at least some of the technologies currently under study by the United States would require deployment in Canada if they are to achieve maximum military effectiveness."[13] "There is virtually no doubt," a sensationalist tract recently released by Canada's most important academic publisher has warned, "that in order to set up a full-fledged space defence system the United States will want to use Canadian soil."[14] "We are reliably informed that northern Canada and Alaska are included in the plans for the Pentagon's star wars and for the components of star wars, such as our becoming the first line of an ABM defense," intoned the foreign affairs critic of the New Democratic Party on the floor of the House of Commons.[15]

The events of a 1985 presidential-prime ministerial summit, held at Quebec City, have left Canadians permanently on guard for the possibility that the United States may want to use Canadian territory for BMD purposes. At the Québec summit, President Reagan, no doubt to the unspoken dismay of his host, delivered a televised address to the Canadian people in which he dwelt on his cherished SDI program. He said, no doubt from the heart, that "the possibility of developing and sharing with you the technology that could provide a security shield, and someday eliminate the threat of nuclear attack, is for us the most hopeful possibility of the nuclear age."[16] Secretary of Defense Caspar Weinberger, who had accompanied the president to Québec, was asked in an interview with a Canadian television network where the "launchers" would be located in a hypothetical, advanced defense system against cruise missiles. His infelicitous, even disrespectful response to the poorly premised question was that some might be put in Canada, some in the United States, some at sea. "It just depends on where is the most effective technical place for them."[17] Clarifications were immediately issued by American officials in Québec to the effect that the United States would never deploy any weapon system in Canada without Canadian permission. But the impression had been created that Weinberger, in an unguarded moment, had really been talking about SDI, not cruise missile defenses, and that, the denials notwithstanding he had tipped the U.S. hand: the United States already had plans for BMD deployments in Canada, Canadian sovereignty also notwithstanding.

Unfortunately, much Canadian thinking about the role Canadian territory would play in BMD is based on analogies with the longstanding role the country has played in continental air defense. Canadian territory lies beneath the flight paths of Soviet bombers. Establishing air defense in depth requires pushing the battle northward into Canada. For that purpose, air defense early warning radars have long been located on Canadian soil, as are fighter aircraft. Canadian territory also lies beneath the paths of ballistic missiles. Therefore, Canadians are often led to conclude, ground-based BMD systems would need to be forward deployed in Canada. Yet, as will be discussed below, this ignores the actual characteristics of many of the systems being explored.

There is, it should be added, one significant Canadian constituency not opposed to cooperation with the United States in the development of BMD. Canadian air force officials worry that they may be shut out of access to the very technology, especially space-base elements, they could put to use to defend Canadian sovereignty. They argue that Canadian opposition can in no way slow the United States, but can in the long run damage Canadian interests.

SDI has been a very tricky issue for the Mulroney government to handle. Repudiation of the program would have been domestically very popular, and in line with the government's own strategic thinking. But as Douglas Ross of the University of British Columbia has put it, "The leadership of any middlepower with even the most rudimentary appreciation of diplomatic prudence would certainly understand clearly that it could dissent from the declaratory 'visions' of a superpower neighbour only with the utmost caution—if it chose to dissent in public at all."[18] That rule may be true for any government. But the Mulroney government has pursued a policy of close ties with the United States. "Good relations, super relations with the United States will be the cornerstone of our foreign policy," is how the prime minister once put it on the campaign trail.

So the Progressive Conservatives have pursued a two-track policy endorsing U.S. SDI research, and at the same time distancing Canada from the program. The endorsement came in a January, 1985 statement by the secretary of state for external affairs, Joe Clark, that was the very model of cautious, limited approval. Canada, he said, found SDI research by the United States "only prudent." He offered no support for President Reagan's vision of a world where nuclear weapons had been rendered impotent and obsolete through the deployment of extensive strategic defenses. Nor did he for a moment suggest that the Canadian government believed that the time had come seriously to consider the strategic desirability of eventually deploying a BMD system to protect North America. Rather, he said, BMD research by the United States had been necessitated by "significant Soviet advances in ballistic missile defence research in recent years and deployment of an actual ballistic missile defence system" [around Moscow]. The West would have to "keep abreast of the feasibility of such projects."[19]

The implication of the Canadian government's stance was that SDI research was necessary only because a Soviet breakout in BMD was a possibility or because it might be used as an American bargaining chip in strategic arms negotiations with the Soviets. Lest there be any misunderstanding, Clark added that actual deployment of BMD and any transgression of the ABM Treaty "could have serious implications for arms control and would therefore warrant close and careful attention by all concerned." Canada, he said, therefore welcomed President

Reagan's pledge "that the U.S.A. would not proceed beyond research without discussion and negotiation."[20]

The distancing between Canada and SDI became policy later in 1985, after the government's refusal to repudiate outright SDI provoked fairly widespread domestic condemnation.[21] The occasion was an invitation from the U.S. government for Canada to participate in the SDI research program. On 7 September 1985 the prime minister announced that Canada's "own policies and priorities do not warrant a government-to-government effort in support of SDI research." However, Canadian private companies and institutions would be free to do so.[22]

In one sense, this has been nothing short of a political master stroke. The endorsement of the prudence of SDI research remains in place and Canadian industry remains free to try pursuing whatever benefits to be had from the program. Yet the "polite no" to official Canadian participation in that research "was treated in fact as a victory of sorts by the anti-SDI forces across the country, and thus that element of the population leaning towards militant rejectionism was mollified."[23] Moreover, the prime minister had demonstrated independence from the United States mitigating, for the moment, charges at home that he followed the American lead too often. Mulroney himself chortled at the time that he had pulled the rug "right out from under" the feet of his critics.[24]

On the other hand, this stance leaves the Canadian government permanently on the political defensive. For reasons also discussed in the previous chapter, Canadian defense efforts on this continent can be politically justified by Ottawa only as contributions either to Canadian sovereignty or to nuclear stability, as understood according to the finite deterrence or Canadian "apocalyptic" perspective. Any Canadian participation in SDI would have failed that test. Indeed, Canadian critics of SDI often cite the very existence of the research program as proof of fundamental, and deepening divergences between United States and Canadian strategic thinking.

Because the Mulroney government has not repudiated SDI outright, any steps it takes in cooperation with the United States for the defense of North America—from modernization of air defenses to renewal of the NORAD agreement—are subject to even more intense domestic scrutiny than would already be the case. The point of such scrutiny is to determine if those efforts are in some fashion linked to the SDI research program, or could in the long run commit Canada to supporting the operation of some future U.S. BMD system. Canadian worries have attenuated since it became clear that nothing would come of the hopes of many in the Reagan administration to move rapidly towards BMD deployment.

U.S. BMD OPTIONS FOR 1991—AND CANADA

President Reagan asked in his 1983 address, "What if free people could live secure in the knowledge that their security did not rest upon the threat of instant retaliation to deter a Soviet attack, that we could intercept and destroy strategic ballistic missiles before they reached our own soil or that of our allies." He therefore called upon the scientific community "to give us the means of rendering . . . nuclear weapons impotent and obsolete."[25]

Whether defenses of such robustness to be, in effect, "leakproof" could ever be developed, while doubtful, remains an open question. But the United States faces the more immediate decision in the 1990s whether to deploy not the perfect or near-perfect defense, but a more limited system capable of destroying only a portion of attacking missiles, possibly as a first step towards a more robust system. The elements of three alternative systems emerged as principal candidates for potential deployment by the end of the 1990s (see Table 5.1).

TABLE 5.1
POTENTIAL FIRST-PHASE U.S. BMD SYSTEMS

Proposed System	Interceptors	Estimated Capability
Phase One (Original) (SDIO, revised, Oct. 1988)	1500 in orbit 1700 ground-based	Destroy 30% of attack by 4700 warheads
"Brilliant Pebbles" (Abrahamson description)	"thousands" in orbit	"more than Phase One"
Accidental Launch Protection System (ALPS) (Lockheed & McDonnell Douglas)	100 ground-based	Destroy small number of warheads

Source: *Congressional Quarterly.*

The first is the original, official "Phase One" system proposed by the Strategic Defense Initiative Organization (SDIO), and involves a combination of ground-based and space-based systems, described below. The SDIO argues that its Phase One system, even though it could destroy only about a third of a Soviet attack of less than 5000 warheads, would strengthen deterrence by "denying the predictability of Soviet attack outcome . . . and imposing on the Soviets significant costs to restore their attack confidence."[26] In other words, it would strengthen deterrence by introducing *uncertainty* into Soviet planning that an attack could succeed. The SDIO at first estimated the cost of deploying the system at $69 billion, although this estimate has been questioned by the General Accounting Office. Follow-on technology to the Phase One system now being researched could allow, according to the SDIO, for an increasingly robust system. Phase Two would not just create uncertainty as in phase one, but actually deny the Soviets the capability to achieve the military goals of a nuclear attack on the United States. Finally, a full-scale, third phase system could assure the survival of American society.

The second system, which would have roughly the same capabilities to destroy Soviet missiles as the official Phase One system, is the entirely space-based "brilliant pebbles" concept, developed by SDI scientists at the Lawrence Livermore Laboratory. Originally a research sidelight, the idea has been championed by the SDIO's former director, Lieut. General James Abrahamson, who has estimated deployment cost at the much lower cost of $25 billion. It also has caught the attention of the Bush Administration. Secretary of Defense Richard Cheney has directed the SDIO to intensify its research on the concept, which now appears to be emerging as the centerpiece of the SDI program. It would consist of thousands of small interceptor missiles in orbit, each equipped with an optical sensor allowing them to home in on and destroy Soviet missiles in the boost phase. Each interceptor would be small and cheap. There would also be no need for an elaborate and expensive control system inasmuch as each "pebble" simply would be programmed to home in on any missile in its detection range.[27]

In 1989, the official "Phase One" system was modified by the SDIO to include "brilliant pebbles." However, in 1990 a strong push was underway in the U.S. Congress to shift SDI research away from space-based elements and towards an emphasis on ground-based systems.

The third, dubbed the accidental launch protection system or ALPS would be the most limited in capabilities. As the name indicates, it would only provide a defense against the accidental or unauthorized launch of a very small number of missiles. Proposed by Lockheed and McDonnell Douglas Corporation at an estimated cost of $9.7 billion, it was originally championed by Sen. Sam Nunn of Georgia. It could rely on ground-based interceptor missiles being developed as part of the official Phase One program. ALPS would have two immediate attractions. First, the 1972 ABM Treaty permits a single-site BMD deployment of not more than 100 launchers. (The Soviet Union currently has a single system around Moscow.) Second, it is already being seized upon by supporters of more extensive BMD deployments. "Politically the nation would have crossed the Rubicon by deploying some kind of defense" is how an official of the Heritage Foundation recently put it.[28]

Today, it is impossible to say with any certainty whether the Bush administration (or its successor) will propose deployment of any system, or just as importantly whether the Congress would be prepared to approve it. No firm policy on the desirability of deployment in the 1990s has emerged in the administration. The American Conservative Union has identified 33 senators and 125 members of the House as staunch opponents of SDI, and 35 senators and 98 as ardent supporters.[29] But this may not be an accurate guide to how the Congress would vote on actual deployment, as opposed to just continuation of research.

Questions will still have to be answered, and not only in the minds of senior administration officials, about the affordability and technical feasibility of any proposed BMD system. Two other obvious questions will also stand out concerning deployment of either the SDIO's Phase One system or the "brilliant pebbles" concept, if they are conceived as anti-Soviet systems. The first is whether deterrence—including extended deterrence—would in fact best be strengthened by the introduction of uncertainty through limited defenses. Yet whether limited defenses would strengthen or weaken extended deterrence already is the subject of debate in the United States. On the one hand, "some argue that the SDI would strengthen extended deterrence because the stronger the shield behind which the United States sits, the more willing it would be, and appear to be, to take measures that might provoke Soviet strategic retaliation on the U.S. homeland."[30] On the other hand, if the Soviets were to match a U.S. BMD deployment with one of their own, striking at Soviet military targets would become more difficult. "The irony of strategic defense is that cities and population centers very likely could move from the bottom to the top of targeting priorities for both the United States and the Soviet Union."[31] Under such circumstances, the credibility could be severely diminished of the U.S. pledge to engage its strategic nuclear arsenal to deter attacks on its allies. Alternatives include further modernization of strategic offensive forces and the further pursuit of arms control agreements with the Soviets, especially in the current climate.

The second concerns the relationship between limited defenses and future offensive and defensive developments. One way for the Soviets to counter the effectiveness of limited defenses would be to increase the number and penetrability of their offensive weapons. This increase could, in theory, be countered by improving the defenses. But "follow-on" BMD technologies may not be proven by the time the debate over first phase deployment begins in earnest. As the Office of Technology Assessment (a Congressional agency) recently observed in a report on SDI:

> a rational commitment to a 'phase-one' development and deployment of BMD before the second and third phases had been proven feasible, affordable, and survivable would imply: a) belief that the outstanding technical issues will be favorably resolved later, b) willingness to settle for interim BMD capabilities that would decline as Soviet offenses improved;

or c) belief that U.S. efforts will persuade the Soviets to join in reducing offensive forces and moving toward a defense dominated world.[32]

But recently, proponents of SDI have shifted direction to emphasize the so-called "n-th country" problem: nuclear armed ballistic missiles in the hands of Third World states, or of "irrational leaders, rogue commanders and terrorists."[33] Indeed, "SDI policy-makers now argue that the threat posed by non-superpower ballistic missiles is the strongest justification for continued SDI spending."[34] President Bush seems to agree. He told the Congress during his January 1991 State of the Union address, "I have directed that the SDI program be refocussed on providing protection from limited ballistic missile strikes, whatever their source. Let us pursue an SDI program that can deal with any future threat to the U.S., to our forces overseas, and to our friends and allies."

It is striking that, Canadian fears notwithstanding, none of the three candidate first-phase BMD systems now being given prominent consideration in the United States would require the use of Canadian territory:

• The "brilliant pebbles" system, being space-based, would therefore obviously not involve Canadian territory.

• The SDIO's original "Phase One" system also included three space-based systems: 6 Boost Surveillance and Tracking System (BSTS) satellites, to detect and track ballistic missiles in the boost stage; 150 Space-Based Interceptor (SBI) satellites, each housing 10 rocket-propelled interceptors intended to acquire, home in on and destroy missiles in the boost phase and reentry vehicles in the mid-course phase; and a Space-Based Surveillance and Tracking System (SSTS), for the mid-course phase. The SSTS and SBI will also have capabilities against Soviet antisatellite weapons (ASATs) in order to protect the space-based elements against attack (see Table 5.2).

Three of the Phase One systems are ground-based: a Ground Based Surveillance and Tracking System (GSTS) which relies on infrared probes that would be launched into space upon warning ("popped-up") to track reentry vehicles in the mid-course and early terminal phase; 1700 small Exoatmospheric Reentry Vehicle Interceptor System (ERIS) missiles to destroy reentry vehicles in the late mid-course phase; and finally a Battle Management/Command and Control, and Communication (BM/C³) system.

The BM/C³ system would necessarily be located in the United States. The ERIS vehicle is expected to have a range of several thousand kilometers, long enough to permit the interceptors to be based in the continental United States, yet still allowing them to attack reentry vehicles in the late mid-course phase. The final ground-based component, GSTS

TABLE 5.2
SDI "PHASE ONE" TECHNOLOGIES

Name	Function	Offensive Weapon Phase
Space-Based		
Boost Surveillance and Tracking System (BSTS)	—Detection of missile launches —Acquisition and Tracking of missiles —Kill assessment	—Boost
Space Based Interceptor (SBI)	—Disabling of boosters, RVs & ASATS —On board sensors for enhanced mid-course capability	—Boost & Midcourse
Space-based Surveillance and Tracking System (SSTS)	—Acquire & track boosters, RVs and ASATS —Discrimination	—Boost & Midcourse
Ground-Based		
Ground-Based Surveillance and Tracking System (GSTS) (pop-up system)	—Acquire and track RVs —Discrimination	—Midcourse & early Terminal
Exoatmospheric Re-entry Vehicle Interceptor System (ERIS)	—Disable RVs in late midcourse	—Midcourse
Battle Management/ Command, Control and Communication System (BM/C³)	—Man-in-Loop Control —Engagement management —Maintaining Track Data —Target Assignment —Communications	—Boost, Midcourse & Terminal

Source: SDIO

sensors atop missiles that would boost them into ballistic trajectory, could also be deployed in the United States. To be sure, moving them northward 1000 km would gain several hundred seconds extension of battle space, time that could be potentially useful in discriminating earlier among RVs, debris and decoys. There appears to be no technical reason, though, why deployment in Alaska or possibly at sea would not be satisfactory.

• Finally, the ALPS system would consist of 100 ERIS-type missiles, based in the United States, probably at the abandoned U.S. ABM site at Grand Forks, North Dakota.

Beyond the first phase, predictions about the utility of Canadian territory well into the next century become highly speculative. The SDIO has more tentatively identified six possible "follow-on" systems. Here the exotic technology appears. Two systems would be space-based: a Neutral Particle Beam Weapon (NPB) and a Space-Based Laser (SBL) to attack missiles in the boost stage and reentry vehicles mid-course. Both would have capability to distinguish between decoys and targets ("discrimination"). Four would be ground-based: a Ground-based Laser (GBL) that would "bounce" a beam off space-based mirrors to destroy missiles in the boost stage; Ground-Based Radar (GBR) to track reentry vehicles in the mid-course and terminal stage; a hypervelocity gun (HVG) to disable reentry in the terminal stage with small projectiles delivered at extremely high speeds; and High Endo-Atmospheric Defense Interceptor (HEDI). HEDI, which would deal with re-entry vehicles in the terminal phase, may have capabilities against low-trajectory submarine-launched ballistic missiles. This could lead to its being added to a phase one system. Finally, one element, the Airborne Optical System (AOS), would be carried in a modified Boeing 767 aircraft and track targets in the late mid-course and terminal phases. Development of the AOS is proceeding apace; it too, might be added to a phase one system.

An analysis by John Pike of the Washington-based Federation of American Scientists (and a critic of SDI) that has been widely reported in Canada and forms the basis of much Canadian thinking about the issue suggests that Canadian airspace might prove necessary for AOS operations, while Canadian territory could be needed for a full gamut of ground-based systems, including GBL. Still, he warns that "it is probably too early to draw firm conclusions as to the political implications for Canada of many of these projects."[35] For their part, officials of the SDIO stress that the technical characteristics of these follow-on systems, much less their feasibility, are still so uncertain that it would be all but impossible to determine with certainty the requirements for potential locations at this stage of ground-based systems beyond the phase one technologies.

In short, the United States does not need Canadian territory for any first-phase BMD system it may choose in the 1990s to deploy. Nonetheless, the deployment of a first-phase system could intensify Canadian concerns that their territory might be needed for any follow-on systems. Moreover, any first-phase BMD system in the 1990s could affect North American air defense efforts, in which Canada and Canadians play central roles. Such a system would also be placed under the command arrangements for North American aerospace defense, which today are jointly maintained by the United States and Canada and which are the subjects of the next two chapters.

NOTES

1. "Politics Holds Key to Pace of Strategic Defense Research," *Aviation Week and Space Technology* 132, no. 12 (19 March 1990), 62.
2. Donald M. Snow, "Is Ballistic Missile Defense a Good Idea?" in *The Technology, Strategy, and Politics of SDI,* ed. Stephen J. Cimbala (Boulder and London: The Westview Press, 1987), 26.
3. John Sloan Dickey, *Canada and the American Presence: The United States Interest in an Independent Canada* (New York: New York University Press, 1975), xi.
4. Leon Sloss and Seymour Weiss, "Strategic Defense: A Third View," in *The Technology, Strategy, and Politics of SDI,* 59.
5. For a full exposition of these views in an American context, see Spurgeon M. Keeney (President of the Arms Control Association of the U.S.), "The Case Against SDI," in Stephen W. Guerrier and Wayne C. Thompson, eds., *Perspectives on Strategic Defense* (Boulder and London: Westview Press, 1987), 60.
6. Canada Senate, Special Committee on National Defence, *Canada's Territorial Air Defence,* January 1985, 54.
7. Ibid., 13 March 1985, 2979.
8. Notes for an address by the . . . Prime Minister before the North Atlantic Assembly, Quebec City, 23 May 1987; text, Prime Minister's Office, Ottawa.
9. See, for example, Michael Vlahos, *Strategic Defense and the American Ethos: Can the Nuclear World be Changed* (Boulder and London: Westview Press, 1986).
10. James Eayrs, *Northern Approaches: Canada and the Search for Peace* (Toronto: Macmillan Company of Canada, 1961), 8.
11. Margaret Atwood, "Canadian-American Relations: Surviving the Eighties," *Second Words: Selected Critical Prose* (Toronto: Anansi, 1982), 383.
12. Address to the Nation on Defense and National Security, 23 March 1983, *Public Papers of the Presidents of the United States, Ronald Reagan* 1883, I (USGPO, 1984): 443.
13. Martin Shadwick, "NORAD, Sovereignty and Changing Technology," Occasional Paper no. 3, Research Programme in Strategic Studies, York University, 1985, p. 3.
14. John Honderich, *Arctic Imperative: Is Canada Losing the North?* (Toronto: University of Toronto Press, 1987), 137.
15. Canada, House of Commons, *Debates,* 31 January 1985, 1864.
16. Presidential address, Quebec City, 18 March 1985. *Weekly Compilation of Presidential Documents* 25 March 1985, 322.
17. Quoted in Peter Goodspeed, "Missile Defense Could be Placed Here U.S. Says," *Toronto Star,* 18 March 1987, 7.
18. Douglas Ross, "Canadian-American Relations and the Strategic Defense Initiative: A Case Study in the Management of Strategic Doctrinal Incompatibilities," paper presented for the 1987 Pearson-Dickey Conference,

Montebello, Quebec, 4–6 November 1987, 5.
19. Canada, House of Commons, *Debates*, 21 January 1985, 1502.
20. Ibid.
21. In addition to objections by others, the two opposition parties together supported a motion in the House of Commons that condemned the government for "its failure to make specific that Canada would not participate in any way in the 'star wars' project of the U.S." Canada, House of Commons, *Debates*, 19 March 1985, 3193–94.
22. Prime Minister's statement, 7 September 1985; text, Prime Minister's Office, Ottawa.
23. Ross, "Canadian American Relations and the Strategic Defense Initiative," 25.
24. *Debates*, 10 September 1985, 6454.
25. Address to the Nation on Defense and National Security, 443.
26. U.S. Department of Defense, Strategic Defense Initiative Organization, *Report to Congress on the Strategic Defense Initiative*, April 1987, II–11.
27. Pat Towell "Political Struggles Over SDI Set to Enter New Phase," *Congressional Quarterly*, April 1989, 702; R. Jeffrey Smith, "Year of Lobbying Turned 'Brilliant Pebbles' into Top SDI Plan," *Washington Post*, 26 April 1989, A16; Fred Barnes, "Pebbles Go Bam-Bam," *New Republic*, 17 April 1989, 12; Theresa M. Foley, "Bush Defense Strategy to Reshape SDI Program," *Aviation Week and Space Technology*, 30 January 1989, 18; "Political Review, Technical Tests Will Set Course of SDI Research," *Aviation Week and Space Technology* 20 March 1989, 61; Pat Towell, "Bush's Revisions May Augur Policy Shifts in Future," *Congressional Quarterly*, 29 April 1989, 976.
28. Quoted in Towell, "Political Struggles Over SDI Set to Enter New Phase," 706.
29. "Politics Holds Key to Pace of Strategic Defense Research."
30. David N. Schwartz, "SDI: The Transatlantic Challenge," in *The Technology, Politics and Strategy of SDI*, 109.
31. Gary L. Guertner, "Nuclear War in a Defense-dominant World," in *The Technology, Strategy and Politics of SDI*, 19.
32. U.S. Congress, Office of Technology Assessment, *SDI: Technology, Survivability, and Software* Washington, 1988, 4.
33. James R. Asker, "Congress Raises ABM Treaty Concerns on Strategic Defense Development," *Aviation Week and Space Technology* 132, no. 26 (25 June 1990): 30.
34. Tim Kennedy, "Missiles, Space and Aviation," *National Defense* 75, no. 459 (July/August 1990): 14. See this piece for a brief overview of the countries with potential or actual capability to produce ballistic missiles.
35. John Pike, "The Strategic Defense Initiative and Canada," staff paper, Federation of American Scientists, 17 March 1986.

VI

North American Air Defense in Transition

Unlike the still very hypothetical options for ballistic missile defense, continental air defense is a current, essential element of deterrence. In fact, after several decades of decline, the continental air defense system is now in the midst of a modest resurgence. The North American Air Defense Modernization Agreement, signed at Quebec City during the presidential-prime ministerial summit of 1985, provides for transitional air defenses to replace those that were on the verge of thorough obsolescence.[1]

Precisely where the transition eventually will lead is unclear, although there is very good reason to believe that further modernization may be necessary in the 1990s. This chapter first describes both the changing Soviet "airbreathing" threat to North America that prompted the 1985 agreement, and the limited capabilities of the modernized system now being put in place by the United States and Canada. It then outlines the factors that may precipitate further modernization. Thereafter it briefly summarizes the technologies being developed under the aegis of the U.S. Air Defense Initiative (ADI), upon which such future modernization would be based.

The final section of this chapter deals with the impact of air defense modernization, current and future, on Canada, and Canadian reactions to it. Here, more than anywhere else, Canada is directly confronted with the paradox of defense cooperation with the United States. Sovereignty concerns strongly militate in favor of Canadian participation in any further modernization of the North American air defense system; such participation could again raise worries about Canadian involvement in what Canadians generally have seen as disquieting strategic trends in the United States.

THE CHANGING SOVIET AIRBREATHING THREAT

The 1985 agreement brought to fruition several years of discussion and study both within the U.S. government and between the United

States and Canada. A 1979 Joint United States/Canada Air Defense Study (JUSCADS) concluded that almost any conceivable modernization of the passive elements of the North American air defense system would pay for itself in less than ten years, mostly through the reduced personnel costs of running modern radars. Despite the study, both countries might have nonetheless gone on for another decade waiting for the arrival of still newer air defense technologies, especially potentially promising space-based systems, and hunting in the meantime for scarce vacuum tubes to service the remnants of radar lines built in the 1950s.

Postponement no longer seemed advisable in the face of immediate and continuing improvements in the Soviet airbreathing threat to the North American continent, especially the earlier than expected development of longer-range strategic cruise missiles. The numbers of weapons carried in bombers has increased, while the capability of Soviet strategic aviation to penetrate—undetected—the North American air defense system has also been enhanced.

The overwhelming majority of Soviet strategic nuclear weapons still rests atop intercontinental ballistic missiles and submarine launched ballistic missiles. But the bomber leg of the Soviet triad of strategic forces is clearly reviving. Today about 12 percent of Soviet strategic nuclear weapons are carried by bombers as gravity bombs or air-launched cruise missiles (ALCMs). Moreover, the rise in the absolute number of strategic nuclear weapons carried in bombers has been fairly dramatic, from under 200 in the late 1970s, to over 1000 today (see Table 6.1).

In all probability, that rise has not come to an end. For over thirty years, a mainstay of Soviet long range aviation has been the Tu-95 *Bear* bomber. The older A, B, C, and G versions of the aircraft carry up to three weapons. The equally aged Mya-4 *Bison,* which just recently passed out of the inventory, carried four. However, the recently introduced *Bear H,* gradually being phased in, probably carries eight subsonic, low-altitude AS-15 *Kent* long-range ALCMs, although some (disputed) estimates go as high as twenty. About fifty *Bear H*s are now operational.

The new supersonic *Blackjack* bomber, roughly similar to the U.S. B-1 bomber and now presumed to be operational can carry twelve to twenty AS-15s. (By the end of 1987, eleven *Blackjack*s had been built; presumably these entered service in 1988.)[2]

So by continuing to replace over the next decade the *Bison*s and older *Bear*s, totalling in 1988 about 100, with *Bear H*s and *Blackjack*s, the Soviets can also continue substantially to increase the number of nuclear weapons carried in long-range bombers without increasing the number of bombers themselves. A realistic prospect is a Soviet longer-range strategic ALCM inventory of several thousand within ten years, although the unclassified predictions have varied substantially. In the meantime,

TABLE 6.1
EVOLUTION OF SOVIET STRATEGIC NUCLEAR FORCES,
1975–1987

Launchers	1975		1980		1984		1987	
ICBMs	1607	64.6%	1398	53.6%	1398	52.8%	1389	51.8%
SLBMs	765	30.3%	989	38.0%	946	35.7%	969	36.1%
Bombers	**155**	**6.1%**	**220**	**8.4%**	**303***	**11.5%**	**326***	**12.1%**
TOTALS	2527	100.0%	2607	100.0%	2647	100.0%	2710	100.0%
Weapons								
ICBMs	1937	67.5%	5002	72.2%	6420	66.9%	6400	60.6%
SLBMs	765	26.7%	1629	23.5%	2122	22.9%	2941	27.9%
Bombers	**165**	**5.8%**	**295**	**4.3%**	**1052***	**11.0%**	**1214***	**11.5%**
TOTALS	2867	100.0%	6926	100.0%	9594	100.0%	10315	100.0%

*These figures include Backfire bombers. An agreed statement accompanying the never-ratified SALT II Treaty states that the Backfire is not strategic and does not fall under SALT limits. However, the Backfire has a range which would allow it to be used for strikes on the United States.

Sources: 1975–1984, John Collins, *U.S.-Soviet Military Balance, 1980–1985.*
John Collins, *U.S./Soviet Military Balance, Statistical Trends, 1977–1986 (As of January 1, 1987)*
John Collins, *U.S. Soviet Military Balance, Statistical Trends 1980–1987 (As of January 1 1988)*

Bear Gs still in service have been rejuvenated by being equipped with shorter-range, but supersonic AS-4 *Kitchen* ALCMs.[3]

The other major element of the Soviet airbreathing threat to North America is the Tu-26M *Backfire* bomber, which can carry several short-range ALCMs. Its status as a strategic bomber is disputed by the Soviets, although its range of 11,000 km allows it to reach North American targets. The counting rules for the strategic arms limitations talks do not recognize it as strategic, while many Western analysts often include as strategic the 160 *Backfire* aircraft assigned to the Soviet air force. They are included in the figures above. (Still other Western analysts count as strategic *Backfires* assigned to the Soviet Navy. These are not included in the figures above.) If no *Backfires* are counted, today just above 7 percent of Soviet strategic nuclear weaponry (or 700 weapons) is carried in bombers.

More worrisome for North American air defenders than the numbers of nuclear weapons carried in Soviet bombers is the fact that the ancient radars built by Canada and the United States in the heyday of continental defense during the 1950s cannot detect cruise missiles. The AS-15, which became operational in 1984, carries a 200–250 kiloton nuclear warhead and has an estimated range of 3000 km. Its small size (on the rough order of 26 feet in length with an 11-foot wingspan) presents a limited radar cross section, while its very low flight altitude can be used to "mask" its presence from ground-based radars whose detection capabilities are seriously limited or completely nonexistent below 500 feet.

Cruise missiles rely on an air-breathing engine, and increasingly accurate, computerized internal guidance systems that can "see" the surface of the terrain over which the missiles fly, match it to electronic memory and adjust the direction of flight accordingly. Their flight paths can be programmed to minimize the chances of radar detection. As NORAD and other air defense officials of both countries would intone in the late 1980s because of radar blindness to modern cruise missiles and bombers, "At the moment, the first warning of cruise missile attack would be the detonation of their nuclear warheads on target."

The latest Soviet strategic bombers can themselves also under fly the current radar system, a task facilitated by the development of in-flight refueling capability based on the II-76 *Midas* air tanker, now beginning to enter service. Refueled, Soviet bombers could also fly an end run around the DEW Line and penetrate North American airspace along portions of the east and west coasts of Canada where no radar coverage recently has existed.

But the 3000-km range of the AS-15 ALCM can make such maneuvers unnecessary. Soviet bombers can "stand-off" to the east, west, and north of the North American continental mainland, beyond the current coverage of conventional land-based radar, and launch hard-to-detect cruise missiles capable of striking targets in Canada and a good deal of the United States.

Raising the prospect of further detection problems is the development by the Soviets of the supersonic AS-X-19 ALCM, also with a range of 3000 km, which could be carried on board *Blackjacks* or in a new bomber, also under development. Deployment could occur in the 1990s.[4]

Sea-launched cruise missiles (SLCMs) are soon to become a greater threat to North America as well. SLCMs have been in the Soviet inventory for decades. Their ranges were quite limited: mostly under 600-km, with one class in the 500–1000-km range. But the SS-N-21 *Sampson* SLCM, recently undergoing what apparently were final sea trials, is of the same engineering family as the AS-15. Western analysts believe that its deployment is imminent. Like the AS-15, the SS-N-21 has a reported range of up to 3000 km. It is capable of being carried in the standard torpedo tubes of virtually any Soviet nuclear-powered attack submarine (SSN), although Western expectations are that deployment will not extend to all classes of such boats. Launched from underwater, such an SLCM could be even more difficult to detect than an ALCM.

A still newer Soviet SLCM, the SS-N-X-24 is also under development. Its range is expected to be longer than the SS-N-21, but whether it will be capable of supersonic flight is not clear. It requires a special launch platform, in the form of a cruise missile-carrying submarine (SSGN), which apparently is under development. The Soviets have tested it from an old, converted ballistic missile-carrying submarine. The number of longer-range SLCMs the Soviets can be expected to deploy is unclear inasmuch as until the deployment of a new SSGN to accommodate SLCMs the number of torpedoes carried in existing attack submarines must be reduced. How willing the Soviets are to do this is not clear.[5] (The problem SLCMs pose for arms control is dealt with below, while the potential problem posed by SLCM-carrying submarines in the waters surrounding Canada is dealt with in chapter VIII.)

Since the 1960s it had been a working strategic assumption that the Soviets probably would use their bomber force to attack North America only after having first struck with ICBMs and SLBMs. A portion of the primary ballistic missile strikes could be used to suppress North American air defenses, thereby facilitating follow-on bomber attacks and allowing for mop-up operations. However, NORAD's inadequate capability to detect cruise missiles and modern bombers has lead to the disquieting possibility that the order of attack could very well be the opposite. The Soviets could be able to use cruise missiles *if undetected* in a no-warning, precursor "decapitation" strike on critical, time sensitive targets in North America as the leading edge of a full-scale nuclear attack. SLBMs and ICBMs would then take the follow-on role.

Such a precursor strike would be intended to create confusion by destroying key decision-making centers, including the U.S. National Command Authority, (the president, the secretary of defense and their successors) and military command, control and communications and intelligence (C^3I) facilities. It would be timed so that the nuclear warheads carried by the cruise missiles would detonate on targets at the same moment that U.S. space-based sensors detected Soviet ICBM and SLBM launches, thereby depriving the United States of the maximum 25 minutes of warning time it would otherwise have before ICBM impact, and the maximum 15 minutes before SLBM impact. In the words of the Special Committee on National Defence of the Canadian Senate, such a raid could leave U.S. strategic forces "decapitated, confused, unable to obtain orders and incapable of retaliating."[6]

John D. Steinbruner of the Brookings Institution suggested in 1981 that fewer than 100 Soviet nuclear weapons on target would so severely damage C^3I facilities that "the actions of individual weapons commanders could no longer be controlled or coordinated." As few as fifty weapons were "probably sufficient to eliminate the ability to direct U.S. strategic forces to coherent purposes."[7] While the Soviets could not be

certain that such a no-warning strike would deprive the United States
of the ability effectively to retaliate, it could at least reduce the probability. Ground-based ballistic missile warning sites and air defense facilities, as well as strategic bomber bases, might also be struck, again,
without warning, until detonation.[8]

THE 1985 MODERNIZATION PROGRAM

The 1985 modernization, now underway, is by no means meant to
re-create the "thick" air defenses of the 1950s and early 1960s. Rather
the intent is to plug (at least partially) the detection gaps, with a view
toward substantially degrading the ability of the Soviets to use bombers
and cruise missiles in an undetected precursor attack.

There are two elements to the modest modernization program, which
is based on a 1980 U.S. Air Force Air Defense Master Plan. The first is to
establish and where possible extend outward low and high altitude,
ground-based radar coverage around the periphery of the North American continent. The second is to facilitate, also at the continent's perim-
eters, operations by airborne warning and control aircraft (AWACS) and
by U.S. and Canadian fighter aircraft (see map—chapter VI).

To provide outward-looking radar coverage aimed at detecting aircraft approaching the continent out of the east, west, northwest and
south, the U.S. Air Force has begun a $2.5 billion program to build four
Over-the Horizon Backscatter (OTH-B) radar systems. OTH-B radar embodies two considerable improvements over the conventional kind: it
is capable of all-altitude aircraft detection, thereby overcoming the troubling absence of coverage at low altitudes, and its range is great, from
roughly 500 to possibly 2000 nautical miles in a broad fan.[9] Current
radar coverage extends to only about 200–250 standard miles from the
radar site.

Each OTH-B system is to consist of a transmitter site and several
receiving sites. The transmitter bounces high-frequency radar waves
off the ionosphere back towards the surface of the earth. "Reflections"
from aircraft bounce "backward" again off the ionosphere and can be
detected at the receiving sites, located 50 to 100 n.m. from the transmitter. The first transmit-receive system, with stations located in Maine,
became partially operational in 1988. A west coast system is to be based
on an Oregon transmitter and receiving stations in northern California.
Two other systems are to be built, one in Alaska, and the other some-
where in the northern portion of the continental United States providing coverage southward—all pending Congressional approval of funding.

While the OTH-B systems are to be paid for and operated by the United
States, the 1985 air defense modernization agreement provides that sta-
tions "with coverage and command and control implications for the
North American Air Defence mission in Canada," that is, the eastern

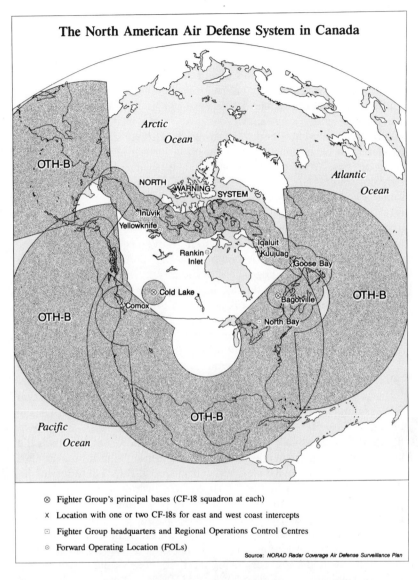

The North American Air Defense System in Canada

⊗ Fighter Group's principal bases (CF-18 squadron at each)

x Location with one or two CF-18s for east and west coast intercepts

▣ Fighter Group headquarters and Regional Operations Control Centres

⊙ Forward Operating Location (FOLs)

Source: *NORAD Radar Coverage Air Defense Surveillance Plan*

and western systems, will be jointly manned by Canadian personnel. Thirty-two Canadians, constituting about a fifth of the personnel are to be sent to each of these two stations, with their costs to be borne by the Canadian government.

Unfortunately, the aurora borealis causes disturbances in the ionosphere that preclude a northward-pointing OTH-B system. Coverage in the north, between the fans of the eastern, western, and Alaskan OTH-B systems, is to be provided by the North Warning System (NWS). The NWS, which relies on enhanced, conventional ground-based radar technology, is by and large to be constructed on the location of the old DEW Line in Alaska and Canada, except that its eastern end will turn down the Baffin Island/Labrador coasts instead of running across southern Greenland as the DEW Line did. It is to consist of fifteen minimally attended long-range radars (eleven of which will be in Canada) and thirty-nine unattended short-range sites (thirty-six in Canada). The expected C$1.6 billion capital acquisition costs and annual operating costs of the NWS are to be shared 60/40 by the United States and Canada. Several coastal radars in both southeastern and southwestern Canada will also be necessary to complete peripheral coverage of the continent.

Modest improvements in air defenses were already being undertaken by each country prior to the agreement. Eleven squadrons of the U.S. Air National Guard are to be equipped with F-16A interceptors, modified for air defense purposes. These squadrons will have normal day-to-day responsibilities for air defense. They can be backed up by two active duty squadrons of the USAF Tactical Air Command (TAC) which have been equipped with F-15 aircraft that, with powerful look-down shoot-down radars, are superior to the F-16s. USAF officials are still hoping that funding can be found to restore a third squadron. The USAF's Alaskan Air Command, whose air defense forces also fall under NORAD's operational control, deploys two squadrons of F-15s.

On the Canadian side, Air Command's Fighter Group contributes two regular-duty squadrons of CF-18s. 441 Tactical Fighter Squadron is stationed at Canadian Forces Base Cold Lake, Alberta, (with one or two fighters on alert at CFB Comox, British Columbia for intercepts in the north Pacific region) while 425 Tactical Fighter Squadron is at CFB Bagotville, Québec (with alert aircraft at Goose Bay, Labrador for intercepts off Canada's northeastern coast). Aircraft at Cold Lake and Bagotville do not normally hold alert. In peacetime these squadrons can be backed up by the other CF-18 squadrons deployed in Canada.

NORAD will also probably have at its disposal eight U.S. AWACS aircraft, co-manned by Canadian personnel. Canada has no AWACS aircraft of its own. In a crisis or during wartime these would play a critical role, for several reasons. The NWS and OTH-B systems are vulnerable to attack and electronic-countermeasures, whereas AWACS is more survivable and incorporates countermeasure resistant technologies.

Of equal importance, doubts persist as to the capabilities of OTH-B technology against cruise missiles, especially against SLCMs whose radar signatures can be obscured by sea-surface clutter. USAF officials have insisted that "OTH-B radars . . . will map cruise missiles although not as well as they do aircraft." At minimum they are expected to be "accurate enough where you can vector in an F-15 close enough so that he can take over with his radar and shoot down whatever you have got out there."[10] But in the absence of operational experience, USAF officials also admit to a lack of certainty, and worry especially about OTH-B's nighttime abilities against cruise missiles. And a former scientific adviser to the U.S. Chief of Naval Operations warns "that reliable day/night detection of cruise missile targets will, at minimum, require significant technological improvements over the already impressive capabilities of current OTH systems, adding, however, "that even very substantial improvements in OTH technology may not ultimately provide us with the kind of reliable early warning required for high-confidence warning of cruise missile attack."[11]

The presence of powerful AWACS look-down radars can significantly alleviate this cruise missile detection problem. In addition, with a combination of AWACS and fighter aircraft operating under AWACS control the air defense battle can be pushed outward in order to "go after the platform," that is, attempt to detect and if possible destroy Soviet bombers before the release of ALCMs compounds the problem by multiplying the number of targets, which are themselves more difficult to detect. Air bases located on the east and west coasts of the United States, and in Alaska facilitate AWACS and fighter deployment.

In northern Canada, an interrelated set of problems surrounds both detecting cruise missiles and "going after the platform." First,the NWS is located to the south of several release points for the AS-15, that is, the missile's 3000-mile range would allow bombers, from points to the north of where they would be detected by NWS radar, to launch AS-15s toward some targets in Canada and the northern United States. SS-N-21's could similarly be launched from some locations in the Canadian Arctic, while their platforms, Soviet submarines, could not be detected by radar. Second, the technical capability of the NWS fully to detect low-flying cruise missiles is also open to question, and its tracking capability and time are limited. Third, immediately to the south of the NWS, and unlike the case with the projected outward-pointing OTH-B fans in the United States, there is an enormous "hole" with no ground-based military radar coverage. The long-range radars of the NWS will provide coverage out to 200 nautical miles. Unless AWACS were operating in the region, attacking bombers and cruise missiles could pass swiftly through NWS coverage into the radar "hole," offering limited time to vector a fighter interceptor towards target on the basis of information provided by the NWS.

Fourth, CF-18s have less powerful radars than F-15s, which would have helped compensate for the absence of ground-based radar in the "hole." Finally, the normal CF-18 operating bases in Cold Lake and Bagotville are too far south to permit ground-based aircraft flying immediately out of those locations readily to go after the platform or from those bases to "chase" cruise missiles or bombers detected by the NWS over far northern Canada.

Compensation for these northward weaknesses is an important element of the 1985 agreement. The five Forward Operating Locations (FOLs) being built on the basis of "minimum essential upgrades" at Inuvik, Yellowknife, Rankin Inlet, Iqaluit (Frobisher Bay) in the Northwest Territories and Kuujjuaq (Fort Chimo) in Québec, will permit the emergency northern deployment of CF-18s (and U.S. F-15s). In addition to small airfields, each FOL will include alert hangers and storage for ammunition, fuel and air-to-air missiles. Each will be capable of supporting operations of a maximum six fighter aircraft and associated personnel for up to 30 days. FOL costs are to be split between the two countries. No armed forces personnel of either country will be permanently stationed at FOLs; nor will aircraft be permanently located there.

From the FOLs, fighter aircraft can attempt immediately to pursue bombers or cruise missiles detected by the NWS just to the north, or optimally, in a crisis, they can operate forward, well to the north of the NWS, in conjunction with USAF AWACS operating out of Alaska. The 1985 agreement also provides for the construction of Dispersed Operating Bases (DOBs) for AWACS in Canada. One will be at Bagotville, the other at CFB Edmonton, Alberta, thus not far from Cold Lake.

The ability of fighter aircraft to operate northward can be enhanced through in-flight refueling. Arrangements therefore also exist to refuel CF-18s either from the very small numbers of Canadian aircraft capable of being outfitted as tankers or from American tankers. In a crisis, relatively sustained U.S. and Canadian air defense operations could be undertaken as far forward as the North Pole.

In the late 1980s, the Soviets increased the number of bomber training flights on the North American side of the Arctic basin in order to familiarize crews with cruise missile operations. The Alaskan Air Command and Fighter Group have responded by pushing peacetime intercepts further north. As of 1988, the most northern intercept was undertaken less than 700 miles from the North Pole by two F-15s from Alaska. The year 1988 also marked the first far northern intercept by Fighter Group, undertaken by three CF-18s and a tanker that had been on training at the Inuvik FOL. However, beginning in 1989 and no doubt reflecting the policies of the Gorbachev era, the frequency of such flights dropped off sharply.

It should be readily apparent that the air defense modernization program "while not inexpensive, is hardly a lavish or overdone system."[12] Under normal circumstances, there are fewer than sixty fighters routinely available that can take to the air in less than twelve minutes;

four of these aircraft are Canadian. AWACS and refueling aircraft are not available continuously.[13]

It is also not quite what U.S. air defenders had hoped for when plans were put together in the late 1970s and early 1980s to overhaul the system. Those original USAF plans called for five active squadrons of F-15s (including aircraft that could serve as antisatellite weapons launchers). Four were deployed in the early 1980s, whereupon the number soon dropped to three and then to two, with day-to-day responsibilities passing to the ANG aircraft. It had been the USAF's strong preference to equip the eleven Air National Guard squadrons with F-15s instead of the less-capable F-16s settled upon. And when hopes faded of acquiring a USAF AWACS inventory of fifty-four, of which nineteen were to be dedicated to continental air defense, NORAD had to make do with only eight "designated" planes and whatever additional ones could be found for its use in an emergency. "Designated" aircraft can be assigned to other roles.

Funding for deployment of the OTH-B systems has been stretched out to the point where the last system may not be operational until the late 1990s, if then. Funding for the United States' share of FOLs, DOBs and the NWS itself has run into Congressional opposition, and is by no means certain. These limitations reflect the traditionally low priority air defense has had in the U.S. defense establishment (including the USAF itself which has always placed greater emphasis on its strategic nuclear and tactical forces), doubts about OTH-B and NWS capabilities, and the conviction held by many in the Pentagon and on Capitol Hill that it remains sensible to wait for the next generation of air defense technology, especially space-based systems, to become available instead of investing heavily in a transition system. Of course, in the absence of a ballistic missile defense system, a high level of active air defense will continue to make little sense.

The strategic utility of the modestly modernized North American air defense system in contributing to deterrence rests on two assumptions. First, in normal, noncrisis peacetime a Soviet surprise attack coming as a complete "bolt from the blue" is considered so unlikely that a far less than entirely leakproof peacetime detection perimeter constitutes an acceptable risk.

Second, in an international crisis the air defense system, having been placed on alert, may have sufficient detection and interception capability to contribute to deterrence through the uncertainty it would create in the minds of Soviet planners. No one believes that the NWS and OTH-B systems, eight AWACS and what is still a very limited number of U.S. and Canadian fighter aircraft would be sufficient to detect, much less destroy all approaching bombers and cruise missiles, even if most of the AWACS and all available fighters were aloft and operating forward at the time of attack. The point of a no-warning "decapitation" or "leading edge" strike with cruise missiles is to increase the probability of the success of the follow-on strike with ICBMs and SLBMs. North American air defense operations could introduce a useful element of randomness, in that the Soviets would not know precisely where AWACS and associated fighter aircraft would be operating. They could not be certain, therefore, that their bombers and cruise missiles would go entirely undetected, and could also not be certain that the cruise missiles essential for a successful decapitation strike would penetrate to target. That uncertainty could lower the probability of a successful strike, thereby bolstering deterrence.

This places, however, a premium on operational effectiveness. As the Commander of Fighter Group summarizes the potential problem posed by "the current weakness of warning of cruise missile attack compared with the high level of confidence we have against ballistic missile attack":

> What we are discovering now, in the cold light of implementation of air defence modernization, and with the reality of a more capable and numerous threat than predicted, is that to get even close to a 'symmetrical' level of confidence on the cruise missile side, the air defence system must function optimally and flawlessly. Clearly, time is the critical factor and we must develop concurrent air defence system response activities which will minimize our reaction times, and thereby maximize the probability of providing unambiguous warning. And this must be accomplished in the austere, remote forward operating locations.[14]

THE POSSIBILITY OF FUTURE MODERNIZATION

A U.S. decision to further modernize the North American air defense system could result from any one of the following factors: BMD deployment, the weaknesses in the 1985 system against the short-term Soviet airbreathing threat, and weaknesses against the longer-term airbreathing threat.

If the United States proceeds in the 1990s and beyond to deploy BMD, the makeshift continental air defense system agreed to in 1985 will probably be found insufficient. The extent to which the United States will be prepared to invest in improved air defenses will no doubt be immediately related to the expected, eventual effectiveness of the BMD system. In the unlikely event that it is expected to be able to destroy a high percentage of incoming missiles, the incentives will be strong to attempt to strengthen North American air defenses to a similar level. In the case of a BMD system with a low attrition rate (such as the ALPS proposal) moderately effective air defenses could be tolerated.

At the same time, BMD deployments by the United States could create strong incentives for the Soviets to build more bombers and cruise missiles and to improve their ability to penetrate air defenses, which in turn could precipitate a stronger U.S. interest in enhanced air defenses. The BMD-air defense relationship was recognized in National Security Decision Directive (NSDD) 178, issued by President Reagan in July 1985, which instructed that a research program be undertaken on strategic air defense "to allow for possible future deployment decisions for defense against low observable air-breathing threats to occur in the same time frame as possible deployment decisions on ballistic missile defense under the SDI program."[15] Pursuant to the directive, the USAF announced the establishment of an Air Defense Initiative (ADI) in 1986.

However, it must be emphasized that even if SDI fizzles out and no BMD deployments occur, the technologies being researched under the aegis of ADI will be relied upon as candidates to replace the makeshift 1985 arrangements. As discussed above, the capability of the NWS and the OTH-B radars to deal with the *current* generation of cruise missiles "is only now being tested."[16] The already admittedly porous system may be found to be too porous.

The arrival of Soviet supersonic cruise missiles, now under development, will complicate the problem. Still more worrisome is the potential development by the Soviets, over the next decade or so, of "stealthy" bombers and cruise missiles, reopening the possibility of a no-warning attack. These are the "low observable air-breathing threats" referred to in NSDD 178. A stealthy cruise missile might rely on a combination of high altitude flight, greater speed, an enhanced internal guidance system and special antiradar shaping. If still greater ranges can also be achieved for cruise missiles, the air defense will find "going after the platform" even more difficult.[17]

The future of air defense may decisively be affected by the outcome of the strategic arms reduction talks (START) between the United States and the Soviet Union. Ironically, a successful agreement will all but certainly make air defense efforts more, not less important. The central focus of the talks has been ballistic missiles, especially the "heavy" Soviet ICBMS which the United States has long seen as being especially threatening to its own land-based strategic arsenal. START, according to Paul Nitze, special assistant to the president and secretary of state on arms control matters, "would require the Soviets to make substantial reductions in their strategic nuclear arms, and would focus reductions on those weapons best suited for conducting a surprise attack: ballistic missiles—in particular, large, fixed, multiple-warhead, land-based missiles."[18] The effect of an agreement to reduce the number of ICBMs and SLBMs in the arsenals of both countries will almost certainly be to increase the relative importance of bombers and cruise missiles, although limits may be put on the number of long-range cruise missiles. Moreover, as Nitze went on,

In addition to the explicit reduction in Soviet ballistic missile forces, START would provide incentives for the Soviets to move away from ballistic missiles toward slower, less threatening delivery systems, such as bombers. Warheads carried on ballistic missiles would be counted under START using rules that reflected the actual number of warheads deployed on each missile type. In contrast, nuclear bombs and short-range missiles carried on bombers would be discounted, i.e. bombers could count as "1" warhead regardless of how many bombs and missiles a bomber actually carried—thereby providing an incentive to retain bomber forces better suited for a retaliatory rather than a preemptive role.[19]

An increase in the relative importance of bombers would lend greater impetus to the development by the Soviets of stealth technology, thus, in the words of a Canadian analyst, "giving rise to difficult future questions about the adequacy of U.S. and Canadian surveillance capabilities against stealthy bombers and cruise missiles."[20] Nonetheless, as Nitze's comments indicate, this trend could be at least somewhat dampened by an agreement that placed a premium on bombers carrying gravity bombs and short-range ALCMs and that created disincentives for carrying long-range ALCMs which could be used in a preemptive role.

How this could work can be seen in the actual numbers agreed to by Presidents Bush and Gorbachev at their June 1990 summit to form the basis of the START accord (which will still need to be ratified by both sides, assuming that a final agreement is eventually signed):

- Each side would be limited to 1,600 strategic delivery vehicles (ICBMs, SLBMS and bombers, not including *Backfires*).
- Each side would also be limited to 6,000 strategic warheads.
- Of the 6,000 warheads, no more than 1,540 will be permitted on "heavy" missiles, which will oblige the Soviets to cut their heavy SS-18 inventory in half.
- Of the 6,000 warheads, no more than 4,900 could be carried on ICBMs and SLBMS.

However, this does not mean that only 1,100 warheads are to be permitted on bombers. The Soviets will be free to deploy well over 3,000, constituting a substantial portion of the overall Soviet inventory. A complicated, arcane formula will apply, which, in keeping with the philosophy outlined by Nitze, "discounts" the numbers of warheads on bombers. In particular, the first 210 Soviet bombers will be counted as having 8 ALCMs, but be permitted to carry up to 12. Bombers carrying no ALCMS will be considered as carrying one warhead, regardless of the actual number of gravity bombs and short-range missiles on board. Thus "the discount rule for bomber payloads means each side could wind up with larger nuclear warhead stockpiles in absolute terms than they have now, despite the accountable warhead ceiling of 6,000 overall."[21]

SLCMs pose difficult problems for arms control. Unhappily, U.S. naval interests and the interests of North American air defense are here at odds. Continental air defense would be simplified by strict numerical and qualitative limitations on Soviet SLCMs. But the U.S. Navy, supported by the Reagan and Bush administrations, places enormous emphasis on the deployment of both antiship and land-attack *Tomahawk* SLCMs in its ships. Eventually about 100 U.S. submarines and 100 surface ships will be capable of carrying the nuclear land-attack variant of the *Tomahawk*. Convinced that the United States has substantial advantages over the Soviets in deploying SLCMs, the U.S. Navy argues, (in the words of the Deputy Chief of Naval Operations for Plans, Policy and Operations) that the development of SLCMs "represents a fundamental change in the nature of naval matters on the order of the advance from sail to steam" and that "the power projection capability represented by U.S. SLCMs is as important to our naval strength as were earlier developments of the aircraft carrier and nuclear submarine."[22]

The Soviets have been slow to deploy their SS-N-21 land-attack SLCMs, and have sought within the context of the START negotiations to limit U.S. deployments. The United States rejected a Soviet proposal to ban all cruise missiles with ranges of over 600 kilometers, which would have required the removal from service of almost all *Tomahawks*.

Verification of SLCM restrictions could be very difficult. The missiles are small. Moreover, there are nuclear and non-nuclear variants of the *Tomahawk*. But the United States firmly rejects any inspection regime which would involve an abandonment of the Navy's longstanding policy of neither confirming nor denying the presence of nuclear weapons on specific ships.[23] The United States has also not accepted a Soviet proposal for a limit of 400 nuclear SLCMs, arguing that short of on-board inspection (which is unacceptable to the United States), there is no adequate means of verification.[24]

President Reagan and General Secretary Gorbachev agreed at their December 1987 meeting in Washington to seek a mutually acceptable solution to the SLCM issue, *outside* the numerical limits the two sides are negotiating in the START talks on offensive delivery systems and warheads. In June 1980, Presidents Bush and Gorbachev agreed on a limit of 880 SLCMs with ranges over 375 miles for each side. As a result, "the Soviets might come to see that SLCMs could provide them with a substantial new strategic nuclear capability. If the agreement, for example, did little more than require the two sides to declare their intentions with regard to deployments, the Soviets would be tempted to put their current SLCM programs to use, especially in missions against North America that would force the United States and Canada to face up to weaknesses in the continental air defense system."[25]

In short, the emerging outline for a START agreement will not only permit an increase in the airbreathing threat to North America, but it substantially shifts the percentage of the overall threat towards bombers and cruise missiles. David Cox of the Canadian Institute for International Peace and Security has concluded:

> For Canada, the START formula continues to pose questions about the impact of future offensive force deployments. The deployment of nuclear SLCMs increases the strategic significance of the maritime approaches to Canada. The relative increase in the importance of ALCMs and the prospect that successive ALCM models will have longer ranges, suggests that the northern approaches to Canadian airspace will increase in importance and be more difficult to monitor.[26]

Finally, a few words need to be added about North American air defense and the interdiction of drugs smuggled aboard illicit flights. In 1989 both the U.S. and Canadian governments agreed that the air defense system would be formally assigned responsibility for dealing with this threat. This affects the U.S. portions of the system more heavily, not only because the United States is the more important destination for such flights, but because many occur in the southern portions of the continent. As well, the same type of problem plaguing detection of cruise missiles affect the detection of small drug-carrying aircraft. In the 1990s the U.S. Department of Defense may invoke these concerns in arguing for funding for air defense.[27]

THE AIR DEFENSE INITIATIVE: A BRIEF SUMMARY[28]

Three features of ADI deserve comment: its relationship with SDI; its relationship to U.S. declaratory nuclear strategy; and the surveillance and weapons detection systems it is researching, at least several of which may be deployed to counter improvements in the Soviet airbreathing threat, regardless of the outcome of the BMD debate. All three features have drawn Canadian attention.

ADI, like its more visible (and far more expensive) research counterpart SDI, has the task of pursuing technologies that would permit deployment of an enhanced "multi-layered defense in depth" that would begin far beyond the periphery of the North American continent and end with point defenses close to American cities and military facilities.[29] Thus, a starting point for ADI is researching systems that could make a "thickening" of continental air defenses an option. Also similar to SDI, ADI has gathered under its wing a number of research projects already underway, although there is no Air Defense Initiative Office that would be parallel to the SDIO. Coordination is through what appears to be a rather cumbersome set of Department of Defense interagency committees. Total spending on ADI-related projects in 1988 was just over $200 million, as compared to the SDI budget of about $4 billion.

While ADI is officially described as being "separate from but complementary to" SDI, there are a number of areas of overlapping research. The results of SDI studies of space-based radar and infrared sensing for BMD could have air defense application. SDI's battle management research will also have to be seriously considered, both for the transfer of applicable technology and with a view toward closely coordinating any future BMD effort with enhanced air defense. SDI's National Test Bed facility will be used to help develop ADI's own air defense battle management system. A more distant possibility is that several SDI-researched weapons systems, such as hypervelocity guns and space- or ground-based lasers could be put to use to destroy aircraft. Finally, as the United States considers the desirability of BMD, the heavy costs of any complementary "thicker" air defense system would have to be put into the equation.

ADI's research mandate is in keeping with current U.S. declaratory nuclear strategy. A major research and development emphasis has been placed on the survivability of air defense systems so that a "survivable, comprehensive air defense" could remain effective as long as possible during a protracted nuclear conflict.[30]

ADI's research and development program centers on surveillance technology, engagement systems, and system architecture. Given the weakness of current radar technology, its self-described "number one priority" is "the development of wide area surveillance systems that can detect carriers at long ranges and track them with sufficient accuracy to allow engagement systems to be employed."[31] Most prominent among the very long-range candidate technologies are those which are space-based.

Expectations in both the United States and Canada for space-based surveillance have been high for a number of years. In 1984 Pentagon devotees of space-based surveillance almost succeeded in killing implementation of the transitional modernization program, arguing in favor of waiting for the arrival of space-based technologies instead of building the NWS. Two such technologies have been under active exploration: space-based infrared sensors and space-based radar. Originally, infrared sensors, which would detect the heat emitted by bombers and cruise missiles, and were being investigated by the United States Defense Department's TEAL RUBY research program seemed to have had the inside track. A satellite carrying experimental TEAL RUBY infrared sensors was to have been launched into orbit from aboard a space shuttle. But the program suffered a major setback when U.S. space shuttles were grounded in the wake of the *Challenger* catastrophe.

Thereafter, officials decided to launch the satellite atop an expendable booster. The satellite launch is now scheduled to take place in the early 1990s. Nonetheless, priority has shifted to the exploration of a space-based radar system, "perhaps augmented with infrared detectors."[32] If the Soviets successfully develop "stealth" technology designed to avoid radar detection, infrared sensing would probably move back up in the scale of North American air defense priorities.

Currently, USAF officials hope to be able to launch a prototype space-based radar satellite by 1993. Contrary to longstanding expectations sometimes expressed in both Canada and the United States, there is little to no chance that within the next ten or fifteen years most, much less all North American air defense radars will be space-based. The cost of space-based radar satellites is expected to be high, running well into the billions of dollars. Moreover, whether such satellites will be able to incorporate reliable capabilities to detect cruise missiles is uncertain. In the short run, "The first elements of a space-based radar system are unlikely to be able to track all small targets, like cruise missiles or light airplanes."[33] The vulnerability of radar satellites may also be an issue.

On the other hand, USAF officials are confident that space-based radar can detect Soviet strategic bombers with their large radar cross sections. By the late 1990s, therefore, a space-based radar constellation of anywhere from three to fifteen satellites could provide very early warning of the approach of Soviet bombers, perhaps as soon as they left home bases and staging areas in and near the Soviet Union itself. Such a system could be, as the then commander-in-chief of both NORAD and U.S. Space Command, General John Piotrowski put it in 1987, "a good point of departure" leading eventually to improvements consisting of extensions in geographic coverage, and acquisition of reliable capability against cruise missiles.[34]

The space-based elements would hand off surveillance and tracking responsibilities to other advanced sensors, although these might very well operate alone if space-based radar is not found feasible and affordable. For long-range operations, ADI is investigating an airborne Advanced Surveillance and Tracking System (ASTS) based on phased-array radar technology which could significantly enhance detection ranges and which would render obsolete AWACS aircraft and the North Warning System. Such phased-array radars are big. One possibility would be to deploy them aboard the frames of very large cargo aircraft, specially equipped with either auxiliary fuel tanks or refueling capability, which would permit extended operations and reliance on remote northern airfields. Another is to deploy them aboard pilotless airships or pilotless aircraft, "drones", in other words. ADI is also investigating improvements in ground-based radars to be used in conjunction with point defenses.

To engage attacking bombers and cruise missiles at very-long, long, and shorter ranges a host of weapons systems are under research or development. Several new air-to-air missiles with longer ranges, higher speeds, greater accuracies and possibly with multi-kill capabilities could soon be available to replace the ones currently carried in North American air defense aircraft. By the 1990s the aircraft themselves could be replaced with supersonic Advanced Tactical Fighters (ATF) being developed by the USAF, and, by the turn of the century with the National Aerospace Plane, which could permit intercepts at very long distances and hypersonic speeds. An enhanced version of the U.S. Army's Patriot surface-to-air missile could provide point defense in the 1990s, and could thereafter be complemented or replaced by a hypersonic, very long-range, (1000–2000 miles) surface or air-launched missile. The final element of the research program is devoted to battle management and command, control and communications (BM/C^3) systems, in order to tie together the possible surveillance and engagement systems.

Air defense systems are expensive to deploy. Detailed cost estimates, comparable to those related to BMD, have not been released; unofficial estimates of a "thick" air defense system complementing a BMD system run above $50 billion.[35] As one Canadian analyst concludes:

> ADI is therefore cost-constrained. . . . Thick air defences are unattractive in the financially tight climate now prevalent in Washington. Funding limitations will ensure that a future air defence network does not include the entire range of systems being complemented. . . . Accordingly, some Canadian officers believe that costs will effectively prevent a return to the fully active air defences of the 1950s and 1960s. Thus, no matter how the BMD deployment decision turns out, ADI will result only in further air defence modernization.[36]

CANADA AND AIR DEFENSE MODERNIZATION

The debate over Canadian participation in the 1985 modernization program and in the ADI research program reveals the deeper dilemma Canada may face when the United States proceeds with the next steps in air defense modernization. That debate has centered on three themes: sovereignty, U.S. nuclear strategy and SDI.

The Mulroney government has taken great pains to emphasize how the 1985 agreement serves Canadian sovereignty. Not only is the North Warning System, unlike the old DEW Line, in Canadian hands, but the FOLs will increase the Canadian military presence in the high Arctic, especially in that CF-18s will be randomly and briefly sent there during peacetime. Canada's military presence in the region—although certainly not its air defense capabilities there—will be bolstered by the *Arcturus* patrol aircraft.

Sovereignty satisfaction with the 1985 modernization is by no means complete, though. Several worries stand out. First, the NWS system is being built to the south of the islands of the Canadian Arctic Archipelago. Two retired Canadian generals argued in 1986 that Canadian sovereignty would be enhanced by building the line to the north, thereby locating the northern radar perimeter along the country's "true perimeter," and including the scarcely populated far northern regions where increased military manifestations of Canadian sovereignty would be useful.[37] While their arguments were widely reported and met with generally sympathetic reception, there was also recognition that the costs of such a far-northern line would be substantially higher than the more southerly location of the NWS, which was to use many already-existent sites of the old DEW Line.

Second, a military radar "hole" in southern Canada has been created by the dismantling (provided for in the 1985 accord) of the thoroughly-obsolete Pinetree Line which was built by the United States and Canada and provided military radar coverage across most of the southern part of the country since the early 1950s. The United States is planning to fill its equivalent "hole" with the southward pointing OTH-B system. As the Standing Committee on External Affairs and National Defence of the House of Commons observed, "Once the Pinetree Line is dismantled, we will have no means of controlling uncooperative air traffic, intruders or stray aircraft in most of our airspace north or south of the 700-km band of territory covered by the radars of the NWS."[38] Third, the dependence on U.S.-owned AWACS for the most effective air defense operations in the high Canadian north has also often been a source of comparatively mild anxiety. This anxiety is mitigated somewhat by Canadian co-manning of AWACS flights and by the fact that control over all air defense operations in Canada is exercised by Canadian NORAD Region Headquarters at CFB North Bay, Ontario. While much of the Canadian authority over AWACS-controlled fighter operations is nominal, a critical aspect is not: in peacetime, according to Canada-U.S. arrangements, permission to destroy a hostile intruder in Canadian airspace would have to come from North Bay.

The short-term solution offered to all three of these sovereignty problems is almost always the same: acquisition by Canada of AWACS, or AWACS-type aircraft. Almost ritualistically the parliamentary committee called for the government to explore such a step. Canadian-owned AWACS could provide radar coverage in the "hole" and to the north of the NWS, serving both air defense and sovereignty-protection purposes. But as the committee members certainly were aware at the time they made their report, it was unlikely that Ottawa would buy AWACS aircraft costing on the order of up to US$200 million apiece. Since April 1989 it has been out of the question.

Again, the "push-resistant" nature of Canadian sovereignty concerns becomes evident. The radar "hole" and the location of the North Warning System are worrisome, Canadians will agree, but not to the point where the Canadian government is prepared to devote resources to remedy the problems. What really drives the commitment of resources to the protection of Canadian sovereignty is the need to undertake efforts which would otherwise be undertaken by U.S. forces.

It did not go unnoticed in Canada that an enhanced air defense system is compatible with, if not logically mandated by, the declaratory nuclear strategy of the Carter and Reagan administrations, with its emphasis on discriminative targeting and the ability to fight a protracted nuclear war. Survivable command and control nodes, essential to such a strategic approach, are at risk in a decapitation strike. Indeed, even in the absence of BMD, some limited active air defenses, that is, the ability not only to detect but also destroy aircraft can make sense within the context of such a strategy. Such air defenses could provide extra minutes of survival for softer C^3I facilities and could limit damage from remaining Soviet bombers after a U.S. strike on the Soviet Union.

Public statements by U.S. officials reenforced the perception. As Richard D. DeLauer, undersecretary of defense for research and engineering in the Reagan administration, told a Congressional hearing a major emphasis of the plan for modernized air defense, as designed at the end of the Carter administration, was "to provide deterrence of a bomber attack through developing a credible capability to limit damage to our strategic retaliatory forces and C^3 nodes in the event that the Soviets would choose to execute a small, precursor bomber strike." That was all fine, he said, as far as it went. But a good deal more was necessary.

> While the plan is responsive to the guidance of the last administration in emphasizing pre-attack warning we feel that strategic defensive forces, and their associated C^3I systems, for North America, must not only provide timely, accurate, and unambiguous tactical warning and attack assessment but must continue to function through all phases of conflict. . . . Pre-attack warning capable of supporting survival actions or the execution of [U.S. nuclear attacks], in the event of an enemy attack, is essential and remains part of our defense objective of deterring nuclear conflict, but it is not sufficient. Our strategic forces should be capable of supporting flexible responses and a protracted conflict as required.[39]

That statement is not exactly accurate: the Carter administration itself set as a goal for U.S. strategic forces the ability to fight a protracted nuclear war, although it never got a chance to try to put the concept into defense budgets. DeLauer promised that the air defense plan would be altered. Yet it is hard to see how, with respect to the hardware of air defense—radars and aircraft—what emerged out of the Reagan administration's deliberations and what was eventually incorporated into the 1985 Canada-U.S. accord was much different from the draft plan prepared in the Carter days. No extra squadrons were added. Plans for new radars were changed only in that AWACS numbers were reduced and the southward-pointing OTH-B coverage added.

On the other hand, the Reagan administration included, as top priority in its Strategic Modernization program, announced in October 1981, substantial sums of money to build in greater survivability for C³I systems.[40] NORAD C³I facilities necessarily were included in the program. As General Robert T. Herres, then NORAD commander-in-chief, put it in 1985, "we are upgrading virtually every part of the warning and assessment system—sensors, communications and processing segment."[41] Largely because of the strict secrecy surrounding the project and C³I systems in general, it is difficult to say whether all these improvements would allow the United States to fight a protracted nuclear war or whether they will simply close vulnerabilities in the C³I architecture that seemed to throw in doubt the ability of the United States to organize an effectively coordinated retaliatory strike.[42]

Canadian defense analysts and "peace" group activists alike labored mightily in the 1980s to warn of the links between North American air defense modernization and the unsettling strategic trends south of the border at variance with the strong Canadian attachment to "apocalyptic" nuclear strategy. "MAD no longer serves as the basis of American nuclear strategy," wrote one of Canada's most respected defense analysts. And, invoking the DeLauer statement, he warned that "the underlying approach of the Air Defense Master Plan . . . was generally compatible with the strategic priorities of the Reagan administration."[43] "The United States wants to have a larger selection of options available to it," accurately observed a spokesman for Operation Dismantle, a leading umbrella organization of the Canadian "peace" movement, and "in NORAD we are contributing to the expansion of nuclear operations."[44]

It is striking, though, that these arguments did not resonate in Canada to the point where the air defense modernization agreement ever became a full political liability for the Mulroney government. There are a number of reasons for this, beyond just the arcane nature of nuclear strategy. Above all, the modest Canada-U.S. air defense modernization program could be motivated and justified by *either* finite deterrence or flexible strategy. Even the most ardent proponent of finite deterrence—or in the Canadian case mutual assured destruction—would have to agree that it would be undesirable, indeed, destabilizing for a condition to persist whereby the obsolescence of radar systems would permit the Soviets to undertake with cruise missiles a decapitating strike. At minimum, radar lines would have to be upgraded, and for positive identification, fighter aircraft deployed. In other words, at bottom, the 1985 modernization restored warning to reasonable standards consistent with the threat. Under these circumstances the question: is a modernized air defense meant for assured destruction or is it meant for a different strategy? becomes moot. It is necessary, whichever the case.

To be sure, the immediate pursuit by the United States of a truly extensive and clearly survivable air defense system with a credible chance of detecting and destroying a very high percentage of Soviet bombers would have challenged Canadian strategic preferences and intensified sovereignty worries. But such a North American air defense system does not exist, at least for the moment. It soon became evident that for all the talk in the United States of air defense master plans and protracted nuclear war the United States really was, for the moment, not all that serious about air defense. The USAF Air Defense Master Plan and the 1985 agreement provided for only small-scale improvements largely aimed at restoring the modest level of air defense that had existed in the 1970s before the advent of the long-range cruise missile threat. It later became equally evident that the USAF was having trouble convincing budget makers in the Pentagon and on Capitol Hill that funding was necessary for even such small-scale efforts. An understandable Canadian conclusion was that "amidst the increasing rhetoric on air defence," the "United States is transmitting some confusing signals."[45]

Finally, SDI had first an intensifying and then a curiously dampening effect on the air defense debate in Canada. In the beginning, the SDI program was often taken as confirmation that the Americans really might be serious after all about strategic defense, and that the air defense modernization proposals could well be or become part and parcel of a broader American plan to move to a posture based on comprehensive defenses.

The debate then became far-fetched. No sooner was the 1985 agreement made public than the opposition parties in parliament began to claim repeatedly that the North Warning System was part and parcel of "Star Wars," by which they seemed to mean, interchangeably, either SDI research or actual BMD deployments. "You cannot have a ground radar tracking system for star wars in Canada that is distinct from the updated NWS," charged, for example, the New Democratic Party defense critic.[46]

Again and again the Progressive Conservatives responded that the NWS could detect only bombers and cruise missiles, not ballistic missiles; that SDI was only a research program that might or might not yield results, which in turn might or might not lead to the actual deployment of new defenses against ballistic missiles; and that in any event the Canadian government firmly supported the ABM Treaty. The U.S. State Department was prompted as well to take the unusual step of releasing via the embassy in Ottawa a press release denying "clearly and categorically" that the NWS was part of SDI.[47] Even if NWS was not literally part of the SDI program, argued the Liberals and NDP, it was all part of the now firmly-established American policy of "pursuing an active defense system" and of "no longer relying upon the deterrent basis for security in North America."[48] This would inevitably lead, in fact it had already begun to lead, they also said, to the "major militarization of northern Canada."[49]

Worried that the opposition's claims might convince a public that could not fully grasp the difference between the various existing, proposed, and utterly hypothetical defense systems, and between cruise missiles and ballistic missiles, the frustrated Progressive Conservatives also overreacted, claiming that "there is absolutely no relationship between the North Warning System and the Strategic Defense Initiative."[50] That went too far. In reality of course, if new BMD systems are ever deployed, they will take their place, along with the NWS and other air defense elements, as part of the North American continent's coordinated defenses. With both sides staking out extreme positions, the debate soon descended into what often seemed a hopeless muddle.

But in the end, SDI focused Canadian attention on future, bigger problems and tended to divert Canadian attention away from the relationship between current air defense efforts and evolving American nuclear strategy, especially when it finally became clear that the 1985 agreement provided for only a minor overhaul. "Current NORAD modernization efforts represent a marginal response to what military planners regard as a marginal threat," concluded the parliamentary committee.[51] Two Canadian fighter squadrons and a Canadian-operated radar line on Canadian soil linked to a not altogether clear American nuclear strategy were of little consequence when compared to the prospect of a future BMD-air defense combination of unknown scope with equally unknown implications for both nuclear stability and Canadian sovereignty. That was really something to worry about!

These three themes, sovereignty, U.S. nuclear strategy and SDI were repeated in the ADI issue. In Canada, the prospect of space-based radar has engendered well-publicized, enticing hopes. The very thought of surveying wide areas from space can be as intoxicating to Canadians ruminating over the difficulties of protecting their sovereignty over the world's second largest land mass as it is to air defenders contemplating the possibility of the ultimate air defense early warning system. Moreover, Canada has a space industry that is doing fairly well.[52] The Special Committee on National Defence of the Canadian Senate permitted itself to imagine a future in which:

> Canada could control the use of its own satellites and make sure that they remained dedicated to passive detection and surveillance needs. Canadian

military satellites over the North could also provide Canadian civil authorities with much useful information about activities in the Arctic and frontier regions. They could, for example, help monitor many forms of air, land and sea movements across the North, keep track of oil spills and other dangers to the environment, or document the impact of development. They could improve communications with remote settlements and facilitate search and rescue operations, while at the same time enabling Canadian industry to remain at the forefront of world technological developments in the space field.[53]

The Mulroney government also spoke powerfully in *Challenge and Commitment* of Canada's interests in space-based surveillance, calling the development of such capability "important for our sovereignty as well as our security."[54]

Thus Ottawa had very strong incentives to participate in ADI. Those in the defense establishment responsible for air defense worried in particular that the United States might not share the fruits of its research on space-based radar and other technology useful to the protection of Canadian sovereignty, if Canada did not contribute to their development. Their case for participation was bolstered by the observation of a professional staffer of the U.S. Senate's Armed Services Committee, (which soon became one of the most-quoted remarks by an American on North American air defense) that "technology and programme choices for upgrading North American air defences appear to be eroding the necessity of Canadian participation."[55]

On the other hand, while the United States might prove entirely willing to share, space-based radar eventually could be deployed as part of air defences efforts complementing a BMD system or in support of a strategy of protracted nuclear war. The Senate Committee was alluding to this concern in remarking on the need to keep Canadian satellites "dedicated to passive detection and surveillance needs." Opponents of any Canadian participation in ADI were quick to cite the infelicitous public comment of an ADI official that "You'd want to conduct a lot of the battle further up north of Canada. I'd rather not fight over Detroit if I could avoid it."[56]

In the face of the strong Canadian interest coupled with nagging worries, the Mulroney government has pursued a two-track policy of trying to maximize its access to U.S. advanced air defense technology, while undertaking relatively small-scale efforts on its own that demonstrate seriousness of intent to the United States and might allow for the deployment of independent Canadian space-based radar satellites, should that prove necessary. Swallowing whatever strategic qualms it may itself have had, and deciding to brave the inevitable domestic political objections, the Mulroney government confirmed in *Challenge and Commitment* Canada's intention "to participate in research on future air defence systems in conjunction with the United States Air Defense Initiative."[57]

To be sure, the government recognized that "Perceptions of the military use of space have increasingly been affected by the American and Soviet research programs into strategic defence and the question this has raised as to the future relationship between the offensive and defensive elements in the nuclear balance."[58] But it called upon Canadians, in turn, to realize that "Failure to meet this challenge could mean forfeiting the responsibility for the surveillance of Canadian airspace to the United States."[59]

A Canadian space-based radar research program was set in motion in late 1986 with an initial budget of C$47 million. Officials of the Department of National Defence have expressed confidence that "given the political decision to do it and the funding," Canada would have the basic capability to deploy an SBR system of four to ten satellites by the mid-1990s, except for the capability to launch the satellites into orbit.[60] But the clear cut preference of Canadian air defense officials, given the enormous costs of space-based radar, is cooperation with the United States, if that proves possible.[61] The C$47 million in that sense can also be seen as earnest money. "Certainly $50 million buys them a seat at the table," agreed the commander-in-chief of U.S. Space Command.[62]

At Canada's behest, the 1985 North American air defense modernization agreement included a pledge by both governments to cooperate on research into advanced technologies. A bilateral Aerospace Defense Advanced Technologies Working Group (ADATS) was formed shortly thereafter to oversee coordination of efforts, including those related to space-based radar and infrared sensing. Cooperation has been extended directly to ADI. Canadian officials are members of the ADI Coordinating Committee and of the ADI Operations Requirements Panel, and serve as technical evaluators to preliminary ADI research and development proposals. A Canadian officer is assigned to the United States' interservice Joint Space Based Radar Office in Colorado Springs, another is to be assigned to the ADI program office in Boston and still another may be assigned to work on ADI matters at the Air Force Systems Command in Maryland. Two Canadian aerospace companies have been designated as subcontractors for the surveillance portions of ADI architecture studies.[63]

Today, it is impossible to predict how extensively the North American air defense system will be modernized over the next decade or so. But unlike the case with BMD, it is hard to imagine an enhanced air defense system which the United States might conceivably deploy over the next ten or fifteen years that did not in some fashion rely upon Canadian territory and airspace. To be sure, much may be undertaken from space-based platforms and, especially with the possible deployment of very long-range air defense fighters and missiles, out of Alaska and the lower forty-eight states. But interceptors and radar aircraft would continue to need access to Canadian airspace and probably to northern airfields, especially if an emphasis is ever placed on a layered air defense. The strategy of "going after the platform" would also seem to imply the necessity of deploying some long-range surface to air missiles with ranges of 1000 to 2000 miles in Canada in order to destroy bombers before the release of cruise missiles.

Thus any further air defense modernization decided upon by the United States will, in consequence, oblige Canada to continue to wrestle with the paradox of defense cooperation with the U.S, with two consequences. First, any substantial expansion of Canadian air defense forces can be expected to doom the Canadian military presence in Germany. The current Canadian contribution in Europe is already rapidly becoming untenable. The need to devote more resources to North American defense in order to protect Canadian sovereignty will hasten the process. It is not too far exaggerated to say that "Basically air defence is going to be a black hole that has a very strong prospect of eating the defence budget entirely by the end of the century."[64]

Second, Ottawa will search for ways to cope with the relationship between Canadian air defense efforts and the overall U.S. strategic posture. A recent study by David Cox, released by the Canadian Institute for International Peace and Security, suggests how this might be done. Cox offers a "pre-war" approach which would

> in effect, limit Canadian involvement to activities which would provide peacetime surveillance and crisis stability, and to desist from programmes which, in the last resort, assume nuclear war-fighting. Hence, for Canada, non-survivable strategic surveillance systems should be considered acceptable, while the move towards survivable air-based or defended space-based surveillance systems should not be considered a high priority for scarce resources. Similarly, active continental defence against cruise missiles, implying an ongoing wartime nuclear exchange, should be avoided by Canada, but a modest northern-based capability to prevent peacetime intrusions should be given priority.[65]

This would not entail a major departure in policy for either the United States or Canada. North American defense has always rested on a division of responsibilities, with the United States taking by far the largest share. Several functions have always been in U.S. hands alone: above all the nuclear deterrent itself, but also ballistic missile detection and space defense operations.

For enhanced North American aerospace defense, Canada could be expected to invest in space-based radars, operated as a Canadian system or as part of a larger, Canada-U.S. effort. It could also be expected to operate a relatively thin, but expensive system of advanced airborne radars and the fighter aircraft needed to help prevent a "no warning" decapitation strike by stealthy cruise missiles and bombers and to confirm that an air-breathing attack had occurred. These systems would undertake peacetime patrol of Canadian airspace, thereby also serving the sovereignty protection mission. A BMD system, if deployed, and the bulk of North American air defenses, perhaps providing the "survivable, comprehensive air defense" the ADI program envisages, would remain in the hands of the U.S. Air Force.

Nonetheless, two problems would have to be faced. First, the distinction between peacetime surveillance and survivable wartime systems is not always clear. AWACS aircraft are an example. Second, by no means would such an approach eliminate tension between Canadian and the U.S. strategic outlooks or sever the relationship between U.S. nuclear strategy and Canada. While the first line of air defense in peacetime Canada would be provided by Canadian forces, the United States elements of an enhanced air defense system would require access to Canadian airspace and possibly Canadian bases. Moreover, while the Canadian government would seek to draw the distinction between Canadian sovereignty and early warning roles on the one hand, and the American roles on the other, it could be faced at home with persistent charges of indirect "complicity" with U.S. nuclear policy.

In fact, even if the most difficult scenarios for Canada-U.S. air defense relations never materialize—if the United States never deploys a BMD system and never tries to enhance substantially the level of air defense effectiveness beyond current levels, improving the system simply to detect any stealthy threats—as long as the United States seeks to engage its nuclear arsenal in the protection of its allies and interests outside North America there will be a certain amount of unease and tension in Canada centering on Canada's North American air defense roles, although it is far from certain at this stage that in the present climate Canadians will be greatly concerned. At the same time, the United States' military preponderance in North America will always present Canada with a sovereignty challenge. From that tension there can simply be no release.

NOTES

1. The agreement itself is titled "Exchange of Notes and Memorandum of Understanding on the Modernization of the North American Air Defense System," 18 March 1985.
2. John M. Collins, *U.S./Soviet Military Balance: Statistical Trends, 1980–1987 (As of January 1, 1988)* (Washington: Congressional Research Service report 88-425 S, 15 April 1988), 22. See also Steven Zaloga, "Tupolev's New Strategic Bomber: Tu-160 *Blackjack*," *Jane's Soviet Intelligence Review,* September 1988, 14.

3. NORAD officials believe that *Bear G*s equipped with AS-4 ALCMs could be used to suppress air defenses in Alaska, opening a pathway to the central regions of North America for other bombers. "New Soviet Bombers, Fighters Heighten Alaska's Strategic Role," *Aviation Week and Space Technology*, 9 May 1988, 43.

4. "Washington Roundup . . . Blackjack Cruise," *Aviation Week and Space Technology* 28 March 1988, 15; "U.S. and Soviet nuclear weapons under development, 1988," *Bulletin of the Atomic Scientists* October 1988, 56; "Airborne Tactical Missiles," *Air Force Magazine*, March 1989, 100.

5. See James P. Rubin, "Sea-launched Cruise Missiles: Facing Up to the Arms Control Challenge," *Arms Control Today*, April 1986, 4, Testimony of Admiral William Studeman, Director of Naval Intelligence to the Seapower and Strategic Criticals Material Subcommittee of the House Armed Services Committee, reported in *Jane's Defence Weekly*, 26 March 1988, 600.

6. Canada, Senate, Special Committee on National Defence, *Canada's Territorial Air Defence*, January 1985, 24.

7. John D. Steinbruner, "Nuclear Decapitation," *Foreign Policy* 45 (Winter 1981–1982): 18.

8. Not all analysts agree with the decapitation scenario. See, for example, Francis J. Furtado, *U.S. and Soviet Land-Attack SLCM Programs: Implications for Strategic Stability*, ORAE Memorandum no. 129 (Ottawa: Department of National Defence, Operational Research and Analysis Establishment, June 1990).

9. OTH-B technology and plans are well described in a manner comprehensible to the layman in Ramon Lopez, "OTH-B Radar Station Nears Completion," *International Defense Review* 20, no. 3 (1987): 341. (As this book went to print the U.S. Defense Department announced that the east coast OTH-B station would be reduced to part-time operation and the west coast station moth balled.)

10. Testimony of the USAF Director of Space Systems and Command, Control and Communications in U.S. Congress, House Committee on Armed Services, *Defense Department Authorization and Oversight*, Hearings before the Committee on H.R. 1872, DOD Authorization of Appropriations for FY 1986, 99th Cong., 1st sess. (1985), 986–88.

11. Theodore A. Postol, "Banning Nuclear SLCMs: It Would Be Nice If We Could," *International Security* 13, no. 3 (Winter 1988–1989): 201.

12. Martin Shadwick, "Canada and North America Air Defense: New Technology, Old Issues?" *Defense and Foreign Affairs* 15, no. 5 (May 1987): 70.

13. Major General J. D. O'Blenis, notes for a presentation, "Air Defence," Fighter Group, North Bay, 1990.

14. O'Blenis presentation.

15. Text. unclassified briefing materials on the Air Defense Initiative, Headquarters, U.S. Air Force, September 1987.

16. Daniel Hayward, *The Air Defence Initiative*, Ottawa: Canadian Centre for Arms Control and Disarmament, Issue Brief no. 9, 1988, 9.

17. Norman Friedman, "Stealth Technology, SDI and the Cruise Missile," *Military Technology* October 1985, 122–26. See as well, David S. Sorenson,

"Defending Against the Advanced Cruise Missile: The Ultimate Air Defense Nightmare?" in *Strategic Air Defense*, ed. Stephen J. Cimbala (Wilmington, Del.: S.R. Books 1989), 139.

18. Paul H. Nitze, "The Case for Cutting Strategic Arms," *Washington Post*, 21 June 1988, A19.

19. Ibid.

20. David Cox, *Trends in Continental Defence: A Canadian Perspective* (Ottawa: Canadian Institute for International Peace and Security, 1987), 16.

21. Paul Mann, "Superpowers Agree to Arms Cuts, But SS-18, Other Disputes Go On," *Aviation Week and Space Technology* 132, no. 24 (11 June 1990): 66–67.

22. Vice Admiral Henry C. Mustin, "The Sea-Launched Cruise Missile: More Than a Bargaining Chip," *International Security* 13, no. 3 (Winter 1988–1989): 184–85.

23. The U.S. position is discussed by Capt. Linton Brooks, Director of Arms Control on the National Security Council Staff in "Nuclear SLCMs Add to Deterrence and Security," in *International Security* 13, no. 3 (Winter 1988–1989): 169.

24. For arguments that a verification regime can be imposed without ship or submarine inspections, based on a recent experiment carried out on a Soviet warship by Soviet and U.S. scientists see Valerie Thomas, "False Obstacle to Arms Control," *New York Times*, 13 July 1989, A23.

25. Rose E. Gottemoeller, "Finding Solutions to SLCM Arms Control Problems," *International Security* 13, no. 3 (Winter 1988–1989): 177. See also Gottemoeller, *Land-attack Cruise Missiles*, Adelphi Paper no. 226 (London: International Institute for Strategic Studies, Winter 1987–1988).

26. David Cox, "A Review of the Geneva Negotiations, 1989–1990," *Background Paper*, no. 32 (Ottawa: Canadian Institute for International Peace and Security, May 1990), 8.

27. See U.S. General Accounting Office, *Drug Control: Issues Surrounding Increased Use of the Military in Drug Interdiction*, GAO.NSIAD-88-156 (executive summary), April 1988; and U.S. General Accounting Office, *Drug Smuggling: Capabilities for Interdicting Private Aircraft are Limited and Costly* GAO/GGD-93, June 1989.

28. This section draws heavily on unclassified briefing material on ADI, provided by the U.S. Air Force. For an excellent, detailed description of the ADI program, see Hayward, *The Air Defence Initiative*.

29. ADI briefing material.

30. Ibid.

31. Ibid.

32. Ibid.

33. Major General Lionel Bourgeois, "Strategic Air Defence of North America: 2000," in *AIRWAR 2000*, ed. Brian Macdonald (Toronto: Canadian Institute of Strategic Studies, 1989), 15.

34. Quoted in *Military Space*, 14 September 1987, 4.

35. U.S. defense analyst Victor Utgoff describes a complementary air defense system, capable of destroying about 70 percent of a Soviet force of 200 bombers with 10 ALCMs each and 700 SLCMs, consisting of a line of 13

early warning aircraft (based on 65 aircraft in service), 80 armed surveillance aircraft, 300 fighter aircraft, and 10 AWACS aircraft, and other elements. He estimates the cost at $55.5 billion. See Hayward, 24. Another set of estimates is to be found in William P. Delaney, "Air Defense of the United States: Strategic Missions and Modern Technology," *International Security* 15, no. 1 (Summer 1990): 181.

36. Hayward, 24.
37. C. E. Beattie and K. R. Greenway, "Offering Up Canada's North," *Northern Perspectives* 14, no. 4 (September–October 1986): 5.
38. Canada, House of Commons, Standing Committee on External Affairs and National Defence, *NORAD 1986,* February 1986, 78.
39. Testimony of Dr. Richard D. DeLauer, Undersecretary of Defense for Research and Engineering, in U.S. Congress, House, Committee on Armed Services, Full Committee Hearing on *Continental Air Defense,* 97th Cong., 1st sess., 22 July 1981, 11–12.
40. See Jeffrey Richelson, "PD-59, NSDD-13 and the Reagan Strategic Modernization Program," *The Journal of Strategic Studies* 6, no. 2 (June 1983): 125.
41. General Robert T. Herres, Address on "Command and Control" to JFK School of Government, Cambridge, Massachusetts, 9 April 1985, text courtesy NORAD Public Affairs Office.
42. As Paul Bracken put it in his landmark work, *The Command and Control of Nuclear Forces,* "One thing emerges repeatedly when we examine nuclear command and control: there are seemingly insurmountable barriers to maintaining political control in a strategic war." *The Command and Control of Nuclear Forces* (New Haven and London: Yale University Press, 1983), 232. John Collins of the Congressional Research Service concluded that the Reagan administration's C^{3}I projects constitute "marginal improvements." He added, "Satellites, large land-based radars, and many other critical components, exposed and unprotected, will be markedly less survivable than the retaliatory and defensive forces whose full effectiveness depends on them for real-time target acquisition, other intelligence, battle management, and war termination instructions." *U.S.-Soviet Military Balance, 1980–1985* (Washington: Pergammon-Brassey's, 1985), 59.
43. R. B. Byers, "NORAD, Star Wars, and Strategic Doctrine," in R. B. Byers, John Hamre, and G. R. Lindsey, *Aerospace Defence: Canada's Future Role?,* Toronto, Canadian Institute of International Affairs, Wellesley Papers 9, 1985, 44, 52.
44. Ernie Regehr, Director of Research, Project Ploughshares, in Canada House of Commons, Standing Committee on External Affairs and National Defence *Minutes of Proceedings and Evidence,* 18 December 1985, 43:6.
45. Martin Shadwick, "NORAD, Sovereignty and Changing Technology," Occasional Paper no. 3, Research Programme in Strategic Studies, York University, 1985, 13.
46. Canada, House of Commons, *Debates,* 5 February 1985, 2014.
47. Press release, U.S. Embassy Ottawa, 7 March 1985.
48. *Debates,* 13 March 1985, 2980.
49. Ibid.

50. *Debates,* 6 March 1985, 2777.
51. *NORAD 1986,* 41.
52. A fine overview of the nonmilitary aspects of Canada's space program, including Canada-U.S. relations in space, is to be found in John Kirton, ed., *Canada, the United States and Space* (Toronto: Canadian Institute of International Affairs, 1986).
53. *Canada's Territorial Air Defence,* 40.
54. Canada, Department of National Defence, *Challenge and Commitment: A Defence Policy for Canada,* Ottawa, 1987, 59. For a recent commentary, see W. C. Weston, "L'importance stratégique de l'espace pour les besoins militaires futurs du Canada," *Etudes Internationales,* 19, no. 3 (September 1988): 493.
55. John Hamre, "Continental air defence, United States security policy, and Canada-United States defence relations,," in *Aerospace Defence: Canada's Future Role?,* ed. R. B. Byers, et al., Wesley Paper 9/1986 (Toronto: Canada Institute of International Affairs, 1985), 27.
56. Quoted in David J. Lynch, "U.S. Considers Defense Shield," *Defense Week* 7, no. 25 (23 June 1986): 12.
57. *Challenge and Commitment,* 56–57.
58. Ibid., 59.
59. Ibid. When Perrin Beatty appeared for the first time before the Standing Committee on External Affairs and National Defence of the House of Commons to defend his white paper, he was probably not surprised that the first question he was asked by the New Democratic defense critic was about ADI: "Why is Canada taking part in plans to fight a nuclear war?" Canada, House of Commons, Standing Committee on External Affairs and National Defence, *Minutes of Proceedings and Evidence* 25 June 1987, 14:10.
60. DND Director of Space Doctrine and Operations quoted in Sharon Hobson, "Canada's Space-based Radar Project," *Jane's Defence Weekly* 7, no. 6 (14 February 1987): 226.
61. "Canadian officials believe that a separate Canadian space-based radar, 'wouldn't make any sense' and that it is logical for SBR to be jointly operated and funded, similar to the North Warning System." Hayward, *The Air Defence Initiative,* 22.
62. Quoted in *Military Space,* 14 September 1987, 4.
63. See Major General R. B. Morton (Chief, Air Doctrine and Operations, National Defence Headquarters), "SDI/ADI and Canadian Sovereignty," in Macdonal, *Airwar 2000,* 17.
64. Douglas Ross, in "The Federal Budget: Defence and Foreign Policy: A Media Roundtable," *Peace and Security,* Summer 1989, 9.
65. David Cox, *Trends in Continental Defence: A Canadian Perspective,* Occasional Papers, no. 2 (Ottawa: Canadian Institute for International Peace and Security, 1988), 49.

VII

Command and Control Arrangements for North American Aerospace Defense

The binational North American Aerospace Defense Command (NORAD), until 1981 named the North American Air Defense Command, has operational control over Canadian and U.S. air defense forces. Its commander-in-chief (CINCNORAD) is a U.S. Air Force general. Americans can readily understand that for any country, not just one like Canada with never-ending worries about sovereignty, relinquishing day-to-day control over home defense forces to a foreign general, even of a friend and ally operating under joint arrangements, would be a serious step.[1] At NORAD's establishment in 1957, a diminution of purely national control seemed to most Canadians a reasonable price to pay as the effective defense of the continent against Soviet bombers appeared to mandate it.

Many Canadians later came to the conclusion that NORAD, being a binational arrangement renegotiated every few years, would also be a useful tool for dealing with the Americans who, in any event, were going to dominate the continent's defenses. As John Holmes put it, "NORAD, which seems a step in the continentalization of North American defense, can be regarded from another angle as a means of preserving a Canadian role and an appropriate degree of sovereignty in a situation in which, if there were no rules, the Americans would simply take over the defense of the continent."[2] Over the years NORAD became a largely uncontroversial, if never universally beloved feature of Canada's military relationship with the superpower to the south.

For the U.S. Air Force, the NORAD relationship with Canada has also been useful. It has provided for the functional integration of United States and Canadian air defense efforts on this continent and has served as a guarantee of access to Canadian airspace and territory for U.S. air defense forces.

Yet the future of that relationship is now in question, in the wake of the growing importance of U.S. military space-based activities. A reflection of that importance was the creation in 1985 by the U.S.

Department of Defense of United States Space Command (USSPACE-COM). While staffed by Americans, and falling exclusively under U.S. command, USSPACECOM is intimately linked in mission and structure to the binationally staffed and commanded NORAD.

Both countries, over the next decade, will be considering the relationship between NORAD and USSPACECOM. To Canadians for whom NORAD, after nearly thirty years of existence, had long become almost synonymous with North American aerospace defense, the creation of the new entirely American space command with responsibilities related to those of NORAD for the defense of the continent was, at the least, confusing. Since then, Canadians have been puzzling out the NORAD-USSPACECOM relationship and debating what it portends, especially if the United States ever decides to deploy a ballistic missile defense (BMD) system. These issues came to the fore in Canada during the extensive 1986 parliamentary hearings on NORAD renewal. They will again have a brief airing in 1991, when the current NORAD agreement expires, and in all probability, a far more extensive one in 1996. Thus in the 1990s the United States may face Canadian proposals for changes.

This chapter, then, has three purposes. First, it will outline the current North American aerospace defense command arrangements, centered on NORAD and USSPACECOM. The seemingly endless confusion in Canada about them is understandable inasmuch as officials of the U.S. defense establishment, still not entirely used to the new structure themselves, sometimes reveal their own confusion about what falls under NORAD's authority and what falls under that of USSPACECOM and its component commands. Second, it will discuss Canadian concerns over their potential implications. Finally it will deal with how the interests of the United States and Canada could be affected by any future Canadian proposals for devolution of the current command structure.

THE CURRENT ARRANGEMENTS

The current command and control arrangements for the aerospace defense of North America reflect Canada's importance in continental air defense and unimportance in military space efforts. Hence NORAD is binational while USSPACECOM is not.

Three features in the Canada-U.S. NORAD agreement distinguish NORAD as a binational entity. First, the command is structured to provide within it a strong Canadian role. CINCNORAD is supported by a Canadian Deputy CINCNORAD and a staff composed largely of officers drawn from both the USAF and Canadian air force, as well as officers from the other U.S. armed services. In the absence of CINCNORAD, Deputy CINCNORAD is empowered to act in his place.[3] Deputy CINCNORAD has usually been appointed to the position after having served in the most senior job in the Canadian air force, currently Commander of Air Command.

Second, NORAD is responsible to the senior military authorities in both countries, who in turn are responsible to civilian political authorities. CINCNORAD reports to the U.S. Joint Chiefs of Staff and the Chief of the Defence Staff in Ottawa, and operates in accordance with formal terms of reference approved by them. His appointment, and that of his deputy must be approved by both governments. Deputy CINCNORAD is also issued terms of reference which provide that he act as CINCNORAD's adviser on Canadian matters and that he ensure in a crisis that consultation is initiated with the Canadian national command authorities.

Third, the agreement seeks to reconcile the effective integration of Canadian and U.S. air defense operations with the retention by Canada of much authority over its own forces and airspace. NORAD has been given "operational control," not command, over United States and Canadian continental air defense forces. Operational control consists of, in the NORAD case, "the power to direct, coordinate and control the operational activities of forces assigned, attached or otherwise made available."[4] Command, on the other hand, remains in national hands. It includes determining the original composition of forces, selecting their permanent stations, maintaining discipline, training and logistics.

In the heyday of continental air defense in the 1950s and 1960s NORAD's authority to operationally control air defense resources was militarily significant. Colorado Springs, in those years, would have used that authority in order to provide for a rationalized air defense battle stretching across the entire continent, drawing upon thousands of fighter aircraft and hundreds of surface-to-air missiles divided over eleven regional air defense centers. The number of such centers has gradually been reduced. Recently, North American air defense operations have been concentrated into three NORAD regions, each headquartered with a NORAD component command that contributes fighter aircraft, radar stations and in the United States, AWACS aircraft. One region covers the continental United States (the component is USAF Tactical Air Command's 1st Air Force, at Langely Air Force Base, Virginia) one covers Canada (Fighter Group of Air Command, North Bay, Ontario) and one Alaska (USAF Alaskan Air Command, at Elmendorf Air Force Base) (see Figure 7.1).

While Colorado Springs still retains nominal operational control, in practice the temporary transfer of fighter and radar aircraft from one region to another is handled by the three regional headquarters. Each region, in turn, retains operational control over air defense aircraft flying in its airspace. This constitutes an additional element of Canadian sovereignty protection inasmuch as Fighter Group at North Bay controls Canadian airspace.

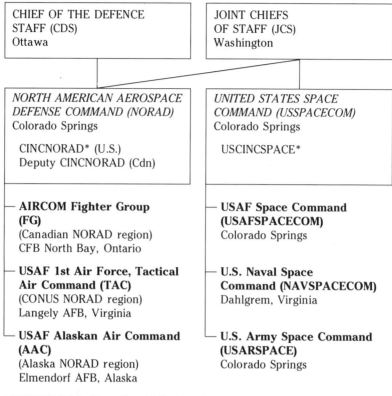

CHIEF OF THE DEFENCE STAFF (CDS) Ottawa	JOINT CHIEFS OF STAFF (JCS) Washington
NORTH AMERICAN AEROSPACE DEFENSE COMMAND (NORAD) Colorado Springs CINCNORAD* (U.S.) Deputy CINCNORAD (Cdn)	*UNITED STATES SPACE COMMAND (USSPACECOM)* Colorado Springs USCINCSPACE*

— **AIRCOM Fighter Group (FG)**
(Canadian NORAD region)
CFB North Bay, Ontario

— **USAF 1st Air Force, Tactical Air Command (TAC)**
(CONUS NORAD region)
Langely AFB, Virginia

— **USAF Alaskan Air Command (AAC)**
(Alaska NORAD region)
Elmendorf AFB, Alaska

— **USAF Space Command (USAFSPACECOM)**
Colorado Springs

— **U.S. Naval Space Command (NAVSPACECOM)**
Dahlgrem, Virginia

— **U.S. Army Space Command (USARSPACE)**
Colorado Springs

*CINCNORAD "dual-hatted" as USCINCSPACE

FIGURE 7.1
NORAD-USSPACECOM COMMAND RELATIONS

Finally, the agreement provides that costs be shared for the operation of NORAD headquarters. The United States, though, pays the major share: 90 percent.

NORAD's original mission, as provided for in the 1958 agreement, was "to counter the threat and to achieve maximum effectiveness of the air defense system."[5] In the absence of active strategic defenses, except for the current thin air defense system, NORAD's chief roles since 1975 have been redefined to that of providing warning and assessment of attack, and protecting the sovereignty of both countries over their respective airspace. It also has the task of "providing for the effective use" of the continent's modest air defenses.[6]

Strikingly unlike the North American air defense system which relies on Canadian territory, Canadian airspace and Canadian air defense forces, all of the systems to detect and track attacking ballistic missiles are American. None has been placed on Canadian soil, or is operated by Canadians. Starting in the 1960s ground-based, long-range, ballistic missile tracking radars were located in Alaska, Greenland, Great Britain and the continental United States. Some Canadians wondered at the time whether the United States chose sites in deliberate avoidance of Canadian territory. But as a glance at the map, or better still, a globe, will show, the Alaskan, British and Greenland locations provide better fan coverage over the polar region towards the Soviet Union. Sites located on the U.S. east and west coasts provide capability to detect submarine-launched ballistic missiles. Later, the United States, without Canadian participation, deployed space-based infrared sensors capable of detecting the hot exhaust plumes of missiles in the boost phase, providing all but instant warning of the beginning of a Soviet space shot or of a ballistic missile attack and other sensors capable of detecting nuclear explosions.[7]

The United States also began, in the late 1950s, to deploy ground-based sensors to track all objects in space.[8] NORAD was given the task of coordinating these efforts, and cataloging all objects in earth orbit. In these space-tracking activities Canadian forces once played a very small role: Baker-Nunn satellite tracking cameras were operated by the Canadian air force in Alberta and New Brunswick. But the obsolete Alberta facility has been closed and the one in New Brunswick is scheduled to be closed at some indefinite date.[9]

Beyond reliance on satellites for warning of ballistic missile attack, space-based operations by the U.S. military have expanded enormously. As Paul B. Stares of the Brookings Institution has summarized,

> The role of satellites . . . is changing in a fundamental way. They are becoming more and more useful for enhancing the war-fighting effectiveness of armed forces. Virtually every type of military operation, from small conventional conflicts to strategic nuclear war, is now likely to involve satellites. Reconnaissance satellites, for instance, are increasingly being located to locate, track and target forces such as naval ships. Communication satellites, by being able to receive and rapidly distribute vital information, can improve in radical ways the command and control of military forces and thus their combat performance. And navigation satellites now make it possible to guide the "dumbest" munitions to their targets with nearly perfect precision. In military terms, satellites have become true "force multipliers."[10]

All three U.S. armed services have space programs and budgets. The USAF, with the most extensive program, organized its own space command (AFSPACECOM) at Colorado Springs in 1982. The U.S. Navy, "the largest tactical user of space-based systems," followed suit with the activation of Naval Space Command at Dahlgrem, Virginia in 1983.[11] The

Army, with the smallest program, was the last, creating in 1988 an Army Space Command, also headquartered at Colorado Springs.

Concern in the U.S. Congress and in the Department of Defense itself about the possible duplication of space efforts by the services, and the need to coordinate those efforts lead to the creation of USSPACECOM. Similar to NORAD, USSPACECOM commands no forces of its own, relying on the assets of its component commands, AFSPACECOM, the Naval Space Command and the Army Space Command.[12] As a unified command, it reports to the Joint Chiefs of Staff. Its commander-in-chief (USCINCSPACE) is a four-star USAF general; his deputy is an admiral, although there is no formal stipulation from which service either is to be drawn. As is the case with other U.S. unified commands, the relationship between USSPACECOM and its service components, especially the division of authority, is the focus of frequent negotiation and adjustment, and sometimes of struggle. Most difficult has been the relationship between USSPACECOM and the often fiercely independent Naval Space Command.

However, (and the sources of a good deal of confusion in both Canada and the United States) USCINCSPACE is "dual hatted" as CINCNORAD, and both USSPACECOM and NORAD are co-located at Colorado Springs, (along with AFSPACECOM and Army Space Command). NORAD and USSPACECOM share the famous complex within Cheyenne Mountain for their central operational facilities, as well as a brand new headquarters building at nearby Petersen Air Force Base. The Canadian Deputy CINC-NORAD is not dual hatted as Deputy USCINCSPACE and the binational NORAD staffs remain distinct from those of USSPACECOM. About 20 Canadians are among the 100 officers on the NORAD combat operations staff, while 23 Canadians are among the 90 officers at NORAD headquarters. By way of comparison, the USSPACECOM combat operations staff numbers 221 U.S. officers, its headquarters 197. (Further complicating matters, there *are* Canadian officers assigned to work with AFSPACE-COM, especially on matters related to space-based air defense.)

USSPACECOM's tasks extend beyond North American aerospace defense. Its first task is to provide, to the extent a unified command can, centralized planning for and coordination of U.S. military space operations, under the rubric of "space support." The first USCINCSPACE described space support as "a summation of all that we do to facilitate execution of the missions of the commands and agencies, namely controlling and maintaining satellites, operating ground stations, managing sensor networks and developing plans to meet future needs."[13] The breadth and vagueness of that description gives some idea of the magnitude of the coordinating problems.

USSPACECOM has four other roles. It is responsible for the protection of U.S. satellites. At the moment, all USSPACECOM's Space Defense

Operations Center can do is detect threats to satellites, and warn their operators so that, to the extent possible, they could undertake passive countermeasures, such as satellite maneuvering. The center would exercise control over AFSPACECOM's proposed antisatellite (ASAT) capability, if it ever becomes operational, which it may now that the Bush administration is attempting to breathe new life into the program.[14]

USSPACECOM has planning responsibilities for the possible deployment of a ballistic missile defense (BMD) system. Research concerning BMD systems remains in the hands of the Strategic Defense Initiative Organization (SDIO). The SDIO recently reported to Congress that it placed a premium on "full interaction with the U.S. Space Command" in order that the United States be in a position to decide whether to proceed with deployment.[15]

USSPACECOM's final two roles touch most directly on its working relationship with NORAD. It has inherited responsibility for coordinating space surveillance; similarly it has inherited the task of warning of ballistic missile attack. USSPACECOM, in turn, provides information to NORAD, and to other commands concerning what is occurring in space (including any attacks on satellites), and warning of ballistic missile attack.

Despite the growing importance of USSPACECOM, NORAD continues to play a central role under the current arrangements. For it has retained what is now called the "Attack Warning/Attack Assessment" (AW/AA) function. NORAD receives information on what is occurring in North American airspace from the Canadian and U.S. air defense systems under its control; from USSPACECOM it receives information on what is occurring in space, and warning of ballistic missile launches. In the event of an attack on North America it would be NORAD that would provide the *integrated* warning and assessment to the United States and Canadian national command authorities and to the Strategic Air Command.

The United States has invested heavily in recent years in overhauling the electronics of the AW/AA system, and centralizing it under NORAD's control. As a recent CINCNORAD explained the program to a Congressional committee, "with the complexity of the threat today it is absolutely essential that all the key decision-makers see the same information at the same time. Hence, we propose pulling all the AW/AA processors under the NORAD umbrella—in creating an integrated architecture for warning of air, space and missile threat."[16]

This updating of the AW/AA architecture forms part and parcel of the broader U.S. program of modernizing C³I facilities, put into place by the Reagan administration, which is intended to allow U.S. strategic forces to survive Soviet strikes, obtain immediate, detailed assessments of those strikes, and respond appropriately. A sophisticated, survivable

AW/AA system would be unnecessary if U.S. strategy were inflexibly based on the immediate, assured destruction of the Soviet Union in the event of Soviet attack. If that were the case, the president or his successor would need know only that a nuclear attack on the United States had occurred in order to authorize the destruction of Soviet cities. Details of the nature of the Soviet attack would be irrelevant. Paul Bracken, in his landmark work, has described the place of assessment in current U.S. strategy:

> . . . many additions to American nuclear doctrine since the 1960s require greater control, precision, and selectivity in the application of forces. A prerequisite for this control is knowledge of battle outcomes that can be concentrated in a single mind, or at least in a single committee or office with easy communications among its members. If this communicated knowledge does not exist or is greatly distorted then the centralized decision makers would have little basis on which to make choices. While the necessary information could probably be gathered eventually, there is unlikely to be much time for data gathering in the course of an attack.[17]

There is one important qualification to the central place NORAD continues to hold as a result of its retention of the AW/AA function. USSPACECOM has been provided with the standby authority to undertake the AW/AA function and to control U.S. air defense forces. This standby authority could be drawn upon in a crisis should the United States decide to go on a higher alert status, and Canada decline to participate. NORAD then would, in effect, cease to function. In other words, NORAD's binational status gives Canada no veto over U.S. actions in the event of an emergency. Twice in its history NORAD has been in precisely such a situation.[18]

To summarize the current division of responsibilities: USSPACECOM coordinates U.S. military space-based efforts and is responsible for providing warning of ballistic missile attack and attacks on satellites; NORAD is responsible for air defense, including the nominal control of air defense forces and would provide integrated assessments of attacks in space, and bomber and ballistic missile attacks on North America.

CANADIAN CONCERNS

Even before USSPACECOM came into existence in late 1985, plans for its establishment were confusing Canadians and producing controversy. Early that year a New Democratic member of parliament stood on the floor of the House of Commons charging "that the US has finalized its plans to establish an integrated command centre at Colorado Springs which will include ballistic missile defences, that is, the SDI as well as offensive nuclear forces," and calling upon the Mulroney government to "agree that, unless we oppose [the new command], Canada will be inexorably drawn into star wars through NORAD."[19]

It was fortunate that the NORAD agreement was scheduled to expire in May 1986, for the occasion afforded the Standing Committee on External Affairs and National Defence of the House of Commons the opportunity to devote a considerable amount of time to figuring out and publicizing the new command arrangements. The hearings (which were the most extensive ever concerning NORAD), and the committee's report are highly revealing of Canadian attitudes and the approaches the Canadian government may take toward NORAD in the 1990s, especially if the United States moves toward BMD deployments. The committee had a firm Progressive Conservative majority; in accordance with the system of fairly strict party discipline observed in the Canadian parliament it could not stray far in its official conclusions from the views held by the Mulroney government.

At the hearings and in subsequent years, it became evident that two groups of Canadians are concerned about the NORAD-USSPACECOM relationship, for opposing reasons. The first consists principally of Canadian airmen and defense officials who worry that USSPACECOM's creation would put too much distance between Canada and U.S. space activities. If NORAD were to become just an air defense command, Canada would be left out. Major General L. Ashley, then chief of air doctrine and operations at National Defence Headquarters in Ottawa, told the committee that "My main concern now is that the division of responsibility may eventually make it difficult to participate in ventures that should be of interest" to Canada, especially space-based radar.[20]

The Canadian military lobbied their U.S. counterparts extensively for the dual hatting of CINCNORAD as USCINCSPACE, in order to have greater access at the top to USSPACECOM. Since 1985-1986, concern within the Canadian military over the USSPACECOM-NORAD relationship has at least temporarily abated. It has been reassured by the CINC's dual hatting and by the central role NORAD, and hence Canadian officers, play in the AW/AA function. Canadian officers at Colorado Springs have also worked hard to establish close relations with USSPACECOM officers, with whom they now work in close proximity. While Canadians are excluded from sensitive information concerning many aspects of U.S. space operations, senior Canadian officials at NORAD apparently no longer worry deeply that in the short run they will be excluded from key information directly affecting Canadian interests, above all, plans related to the development of space-based air defense radar. The creation of the small Canadian program to develop space-based radar has also given the Canadian military something to bargain with as the United States continues its larger program. In the long run, though, Canadian airmen and defense officials can be expected to resist any attempts to put even greater distance between Canada and USSPACECOM.[21]

The second group consists of Canadians strongly opposed to the SDI research program and the general trends in U.S. strategy. They argue that the NORAD-USSPACECOM link either already brings Canada much too close to those programs or could do so in the future.[22]

The hearings revealed the extent of the confusion over the division of authority between USSPACECOM and NORAD, and the relationship between the two, especially as to where BMD, and even the control of U.S. strategic nuclear weapons all fit into the structure. Surveying that confusion, the committee later noted of its hearings that:

> Some of the disarmament group representatives, and even academics seem to be under the impression that [Deputy CINCNORAD], a Canadian officer whom the agreement designates to take over command of NORAD in CINCNORAD's absence would (or might) also act as deputy commander of the two other commands located at Colorado Springs even though these are strictly U.S. national commands. An even larger number of witnesses seem to assume that, given a single commander, some of the functions of all three commands—NORAD, AFSPACECOM and USSPACECOM— are bound to become integrated to the point where they become indistinguishable in fact, if not in organization. Other observers have gone further and forecast that the same U.S. officer might eventually be put in charge of the nuclear offensive systems as well as of the defensive systems of the U.S.[23]

These misunderstandings could have serious political implications, for no Canadian government can afford being seen as directly linking Canadian defense efforts to BMD or U.S. offensive nuclear operations. To deal with this confusion, the committee took several steps, including an invitation to General Robert Herres, then CINCNORAD to testify. General Herres' appearance was the first ever by a CINCNORAD, producing a packed committee chamber. He emphasized that BMD planning and ASAT were exclusively U.S. activities outside NORAD's purview, and that they could only become NORAD responsibilities with the explicit consent of both the United States and Canadian governments.[24]

Fueling suspicions has been the seemingly innocuous yet controversial issue of NORAD's 1981 name change to the North American *Aerospace* Defense Command, which seems to imply that the command would be responsible for BMD. The committee chairman, calling the change "unfortunate" suggested that a better name would have been the "North American Air Defense and Aerospace Surveillance Command."[25] Actually, after 1985, when space surveillance and ballistic missile detection facilities were placed under the control of USSPACECOM, a still more accurate, if even more unwieldy name would have been

the "North American Air Defense and Aerospace Attack Warning/
Attack Assessment Command."

Another source of suspicion is the so-called "ABM clause." That clause
had been inserted in the NORAD agreement in 1968 at a time when
the United States was moving towards the deployment of a "thin" ABM
system. It specified that NORAD participation would "not involve in any
way a Canadian commitment to participate in an active ballistic missile defense,"[26] although the United States never had the intention of
involving Canada. The clause had no legal implications. Rather it served
the political need of the Canadian government to distance itself from
the U.S. ABM system. It had been removed from the accord in 1981,
well after the United States had decided not even to deploy the single
site permitted it under the protocols to the 1972 ABM Treaty.

Officials of both governments stressed in 1985 that not only was it
unnecessary to protect Canada but it had been, "deleted precisely to
avoid any suggestion that either Canada or the United States might take
actions which would breach the ABM Treaty."[27] Opponents of NORAD
renewal suggested that as early as 1981—two years before President
Reagan's surprise address—U.S. officials already had wanted to avoid
foreclosing any future options, and thus had quietly removed the clause
from the agreement. Without it, they said, Canada had no protection
against being dragged into SDI through NORAD.

The committee agreed that the clause was unnecessary, but "to help
allay public concerns" it recommended that the government invite the
United States at the time of NORAD renewal to issue jointly a declaration "reaffirming both countries' commitment to deterrence and strategic stability, as well as their support for the integrity of the ABM Treaty
and a negotiation process leading to verifiable reduction of armaments."[28] The Mulroney government, apparently feeling that such a step
also was unnecessary simply renewed the agreement in 1986. With the
SDI program still alive under the Bush administration, the issue of the
"ABM clause" may well reemerge in the 1990s.

Public confusion in Canada about the NORAD-USSPACECOM arrangements has by no means disappeared, though. A good example is to be
found in an otherwise first-rate study of North American defense
released by the influential Canadian Institute for International Peace
and Security in 1987 which included the inaccurate observations that
NORAD had become "a very small adjunct to Space Command," that
the U.S. military had "subsumed NORAD . . . under a unified national
command system," and that "the logic of the organization chart is that
the NORAD commander reports to the Unified Space Command."[29] The
quality of debate over Canada's involvement, real and potential, in any
BMD deployment continues to suffer accordingly, for the impression
lingers that the United States is inexorably building a command structure

that would bring Canadians into the operation of a BMD system. This impression, in turn, continues to generate pressure on the government to show that there exists real distance between Canadian air defense efforts and U.S. planning for BMD.

For the moment, the NORAD issue in Canada simply is unresolved, pointing to more rounds of scrutiny in the 1990s.[30] Thus what is most striking about the outcome of the parliamentary committee's deliberations is its reflection of the unresolved tension in Canada between the worry that the link between USSPACECOM and NORAD is too *loose* and the worry that it is too *tight.* Certain Progressive Conservative members of the committee said that their concern "is not that the integration of Canadian and U.S. aerospace defence forces has progressed too far but rather that some of NORAD's traditional functions may be turned over to (USSPACECOM). . . . This could diminish the scope for Canadian involvement and would become especially serious if the United States decided to put different officers in charge of USSPACECOM and NORAD."[31]

On the other hand, the committee concluded that the fundamental objections raised by opponents to NORAD renewal were "premature" and might therefore have to be dealt with directly in the 1990s. "NORAD is the here and now;" the committee concluded, "for the foreseeable future SDI will be nothing more than a research program."[32] At the same time, the committee was "unconvinced that U.S. strategy has changed to the extent that it no longer relies on offensive retaliation and MAD as the basis for deterrence."[33] However, in the 1990s, the situation could be very different for,

> this Committee or its successor should have in hand answers to important questions concerning (USSPACECOM) and SDI. It will also have the benefit of hindsight about U.S. directions under a new administration and the progress or outcome of East-West negotiations at Geneva. It may conclude that changes in strategies and policies require Canada to examine closely the value of both the Strategic Defence Initiative and NORAD. It may have to choose between NORAD and (ballistic missile defense).[34]

Should Canada decide sometime in the 1990s against NORAD, "other, less integrative arrangements are conceivable and functioned quite satisfactorily until 1957. This option is always available to Canada, should it feel uncomfortable with directions taken in the United States."[35]

THE UNITED STATES AND "OTHER, LESS INTEGRATIVE OPTIONS"

If, for whatever reason—assertion of sovereignty, aversion to U.S. strategy, fear of being dragged into BMD—the Canadian government opts in the 1990s for "other, less integrative arrangements" it is likely to encounter little opposition from the U.S. military. The fears of many Canadians notwithstanding, U.S. officials have absolutely no more interest than the New Democratic Party in integrating Canada into US-SPACECOM or directly involving them in the operation of any BMD system. There is no incentive for the United States to do so, given the paucity of Canadian military efforts in space, and the availability of alternative means of coordinating Canadian and U.S. air defense efforts which would meet the security needs of the United States.

On the contrary, the U.S. military has sought to preserve a distance between Canada and U.S. space operations, to the point where it considered moving the Canadians and control over air defense operations out of Cheyenne Mountain and away from the new space command. During the planning for USSPACECOM, the USAF headquarters staff in Washington seemed ready to support the relocation of NORAD to Langley Air Force Base, headquarters of the continental U.S. air defense region. There, NORAD would have reverted to being the North American *Air* Defense Command, and would have supplied information on what was occurring in North American airspace to USSPACECOM at Colorado Springs, where the AW/AA function would be undertaken by U.S. officers alone.

Even once it was determined that the new space command would be co-located with NORAD at Colorado Springs, it was not decided until the last minute that USCINCSPACE would be dual-hatted as CINCNORAD. Such a step was opposed by the U.S. Navy, which feared that dual hatting would entail reserving the CINCNORAD/USCINCSPACE slot for a USAF officer, because of NORAD's responsibilities for air defense. Dual hatting was eventually agreed to upon the lobbying of the Canadian air force and at the insistence of General Herres. To meet the U.S. Navy's objections, the Joint Chiefs of Staff ended the long-standing stipulation that CINCNORAD be a USAF officer, leaving open the possibility that a future CINCNORAD/USCINCSPACE could be an admiral. It was no coincidence that the first Deputy USCINCSPACE was a naval aviator.

It is hard to see how the U.S. military would ever want to involve Canada in operating a BMD system to whose development it had contributed nothing. This will be all the more the case if, as seems most likely and as discussed in chapter V, Canadian territory and airspace is not needed for the operation of a phase I SDI-type system.

For North American air defense, on the other hand, Canadian territory and airspace, as well as the cooperation of Canadian air defense forces will remain essential in the years to come. Linkage between air defense efforts and any future BMD operations would also be essential, so that those responsible for each would know that an attack on North America had begun, and so that complete assessments of Soviet attacks could be undertaken.

But a single command which many Canadians fear will be given control over both air defense and BMD and charged with AW/AA is not only unnecessary, it is unwanted by the U.S. military. The U.S. Army and U.S. Navy have been quietly arguing that still another U.S. unified command would have to be established to control a BMD system, while the USAF is determined to have any such system placed under the control of USSPACECOM, without giving it control over air defense.

Simply giving BMD to USSPACECOM, and leaving the relationship between it and NORAD further untouched might provide enough distance between Canada and a BMD system to satisfy the Canadian government and public, as well as the U.S. military. However, devolution of the USSPACECOM-NORAD relationship could be arranged to put even greater distance between Canada and BMD, yet still provide the essential linkage between air defense and ballistic missile defense operations. Two steps would be fairly easy to achieve:

1. The AW/AA function could be shifted from NORAD to USSPACE-COM (which, as discussed above, already is prepared to undertake it under certain circumstances). This would, in effect, reduce NORAD's sphere of operations to air defense. NORAD would provide information as to what was occurring in North American airspace to USSPACE-COM. It would not become a subordinate, component command of USSPACECOM, but rather a supporting command, much as USSPACE-COM now is a supporting command of NORAD.

This step could in the future become attractive to Canada even if BMD deployments never occur, for it would remove Canadians from direct participation in a function that is essential for the retention of flexible nuclear options by the United States.

2. The dual hatting of USCINCSPACE as CINCNORAD could be terminated. This would end much of the confusion that still persists today and provide a clearer distinction between binational air defense operations and U.S. BMD efforts. To repeat, a two-CINC arrangement almost emerged in 1985.

Yet two more far-reaching forms of devolution are also conceivable:

1. The "Langley option" could be taken up: the joint air defense command would be moved away from Colorado Springs; and

2. Finally, and more dramatically, it is far from clear that a North American air defense command, although desirable, is necessary. Already, most of the day-to-day coordination of North American air defense has been decentralized from Colorado Springs into the hands of the regional headquarters at North Bay, Langely, and Elmendorf. As long as air defense plans are jointly formulated, information, including radar data, continually shared, and open access to each other's airspace guaranteed, an effective air defense could probably be mounted without a central command.

While these options will be available, Canadians would have to think long and hard before availing themselves of any of them, with the Canadian defense establishment firmly in opposition. A U.S. decision on BMD is not going to be affected by whether Canada remains in an integrated command or not. Nor is the future of U.S. nuclear strategy going to be affected by Canadian participation in NORAD. Moreover, no matter how devolved the command structure, any air defense efforts Canada undertakes will necessarily always be linked with the U.S. strategic posture. As the parliamentary committee forcefully put it, "Most Canadians recognize that Canada can no more abstain completely from planning its defence jointly with the United States than alter the facts of geography which place it in a location of critical significance for the U.S."[36]

A devolution of the joint command structure in order to put some measure of political or symbolic distance between Canadian efforts and those of the United States could cost Canada the advantages it has enjoyed through NORAD participation. These include, particularly, fairly easy access to information on U.S. plans, access to U.S. technology and great savings in the costs of air defense command and control facilities. So once again the paradox appears. Opting out in order to preserve Canada's sovereign right not to be directly tied to activities of which it does not approve, would come at other costs to its sovereignty.[37]

NOTES

1. Ironically, the prime minister in 1957, John Diefenbaker, did not grasp the seriousness of the step when he used an informal, if not irregular, procedure to approve the agreement. The result was great controversy. See chapter 5, Joseph T. Jockel, "The Creation of NORAD," in *No Boundaries Upstairs: Canada, the United States and the Origins of North American Air Defence,* (Vancouver: University of British Columbia Press, 1987).
2. John W. Holmes, *The Shaping of Peace: Canada and the Search for World Order, 1943–1957,* vol. 2 (Toronto: University of Toronto Press, 1982), 291.
3. There have been exceptions to this authority, most notably concerning the release for use of U.S. air defense nuclear weapons, when those were part of the inventory.
4. 1958 Agreement: "North American Air Defense Command: Agreement effected by exchange of notes," 12 May 1958, *U.S. Treaties and other International Agreements Series,* 4031 (9 United States Treaties, 538).
5. Ibid.
6. *Exchange of Notes between Canada and the United States of America, Canada Treaty Series* 1975, no. 16; and subsequent renewals in 1980, 1981, and 1986.
7. For a description, see Paul B. Stares, *Space and National Security* (Washington: The Brookings Institution, 1987), 24–29.
8. Ibid., 204–7.
9. It has been scheduled to be closed for quite some time. Currently, it may

be kept in service simply to provide the Canadian Armed Forces with a space sensor, albeit an ancient one which it can contribute to the continent's defenses.

10. Ibid., 4.

11. Brendan M. Greeley, Jr. "Navy Expanding its Space Command to Bolster Readiness," *Aviation Week and Space Technology* 124, no. 6 (February 1986): 54.

12. The U.S. armed services have relied on the term "operational command" to describe the relationship between USSAPCECOM and the service components. The concept is in essence the same as "operational control." Based on interviews in the Pentagon and at Colorado Springs, it is evident that U.S. officials have managed often to confuse themselves with the distinctions between operational control, operational command, and command.

13. Testimony by General Robert T. Herries, USAF, Hearings before the Strategic and Theater Nuclear Forces Subcommittee of the Senate Armed Services Committee, 26 March 1986). Text courtesy NORAD/USSPACECOM public affairs office.

14. The USAF has been developing an ASAT system since 1977. It was based on a small terminal warhead that would home in on the heat emitted by a satellite and destroy it by the force of the collision. The warhead would be boosted from the air into space by a small two-stage rocket. The rocket and warhead were designed to be carried by an F-15 fighter. The USAF had originally planned to acquire over one hundred warheads and equip 40 F-15 aircraft with launch capability. But Congressional objectives, based on cost overruns and arms control concerns, have left the system in limbo. The Bush administration, in its first budget, asked Congress for $95 million to develop "a new kind of ASAT missile" and $20 million to adapt an experimental laser to ASAT purposes. *Congressional Quarterly*, 13 May 1989, 1138.

15. U.S. Department of Defense, Strategic Defense Initiative Organization, *Report to Congress on the Strategic Defense System Architecture*, January 1988, 21.

16. General Robert T. Herres, Address on NORAD Modernization, SAIC Luncheon, Colorado Springs, 6 March 1985. Text courtesy NORAD public affairs office.

17. Paul Bracken, *The Command and Control of Nuclear Forces* (New Haven and London: Yale University Press, 1983), 121.

18. During the Cuban Missile Crisis of 1962 the Canadian government hesitated before putting its forces on the same status as those of the United States. During the 1973 Arab-Israeli War the United States sought to signal the Soviet Union by placing its forces, including those committed to NORAD, on higher alert. Canada did not participate. For an overview of the unilateral authority the United States has retained, see David J. R. Angell, "NORAD and Binational Nuclear Alert: Consultation and Decisionmaking in the Integrated Command," *Defence Analysis* 4 (June 1988): 129. This piece is slightly dated, however, with respect to the role of USSPACECOM.

19. Canada, House of Commons, *Debates,* 29 May 1985, 5189.

20. Canada, House of Commons, Standing Committee on External Affairs and

National Defence, *Minutes of Proceedings and Evidence* 52 (6 December 1985): 11.

21. This paragraph is based on interviews with senior Canadian officers at NORAD.

22. ASAT was also an issue. Opponents of renewal pointed to Canada's strong stance in favor of limitations on arms in space and USSPACECOM's potential ASAT responsibilities. The issue has faded as a result of the Congressionally-imposed moratorium on ASAT. If the Bush administration succeeds in getting development underway, the issue will probably resurface.

23. Canada, House of Commons, Standing Committee on External Affairs and National Defence, *NORAD 1986*, 1986, 63–64.

24. Canada, House of Commons, Standing Committee on External Affairs and National Defence, *Minutes of Proceedings and Evidence* 54 (11 December 1985): 4–39.

25. *NORAD 1986*, xi.

26. *Agreement between Canada and the United States of America, Canada Treaty Series*, no. 5 (1968).

27. Canada, House of Commons, *Debates*, 4 February 1985, 1961.

28. *NORAD 1986*, 78.

29. David Cox, *Trends in Continental Defence: A Canadian Perspective* (Ottawa: Canadian Institute for International Peace and Security, 1987), 34.

30. One other issue bound to arise in 1991 is whether formally to assign NORAD with drug interdiction tasks. While this may make sense politically, the existing NORAD mission of protecting the sovereignty of both countries over their airspace has already been interpreted to include drug interdiction.

31. *NORAD 1986*, 75.

32. Ibid.

33. Ibid. This surprising conclusion, at variance with the facts, may simply have reflected a decision to duck the issue.

34. Chairman's forward, *NORAD 1986*, xii.

35. *NORAD 1986*, 76.

36. Ibid., 71.

37. In late 1990 and early 1991, with a U.S. decision on BMD deployment still at least several years away and with attention fixed on the Persian Gulf, the process of NORAD renewal was proceeding very quietly in both Canada and the U.S. However, U.S. press reports indicated that the Pentagon seemed to be considering the restructuring of its major commands to include a new "strategic force command" with authority over strategic nuclear assets and elements of North American surveillance. In the still quite unlikely event that the U.S. proceeds in the 1990s with such a restructuring, "other, less integrative options" to NORAD probably would be inevitable.

VIII

The United States, Canada, and Arctic ASW: The Issue that May Not Go Away

"Over the past two decades," the Mulroney government observed in *Challenge and Commitment*, "with the development of nuclear power, the Arctic has become an operating area for submarines . . . the Canadian navy must be able to determine what is happening under the ice in the Canadian Arctic and to deter hostile or potentially hostile intrusions."[1]

The April 1989 cancellation of the SSN acquisition program put an end, for the moment at least, to plans to equip the Canadian navy with under-ice operating capability. The cancellation, again for the moment at least, also pushed off the Canada-U.S. agenda which had become, for the United States, the most unsettling Canadian defense development since the Trudeau government halved the Canadian contribution to NATO Europe two decades ago. Quite simply, the U.S. Navy does not welcome the prospect of partners in Arctic antisubmarine warfare (ASW) and is more than willing to be relied upon alone in Canadian Arctic waters.

The issue, however, may not disappear along with the plans for Canadian SSNs. Ottawa apparently intends to proceed with the deployment of a fixed, under-ice, submarine detection system in the Canadian Arctic based on sonar technology. It could also decide to develop in the 1990s "air independent propulsion" (AIP) technology for "hybrid submarines" as they are called, and to begin equipping the Canadian navy with them at the end of the decade for under-ice operations.

Naval arms control may be placed on the international agenda during the 1990s, although at the moment there has been little interest on the part of the United States. The focus of U.S. naval planning will shift towards contingencies in the third world, and away from the Soviet threat.

But the Soviet navy will remain a major concern. At least throughout the decade, the U.S. Navy clearly will retain the tasks, among others, of patrolling the seaward approaches to the North American continent and being able to keep the sea lines of communication to Europe open in a crisis. This latter task could take on new importance as the United States reduces its conventional forces in Europe and shifts toward a posture based on reinforcement.

This chapter first records the strategic significance of Canadian Arctic waters, especially to the U.S. Navy, even as coping with the Soviet navy declines in relative importance. It then describes the impediments to Canada-U.S. naval cooperation in the region. Finally, it introduces the two Canadian options there, the fixed under-ice system and the hybrid submarines and then assesses their impact on U.S. interests.

THE STRATEGIC SIGNIFICANCE
OF CANADIAN ARCTIC WATERS

It is important not to overrate the importance of Canadian Arctic waters, a tendency that sometimes emerged in the Canadian SSN debate. The strategic significance of Canadian Arctic waters is threefold: they contain potential launch points for new Soviet long-range SLCMs (should the Soviet Union opt for such a strategy), they might be relied on as a "back door" to the Atlantic by Soviet SSNs, and they might also serve as a "back door" to the Arctic basin for U.S. SSNs.

Up until now, Soviet SLCMs, because of their short ranges (all 1000 km or under), could strike at targets in the United States or southern Canada only from fairly close-in stations along the Atlantic, Pacific and Gulf of Mexico coasts. But the SS-N-21 SLCM with its up to 3000 km estimated range could also be launched by Soviet submarines at targets in Canada and the northern United States from points in and near the Canadian Arctic Archipelago, and off the Labrador/Baffin Island coast. To be sure, such missiles could be launched from off the Atlantic and Pacific coasts of North America, although this is an area of intense ASW surveillance.

The strategic role the Soviets have assigned or will assign long-range SLCMs is not clear, and has been the subject of relatively intense debate in the West. They could be dedicated to a theater role in Europe in order to outflank NATO air defenses and reduce the need for long-range ground interdiction aircraft.[2] To the extent they are targeted on North America, because of their relatively slow speed they could be reserved for follow-on strikes. Nonetheless, "in addition to their potential as second-strike weapons, there is now a very small but still identifiable possibility that SLCMs launched from the Arctic archipelago could be used in a first-strike capability."[3]

Arguments for assuming that the Soviets could use SLCMs in a precursor "decapitation" strike on North America depend heavily on the problems the North American air defenses could have detecting cruise missiles. This would especially be the case with SLCMs launched from submarines in the Canadian Arctic and off the Labrador/Baffin Island coast. Rising out of the water, SLCMs could be especially hard at first to detect by NORAD AWACS and fighter aircraft. If these aircraft were not operating in the vicinity, the missiles might or might not be detected by OTH-B radar or the North Warning System, depending upon the capabilities against cruise missiles these radars are found to have. In the case of the North Warning System, the missiles would pass through the system's radar envelope into the Canadian radar "hole."[4] Unlike the case with bombers carrying air-launched cruise missiles there would be, prior to launch, no radar warning of the presence of the platform, that is, a submarine.[5]

To the north, there are very substantial limitations to the firing positions SLCM-carrying submarines could take up. In particular, the SS-N-21, which will be carried in standard SSN torpedo tubes, cannot be fired through ice. Entry to submarines in many areas is difficult. Mountain ranges between potential launch points and targets form another barrier. Taking these limitations into consideration there are, according to Commander Peter Haydon in a study released by Directorate of Strategic Policy Planning of the Canadian Department of National Defence, only five realistic SLCM launch points in the Canadian Arctic and Labrador/Baffin Island coast regions. These points vary in utility due to the extent of summer and winter ice cover, and difficulty of entry for submarines (see map on page 164).

Haydon invites particular attention to the waters off the Labrador/Baffin Island coast, as "a particularly attractive cruise missile launch area." It not only is accessible to submarines entering from the Arctic or the Atlantic, but contains a good deal of open water as well as light ice cover for much of the year. All of eastern Canada and most of the eastern United States would be in range of a 3000-km SLCM launched from there. "Control of this huge area presents many problems and would require a coordinated ASW operation using submarines, aircraft, fixed sensors and, on occasion, surface ships in order to provide complete control."[6]

The Arctic might become an attractive region for the Soviets to position SLCM-carrying submarines if SLCM ranges can be extended beyond 3000 km; if long-range SLCMs are deployed on boats especially designed to carry them (SSGNs), thereby eliminating the need to rely on SSN torpedo tubes as launchers; or if Soviet submarines are equipped with the capability to launch them through heavily ice-infested waters. The number of available launch points would be multiplied and more areas in the United States would come in range. As discussed in chapter VI, two of these possibilities may already be materializing; the Soviets have rebuilt one old *Yankee* class SSBN as a trials SSGN for twelve SS-NX-24 SLCMs, and are expected to produce an entirely new class of SSGN

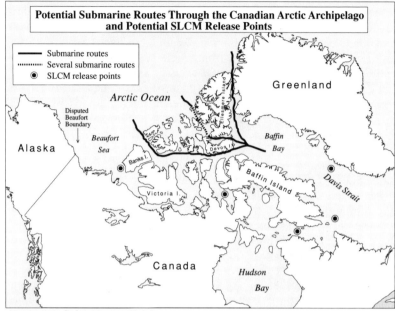

Potential Submarine Routes Through the Canadian Arctic Archipelago and Potential SLCM Release Points

Adapted from Haydon, *The Strategic Importance of the Arctic*

capable of carrying up to twenty-four of the new missiles. If a new launch tube is also being developed, it probably embodies improved capabilities through ice. The range of the SS-NX-24 is also about 3000 km. As pointed out in chapter VI, the outline for a START agreement approved by Presidents Bush and Gorbachev in June 1990 was accompanied by a tentative parallel accord permitting each side to deploy 880 long-range SLCMs.

The ranges of Soviet submarine-launched ballistic missiles (SLBMs) have increased dramatically, to above 8000 km. Submarines carrying them (SSBNs) also need no longer be stationed off the U.S. coasts for the missiles to be able to reach their targets. Western analysts believe that the Soviets, in a crisis, would in all probability take advantage of those ranges and withdraw almost all of their modern SSBNs into "bastions" where they will be protected by the bulk of the SSN fleet against U.S. strategic ASW (attempts to destroy SSBNs). These bastions would be located on the Soviet side of the Arctic basin (especially in the Barents Sea), and in the Sea of Okhotsk, close to SSBN home ports in Murmansk on the Kola Peninsula and Petropavlovsk on the Kamchatka Peninsula. Locating bastions under or at the edge of ice fields could allow defensive advantage to be taken of acoustic conditions that make it harder to detect submarines.

Executing the bastion strategy, however, would impose a severe limitation on the number of SSNs the Soviets would have available to attack commercial shipping and allied warships. It also means that the wartime deployment of Soviet SSBNs to the Canadian Arctic region is unlikely.

Still, even a few Soviet SSNs operating in wartime off the east coast of the United States could wreak havoc, tying down ASW forces vastly out of proportion to their size and disrupting the reinforcement of NATO Europe by the United States. The Soviets could have strong incentives to attempt to introduce those SSNs into the North Atlantic through the "back door" provided by passages through the Canadian Arctic Archipelago—if they were not adequately defended—especially since the "front doors" through the Greenland-Iceland-United Kingdom (G-I-UK) Gap and the North Cape-Bear Island Gap are areas where NATO deploys extensive naval forces and would in wartime swiftly establish choke points. There are three relatively narrow passages through the Canadian Arctic Archipelago between the Arctic Ocean and Baffin Bay accessible to submarines:

- the Northwest Passage through M'Clure Strait, Barrow Strait and Lancaster Sound;
- via Nares Strait between Greenland and Ellesmere Island;
- via several channels through the Sverdrup Islands and Jones Sound.

Moreover, while much of the United States Navy's (USN) current planning "is fixed on the notion that the Soviets will automatically withdraw their SSBNs into bastions and protect them with virtually their entire SSN force, this might not be the case."[7] Soviet options would include dispersing their SSBNs under the protection of fewer SSNs or leaving them in the bastions, also protected by fewer SSNs, and relying on their improving air and surface ASW forces to defend them there against attacks by US SSNs.[8] Under such circumstances more Soviet SSNs would be freed to attempt to enter the North Atlantic through the front or back doors, what the USN has called "the SSN flush." (If the SSBNs are dispersed, some could be deployed nearer Canadian Arctic waters, although because of their large size, probably not into the narrow and shallow passages between the islands of the archipelago. If the Soviets are seriously considering dispersal as an alternative option, they may from time to time send SSBNs to probe the Canadian Arctic region in order to gain navigational experience.)

Considering alternatives to the bastion strategy may have become attractive to the Soviets in reaction to the heavy emphasis being placed publicly, until recently, by the USN on bastion attacks. Strategic ASW is nothing new for the USN. "Indeed, the destruction of Soviet SSBNs was listed as a key wartime objective as far back as 1964—soon after the Soviets deployed their first SSBNs."[9] The Soviets have almost equally as long planned to attack U.S. SSBNs, to the extent they would have been able to do so with their markedly inferior ASW capabilities pitted against quiet U.S. boats. For years, the USN was most reluctant to discuss in public its plans for strategic ASW, as well as naval strategy in general. That naval silence began to be broken in 1984 and then was wholeheartedly abandoned with the January 1986 public release by the U.S. Naval Institute, a private professional association, of 150,000 copies of a remarkable document, *The Maritime Strategy*. Billed as "the nearest thing to a British 'White Paper'—that is, an official statement of policy," it contained articles signed by the Secretary of the Navy, the Commandant of the Marine Corps and a lead article signed by Admiral James D. Watkins, then Chief of Naval Operations. Admiral Watkins' piece provided an unclassified overview of what the USN calls "the Maritime Strategy."[10]

The Maritime Strategy was reported to be the outcome of extensive debate and discussion within U.S. naval circles and to reflect the professional consensus of the leadership of the USN and Marine Corps as to how war with the Soviet Union could best be deterred and, if deterrence were to fail, won. As such, it was to provide "a common frame of reference for Navy and Marine Corps officers, a way of considering the purpose of their profession, and a catalyst for strategic thought."[11] It postulated three phases of confrontation between the West and the Soviet Union, and described the roles U.S. maritime forces ideally would play in the struggle. During each phase, strategic ASW with conventional (i.e. non-nuclear) weapons would play a central role. During the first, which is concerned with the deterrence of and preparations for, open conflict, the USN would move its ASW forces aggressively forward. This would force Soviet SSNs into bastions to protect SSBNs, limiting the number of SSNs available to attack allied warships and merchant vessels.[12] In the second phase, at the outbreak of war, the USN would, in Admiral Watkins' words, "seize the initiative."

> One of the most complex aspects of Phase II of the Maritime Strategy is antisubmarine warfare. It will be essential to conduct forward operations with attack submarines, as well as to establish barriers at key world checkpoints using maritime patrol aircraft, mines, attack submarines, or sonobuoys, to prevent leakage of enemy forces to the open ocean where the Western Alliance's resupply lines can be threatened. Maritime air and anti-submarine warfare units will be involved, along with offensive and defensive mining. As the battle groups move forward, we will wage an aggressive campaign against all Soviet submarines, including ballistic missile submarines.[13]

The navy would "carry the fight to the enemy" during the final phase. Its goal "would be to complete the destruction of all the Soviet fleets which was begun in Phase II," permitting it "to threaten the bases and support structure of the Soviet Navy in all theaters with both air and amphibious power." Its ASW forces "would continue to destroy Soviet submarines."[14]

The Maritime Strategy was not itself a fixed timetable or a set of plans to which the United States would be committed to execute in wartime. Rather, it specified "how the navy, in concert with its allies, would *prefer* to fight a war against the Soviet Union and its allies" (emphasis added).[15] To be sure, in 1986 the Secretary of Defense and the Chairman of the Joint Chiefs of Staff both endorsed the strategy's broad elements, especially the desirability of attacking SSBNs.[16] But such a step could be taken only with the permission of the president of the United States. "No one knows whether a president would even authorize an attack on Soviet SSBNs in these circumstances."[17]

Moreover, the USN has been for the past couple years seriously rethinking elements of the Maritime Strategy, although in doing so it largely has returned to its tradition of public silence. Apparently at issue was not so much—within the USN—the desirability of attacking SSBNs, but rather whether striking ports and other facilities in the Soviet homeland would make sense. Such attacks could expose American forces, especially aircraft carrier battle groups, to unacceptable risks by bringing them close to the Soviet Union and could provoke the Soviets into escalation in a way that the destruction of their SSBNs might not. Fairly extensive debate has also been occurring about not only the technical feasibility of the Maritime Strategy, but also whether from a strategic point of view it would be wise to confront the Soviets with the destruction of their SSBNs.[18]

The sweeping improvements in Soviet-American relations, and cuts in the U.S. defense budget, are accelerating this rethinking of the Maritime Strategy. However, the USN may argue that an emphasis on an approach not unlike the Maritime Strategy might mesh well with the draw down of U.S. forces from Europe, as a way of deterring the residual Soviet threat to Europe.

Still, an abandonment of a strategy based on going after SSBNs in bastions would not eliminate entirely the strategic significance of the Canadian Arctic. Regardless whether the USN were to receive permission to enter the Soviet bastions it can be expected to retain the ability early in a conflict to seal off with SSNs the "back door" into the Canadian Arctic Archipelago. This would prevent the transit of Soviet SSNs into the North Atlantic and would prevent Soviet SSNs and SSGNs from taking up SLCM firing positions. U.S. SSN patrols would also seek out and destroy all Soviet submarines in the entire Canadian Arctic region, where mines could also be sowed. While it is unlikely that Soviet SSBNs would be in the area, authority would almost certainly be granted readily to American forces to destroy any ones that were so close to the American homeland, whether or not authority were granted the USN to enter the Soviet bastions.

In a crisis or war, the presence of U.S. submarines in the waters of and adjacent to the Canadian Arctic region would allow for better use to be made of NORAD's air defense resources, especially the small AWACS inventory. Information on the location of Soviet SSNs and SSGNs and their destruction by U.S. forces would be passed on to NORAD. AWACS and fighter aircraft operating in the Arctic could be directed then to "sit" above or near the most probable release points for SLCMs in order to enhance the chances of detection and interception.

The Soviets, to the extent that they would be able to free sufficient numbers of SSNs from the task of bastion protection, might also try to close the Canadian Arctic back door from the Atlantic to U.S. SSNs. More limited Soviet options would include destroying parts of the fixed, under-ice detection system the Canadian government is planning to deploy in the waters of the Arctic archipelago, trying to position SSNs near the Arctic entrances to monitor quietly the movement of U.S. boats heading towards the flank of the Soviet bastions, and laying mines in those same entrances.

"Just as Soviet nuclear attack submarines might attempt to circumvent the GIUK Gap via a Polar transit, so U.S. Navy submarines could follow the same route in reverse and confront the Soviet northern fleet with another 'threat axis.' "[19] Having been given presidential authority to enter the bastions and destroy Soviet SSBNs, and, if necessary, having forced open the "back door," the USN could also use the Canadian Arctic region as a backup staging and emergency logistic resupply area for its SSNs. The Canadian Arctic would provide access to the Arctic Ocean; yet it is located far from Soviet air forces in the Kola and Kamchatka regions that might readily observe and interfere with such operations. If there have been discussions between the U.S. and Canadian navies about this possibility, they have been shrouded in secrecy.

As the SS-N-21 SLCM becomes operational, the USN can be expected to step up whatever peacetime patrolling of Canadian Arctic waters it already has been undertaking. Such patrols would also be useful to ascertain the extent to which Soviet SSNs, SSGNs, and possibly SSBNs have been probing the area. No unclassified information is available concerning the current extent of U.S. submarine operations in the Canadian Arctic region. However, as a former senior Canadian naval official recently observed of Arctic waters, "it is highly probable that the strategic game of marking (Soviet) submarines by American nuclear attack submarines and counter marking by Russian SSNs has already begun."[20]

CANADA-U.S. NAVAL COOPERATION—AND ITS LIMITS

The U.S. Navy has rarely been enthusiastic about the development of naval power by America's allies, tending to "consider itself as the sole adversary of the Soviet navy."[21] Nonetheless, there is a long history of fairly close cooperation between the Canadian and American navies; "the overwhelming NATO/Atlantic orientation of the Canadian navy has meshed well with Canada-U.S. bilateral maritime cooperation."[22]

Canada's commitment of ASW forces to the North Atlantic (and to a far lesser extent to the Pacific), has tended to free U.S. naval resources for other commitments. Maritime Command (MARCOM) undertakes peacetime surveillance of Soviet submarines, and in wartime would engage in strategic ASW in defense of North America, as well as ASW operations intended to protect the sea lines of communication between North America and NATO Europe. The U.S. Navy has also approved of the traditional Canadian policy of limiting the Canadian navy to smaller, less expensive vessels, namely destroyers and now patrol frigates, while leaving the aircraft carriers and nuclear-powered submarines to the United States.

Canadian naval operations are well integrated with those of the United States, especially in the western Atlantic where there are no other allied fleets active. In wartime, MARCOM's Atlantic forces, along with those of other allied countries would be placed under the operational control of NATO's Allied Command Atlantic (ACLANT) and its Supreme Allied Commander, (SACLANT), a U.S. admiral located at Norfolk, Virginia, who commands the U.S. Navy's Atlantic fleet, the 2nd Fleet.

SACLANT would delegate authority over those forces assigned to him to the appropriate NATO area commanders. Among them are the Commander MARCOM as commander of the Canadian Atlantic (CANLANT) area (COMCANLANT); and submarine commanders, including Commander Submarines Western Atlantic (COMSUBWESTLANT), also located at Norfolk. NATO arrangements also exist whereby SACLANT could also delegate wartime command over all NATO forces in the western Atlantic to the Commander MARCOM as interim commander-in-chief. This step would be taken when the bulk of United States and allied forces were operating forward in the Northeastern Atlantic and the Arctic.

In the Atlantic there are also bilateral arrangements between the U.S. and Canadian navies, providing for coordinated ASW surveillance and joint exercises in peacetime; and in crisis or wartime, joint operations, should the NATO command arrangements not be activated.[23] Although Canadians are fond of pointing out, accurately, that North American Pacific waters are part of the North Atlantic Treaty area, the NATO command structure does not extend to the Pacific. On the west coast, exclusively bilateral arrangements provide for relatively close-to-shore ASW co-operation between the small forces of MARCOM's west coast subordinate, MARPAC, and the USN'S Third Fleet.[24]

The Canadian government and navy forcefully argued that the U.S. Navy should welcome Canadian SSNs as an augmentation of Canadian ASW efforts in the Atlantic and the Pacific, as well as their extension into the Arctic, an area of growing strategic importance. The USN's ensuing deep opposition to the Canadian boats was partially motivated, as discussed in chapter III, by concern over the financial impact of the SSN program on the rest of the Canadian defense effort. U.S. naval officials also doubted the ability of their Canadian counterparts to build and operate an SSN fleet effectively and safely. But a third concern, and one that remains relevant to the future of a Canadian presence of some sort under the Arctic ice, was related to the sharing of information on the movement of U.S. submarines.

Few secrets are as closely held by the U.S. defense establishment as the location of U.S. SSNs and SSBNs. Within NATO, there is an extensive system of "water space management" to coordinate peacetime submarine movements. The system is largely operated by the USN, which garners information from allies on the planned movements of their boats and from the bewilderingly extensive global array of sensors operated by U.S. and allied (including Canadian) forces to detect the movement of Soviet subs. The USN parcels out very little information to its allies concerning U.S. movements, preferring instead to simply guarantee, having heard from them where their submarines are to be, that American boats will not be in the way.

The limitations on Canadian access to information on U.S. movements vary from the Atlantic to the Pacific to the Arctic—from scarce to all but non-existent. In peacetime, COMSUBWESTLANT acts as the Submarine Movement Advisory Authority (SMAA) for the Western Atlantic. While Canadian naval officers serve on the ACLANT staff and on those of several subordinate commands they do not, however, serve on the COMSUBWESLANT operational staff. COMSUBWESLANT's operational staff consists entirely of the officers of a purely U.S. command, COMSUBLANT, who simply "don another hat" for NATO purposes. COMSUBLANT is the principal U.S. submarine command, with peacetime and wartime responsibility for control of all U.S. submarines, including SSBNs, in the Atlantic.

MARCOM, as a NATO submarine operating authority (SUBOPAUTH) informs the SMAA of all movements of the three Canadian submarines in the Atlantic. "The SMAA monitors submarine movements in his area of concern and informs the SUBOPAUTH and units concerned of any mutual interference. In the event that a possibility of mutual interference exists, the SMAA relies upon the SUBOPAUTH to resolve the interference problem."[25] Thus, while Canada continually reports the peacetime movements of its three subs in the Atlantic to the SMAA, MARCOM is not usually informed of the movements of other allied subs, except where necessary to avoid interference.

On the Pacific coast, where Canada has no submarines, there is no SMAA. Because of its small ASW force there, a certain amount of information is necessarily shared between U.S. and Canadian naval forces. While its exact nature is classified, it is clear that Canadian naval officials, although guarded in their comments, are unhappy with its extent, especially the limitations placed on Canadian access to data from the U.S. underwater submarine detection system (SOSUS). Thus "Canada is the beneficiary of much more information from the USN SOSUS system in the Atlantic than it is in the Pacific. The message is clear: participation in joint operations opens doors to intelligence that would otherwise be closed to Canada."[26]

In the Arctic, of course, Canada currently has no under ice capability and thus no claim to information on the movement of U.S. boats, or for that matter U.S. information on the movement of Soviet boats. Obliging the U.S. Navy to provide such information was an important motivation behind the Canadian SSN program. As the Department of National Defence explained:

> Increasing the number of Canadian submarines will increase the need to coordinate sub-surface waterspace management among NATO countries and to exchange timely information on transits and exercises involving sub-surface vessels. Thus far, Canada has had relatively little influence on NATO waterspace management because we have had so few assets. With the introduction of submarines capable of patrolling the Arctic, Canada will become a full partner under the sea as well as above.[27]

The Commander of MARCOM, Vice Admiral Charles Thomas, explained it more bluntly: "When we have submarines of the force that we are talking about, we will be a full participant. . . . I suspect that anybody operating in waters of interest to Canada will make sure Canada knows about it, because the prospect of blue bumping into blue in the night at 600 feet is not entertaining."[28]

The U.S. Navy was irritated at the prospect of what it saw as Canadian coercion and so all the more pleased when the SSN program was canceled. But the Canadian motivation remains: the Canadian Arctic, is, as the White Paper put it, "an operating area for submarines." And if possible, the Canadian government will still want to know "what is happening under the ice."

THE CANADIAN OPTIONS UNDER THE ARCTIC ICE

Very little public information is available concerning the Canadian government's plans for a sonar under-ice detection system in the Arctic, given the generally high level of secrecy cloaking such technologies. No details at all were provided in *Challenge and Commitment* or have been released since.

The idea for such a system is not new, being first proposed in the Liberal government's 1971 white paper, *Defence in the 70s.* One reason it was never put in place was the government's conclusion that it would require submarines to maintain it. Presumably this technological hurdle has now been overcome, or is expected to be. It can only be presumed, as well, that the sonar technology under consideration and at the disposal of the Canadian government would in fact be capable of detecting future classes of submarines, despite the recent advances in quieting them that threaten the utility of passive sonar devices, including the U.S. SOSUS system.[29] It is not at all clear whether a Canadian sonar system, if it were able to detect the latest submarines, would be able to distinguish the acoustic signatures of Soviet boats from those of U.S. boats.

Recently, Rear Admiral F. W. Crickard, just retired as the Deputy Commander of MARCOM, described what a passive acoustic system in the Arctic "might consist of." Coverage would not extend throughout the navigable waters of the Canadian Arctic Archipelago. Rather, it would be established in three control areas at its western and eastern ends. Two would be in the west: one at the entrance to Amundsen Gulf, thereby covering one of the potential SLCM release points, and one at M'Clure Strait at the entrance to the Northwest Passage. One would be in the east, at Lancaster Sound, covering the eastern entrance to the passage as well as portions of the routes which lead through Jones Sound and the Neves Strait to the north. The Canadianization of the old DEW Line into the North Warning System will provide sites, operated by Canadians, where data from the three control areas could be preliminarily assessed and transmitted to operations control centers in southern Canada. In the summer months the under-ice system would be backed up by Canadian *Aurora* long-range patrol aircraft.[30]

With MARCOM's three *Oberon*-class submarines on the verge of obsolescence, its highest priority is the acquisition of three or four new conventional submarines (SSKs) to replace them in Atlantic roles. There is a very good chance that once the acquisition is underway, the Canadian government will pursue in the 1990s the development of air-independent propulsion technology for hybrid submarines which could operate in tandem with the fixed sonar system in the Arctic. One strong possibility would be to proceed with the acquisition of SSKs and with the development of hybrid technology with which the SSKs could be "retrofitted."[31] The Department of National Defence has been planning to let a contract for a two-year study of AIP technology which could in fact be "retrofitted." Future Canadian submarines could then also be acquired with AIP technology in place.

It is striking that the Canadian navy and the influential Canadian Centre for Arms Control and Disarmament, which were on opposing sides of the SSN question, have supported such a program. The navy rejected alternative submarine technologies as long as the possibility of acquiring the far more capable SSNs was alive. Hybrids are now the navy's only option for ever acquiring Arctic capability. Many of the objections Canadian arms control and disarmament groups had concerning SSNs, including cost and impact on nuclear nonproliferation do not apply to the hybrids. In fact, the Arms Control Centre took the lead during the debate over the SSNs in publicly championing hybrid technologies.[32]

There are several hybrid technologies under development. Each is intended to allow a conventional submarine to be fitted with an air independent propulsion system, eliminating the need for snorkling and permitting under-ice operations. Hybrids cannot match the speeds and endurance of SSNs, and are thus not suited for open-ocean and distant water operations. However, they are expected to share the quietness of SSKs and thus could be "highly effective operating in or near oceanic straits and other restricted areas where enemy submarines . . . might be expected to pass."[33] In other words, if the technology proves to be effective, they could be ideal for operations in the narrow passages of the Canadian Arctic Archipelago.

If Ottawa does proceed with intensive development, the most attractive technology appears to be that for a diesel electric/nuclear hybrid submarine, or SS*n*, also called the "budget-conscious nuke." An SS*n*, similar to an SSK, is propelled by an electric system, powered by a storage battery. The battery, in turn, is charged by a diesel system and by a small nuclear reactor. Reliance on the nuclear reactor, when required, eliminates the need for snorkling.

SS*n* technology has been under development in Canada for several years at two locations. Atomic Energy of Canada, Limited, a Crown (government-owned) corporation has developed a "concept design" for what it calls a "nuclear battery," which would be a small nuclear reactor sealed for its lifetime of thirty years. Refueling would thus be unnecessary. The nuclear option study team in the Department of National Defence which eventually recommended acquisition of SSNs called the nuclear battery "the most promising" of all the hybrid technologies, although it warned that the idea was no more than a concept and would require "substantial development of potentially difficult technologies."[34]

A private Canadian concern, the ECS Group of Companies has been aggressively exploring SS*n* technology since the late 1970s, and is developing an "autonomous marine propulsion system" (AMPS), which it describes as "a low-power nuclear reactor embodying features of intrinsic safety, low complexity and extremely high reliability, while requiring minimal operator attention."[35] It has recently entered into an information exchange with the Netherlands manufacturers of the *Walrus*-class submarines to exploring mating AMPS to *Walrus* boats.

Thus development of SS*n* technology could be especially attractive to the Canadian government as support for domestic industry. Indeed, there might be an export market in countries looking for an alternative to expensive SSNs. The costs of a Canadian SS*n* fleet could also be attractive. Six SS*n*s using AMPS propulsion could cost on the order of C$2.7 billion, excluding any special shore infrastructure for the propulsion systems.[36] Nuclear-nonproliferation would not be a major issue in the case of Canadian SS*n*s, as the technology and fuel sources would be Canadian.[37]

Yet it must be stressed that hybrid technologies, including those for SS*n*s, are by no means proven. Atomic Energy of Canada's "nuclear battery" scarcely passed beyond paper when the 1987 decision to acquire SSNs put an end, at least temporarily, to its development. And "no fully operational AMPS system has yet been built, much less been submitted to vigorous at-sea testing [although] many of the system's technological 'building blocks' have been thoroughly tested by ECS. No real resolution of the claims made for the system can be achieved, obviously, until a full-sized prototype is constructed and tested."[38] Moreover, with the SSN debacle in mind, the Canadian government might be afraid that the public would not be able to distinguish between SSNs and SS*n*s.

IMPLICATIONS FOR THE UNITED STATES

The argument can certainly be made that an effective Canadian under-ice system operating alone or in tandem with Canadian SS*n*s or other AIP submarines not only would serve to protect Canadian sovereignty but would mesh well with U.S. strategic interests. The Canadian navy would in peacetime assume responsibilities for monitoring the presence of Soviet submarines in the Arctic. In a crisis Canadian boats would join in operations to close the "back door," and destroy SLCM-carrying SSNs. These peacetime and wartime efforts would free the U.S. Navy to devote resources, especially SSNs elsewhere, including the Arctic basin. Canadians are involved in the operation of a portion of the U.S. Atlantic SOSUS system; similar cooperative arrangements could be extended to the Canadian Arctic system.

In addition, hybrid technology developed by Canada might eventually be put to use by the U.S. Navy. The construction of some expensive SSNs could be foregone through the acquisition of cheaper SS*n*s.[39]

Nonetheless, significant problems will arise for the United States if Canada proceeds with the development of ASW capabilities in the Arctic. The first is obvious. Canadian Arctic under-ice capabilities will reopen the sensitive problem of Canadian access to information on the movement of U.S boats through the region. No doubt some arrangement could be hit upon, for as was pointed out during the SSN debate, "The prospect that submarines from both countries will engage in uncoordinated activities in the Arctic is sufficiently bizarre that a negotiated agreement will surely be necessary before operational patrols actually begin."[40]

In attempting to reach such agreement with the United States, Canada could yet again be faced with the paradox of its defense relationship with the United States, akin to that caused by U.S. nuclear operations in the continental air defense arrangements. Canadians, for the most part, have been no more enthusiastic about U.S. plans to destroy Soviet SSBNs than they have been about U.S. flexible nuclear operations. As the SSN debates made clear, Ottawa will need to show that Canadian efforts in the Arctic will protect Canadian sovereignty yet not directly support U.S. plans to enter the Soviet SSBN bastions, should the United States retain such an approach.[41] It is not obvious how this could be reconciled in domestic politics with a close working relationship with the U.S Navy to close the Arctic "back door."

Even if a cooperative arrangement can be worked out which meets Canadian sovereignty needs and overcomes the objections of the U.S. Navy, it is doubtful that U.S. interests would be served by Canada's devoting defense resources to Arctic ASW. Those resources remain meager at best, while the sonar and hybrid submarine technologies for Arctic ASW are both rapidly changing and expensive. Even the $2.7 billion needed for an SS*n* fleet, while far less than the cost of the SSNs, would constitute a serious drain on future Canadian defense efforts. Moreover, "the unforeseen problems of an independent weapons development programme weigh heavily in a context where budget pressures allow little room for experiment or misjudgement."[42]

From the United States' perspective, it would be far better for MARCOM to avoid launching out on the development of Arctic capabilities based on what are still uncertain technologies, but rather to build upon its traditional ASW roles in the Atlantic and the Pacific where it still will meet U.S. and NATO needs. In those regions MARCOM has the necessary training, expertise, shore facilities, ships and aircraft. Thus, for the United States, it would be far better for Canada to restrict itself to the acquisition of additional patrol frigates, long-range aircraft and conventionally powered submarines, leaving Arctic operations to the U.S. Navy. But, of course, Canadian sovereignty arguments may continue to militate otherwise.

NOTES

1. Canada, Department of National Defence, *Challenge and Commitment: A Defence Policy for Canada* (Ottawa: Minister of Supply and Services, 1987), 50.
2. Michael MccGwire, *Military Objectives in Soviet Foreign Policy* (Washington, D.C.: The Brookings Institution, 1987), 501–2.
3. David Cox, "Living Along the Flight Path: Canada's Defense Debate," *The Washington Quarterly* 10, no. 4 (Autumn 1987): 101.
4. For a discussion of decapitation strikes and the limitations of the North American air defense system, see chapter VI.
5. For a strongly dissenting view on the role in SLCMs in a "decapitation strike," see Francis J. Furtado, *U.S. and Soviet Land-Attack SLCM Programs: Implications for Strategic Stability,* ORAE Memorandum no. 129. Ottawa: Department of National Defence, Operational Research and Analysis Establishment, June 1990.
6. Commander Peter T. Haydon, *The Strategic Importance of the Arctic: Understanding the Military Issues,* Ottawa, Department of National Defence, Directorate of Strategic Policy Planning, Strategic Issues Paper no. 1/87, March 1987, 16.
7. James Stavridis, "Creating ASW Killing Zones," U.S. Naval Institute *Proceedings* 113/10/106 (October 1987): 42.
8. For an extensive discussion of alternatives to the bastion strategy, see Stavridis, ibid.
9. Ronald O'Rourke, *Nuclear Escalation, Strategic Anti-Submarine Warfare and the Navy's Forward Maritime Strategy,* Congressional Research Service Report no. 87-138F, 27 February 1987, 61. The following few pages draw heavily on this fine piece of analysis.
10. Admiral James D. Watkins, "The Maritime Strategy," in *The Maritime Strategy,* supplement to the January 1986 edition of the U.S. Naval Institute *Proceedings,* 2.
11. Linton F. Brooks, "Naval Power and National Security: The Case for the Maritime Strategy," *International Security* 11, no. 2 (Fall 1986): 60.
12. Watkins, 9.
13. Ibid., 11.
14. Ibid., 13.
15. Barnett, 31.
16. U.S. Congress, Senate, Committee on Armed Services. Hearings, *Department of Defense Authorization for Appropriations for FY 1987,* 99th Cong., 2d sess., part 1, 1986, 83.
17. William W. Kaufmann, *A Thoroughly Efficient Navy* (Washington: The Brookings Institution, 1987), 104.
18. An exhaustive bibliography of public materials related to the Maritime Strategy, edited by Captain Peter M. Schwartz, USN, was released in mimeo form in August 1987 by the Strategy, Plans and Policy Division, Office of the Chief of Naval Operations, department of the Navy, Washington, D.C. 20460-2000. For a recent, critical assessment of the feasibility, see Mark Sakitt, "Is the New Maritime Strategy Dead in the Water? An Evaluation of Arctic Warfare and Soviet Countermeasures," paper presented at the

Conference on Maritime Security and Arms Control in the Pacific Region, University of British Columbia, 19–21 May 1988; see also Sakitt's "Submarine Warfare in the Arctic: Option or Illusion" (Stanford, Calif.: The Center for International Security and Arms Control, May 1988).

19. Jan S. Breemer, "The U.S. Navy Plans for a Different Type of Cold War," *Sea Power* 27, no. 9 (August 1984): 25.

20. Rear-Admiral F. Crickard, "The Canadian Navy: New Directions," *NATO's Sixteen Nations* 33 (special issue) (January 1988): 57.

21. Kaufmann, 71.

22. Joel J. Sokolsky, *Defending Canada: U.S.-Canadian Defense Policies* (New York: Priority Press Publications, 1989), 71.

23. These arrangements are codified in the (classified) Canada-United States Maritime Operation Plan-East (CANUS-MAREASTOP).

24. These arrangements are codified in the (classified) Canada-United States Maritime Operation Plan-West (CANUS-MARWESTOP).

25. Unclassified briefing note, "Submarine movements and waterspace management," Ottawa, Department of National Defence, n.d.

26. "The Canadian Navy: New Directions," 58.

27. Canada, Department of National Defence, Directorate of Information, *Canada's New Submarines,* 1988, 11.

28. Canada, House of Commons, Standing Committee on National Defence, *Minutes of Proceedings and Evidence,* 7 March 1988, 29:26-27. To this the Minister of National Defence, who was also present, added: "We expect to have full cooperation from our allies . . . we expect our allies to respect our sovereignty and our territory." Ibid., 29:36.

29. For a recent summary of this problem see *Report of the Advisory Panel on Submarine and Antisubmarine Warfare to the House Armed Services Subcommittees on Research and Development and Seapower and Strategic and Critical Materials* (unclassified edition), 21 March 1989.

30. F. W. Crickard, "An Anti-submarine Warfare Capability in the Arctic: A National Requirement," *Canadian Defence Quarterly* 16, no. 4 (April 1987): 24. An official of the Department of National Defence also publicly discussed a system based on three locations. *Globe and Mail* (Toronto), 8 July 1989, A7.

31. *Jane's Defence Weekly* 21 April 1990, 739.

32. See in particular, Daniel Hayward, "Hybrid Submarine Technologies," Canadian Centre for Arms Control and Disarmament, *Arms Control Communique,* no. 53 (12 September 1988).

33. Don Walsh, "Is It Time for the SS*n*?: Hybrid Reactor Boats Could Augment the Navy's *Seawolf* Fleet," *Sea Power,* April 1989, 4.

34. Canada, Department of National Defence, "AIP Technology Evaluation," *SSN Fact Sheet,* no. 5 (Ottawa: Department of National Defence, 1988).

35. A. F. Oliva and R. J. Gosling (ECS-Power Systems Inc.), "The SS*n:* An Affordable Platform for Enhancing Undersea Naval Capability," originally presented at Underseas Defense 88, San Diego, California, October 1988, available from the ECS Group of Companies, 1500-112 Kent St., Ottawa, Ont. K1P 5P2.

36. Canadian Centre for Arms Control and Disarmament, based on data

supplied by the ECS Group of Companies. See *Jane's Defence Weekly* 21 April 1990, 739.

37. If Canada ever exported the technology, then of course the non-proliferation issue would arise.

38. Walsh, 3.

39. On this point, see Walsh.

40. David Cox, "Canada's Defense Debate," *Washington Quarterly* 10, no. 4 (Autumn 1987): 104.

41. It was understood during the SSN debates by all concerned that Canadian SSNs themselves would not have been sent into Soviet bastions. Canadian opponents of bastion attacks and of the SSN program argued instead that Canada risked "becoming an adjunct" to, or being "inextricably caught up" in, or becoming partners" in dangerous U.S. naval plans by simple virtue of possessing SSNs. John Lamb of the Canadian Centre for Arms Control and Disarmament, and David Cox of the Canadian Institute for International Peace and Security, quoted in the Ottawa *Citizen,* 9 May 1987, B4; and "Canada's Stake in Common Security," report by the International Affairs Committee of the New Democratic Party of Canada, April 1988, 18.

    General Paul Manson, Chief of the Defence Staff, pressed while testifying before a House of Commons committee to outline the official position of the Department of National Defence on the USN's Maritime Strategy, equivocated at length, eventually concluding that "the important fact is that Canada is not obliged in any way to follow American strategy whether it is good or bad." Canada, House of Commons, Standing Committee on National Defence, *Minutes of Proceedings and Evidence,* 3 February 1988, 25:13. The Minister of National Defence, Perrin Beatty, went so far as to assert at one point that the USN really had no plans to hunt out and destroy SSBNs in bastions, that it was all a misunderstanding! Ibid., 18 June 1987, 13:26.

42. David Cox, *Trends in Continental Defence: A Canadian Perspective*, Ottawa, Canadian Institute for International Peace and Security, Occasional Papers, no. 2, 1986, 44.

IX

If Canada Breaks Up: Thinking About the Military Implications

In the summer of 1990, Canada entered the most difficult period in its history, from which it will almost certainly emerge profoundly altered. Centrifugal forces, now set loose, are bound to alter the Canadian confederation over the next several years with a referendum on Québec independence now scheduled for Autumn, 1992.

Not all of the potential consequences of the current crisis would have direct implications for the Canadian Armed Forces or for Canada-U.S. defense relations. But some would, most importantly for North American air defense operations. What follows is a survey of those potential consequences and an assessment of their potential impact.

THE POLITICAL SITUATION IN CANADA

The immediate cause of the Canadian crisis was the death, in June 1990, of the 1987 "Meech Lake" accord between Ottawa and the ten provincial governments, named after a government conference center north of Ottawa where the deal was struck. The accord would have provided for a formal amendment to the Canadian Constitution which, among other things, would have entrenched recognition of Québec as "within Canada a distinct society." This recognition would have conferred legislative powers on the Québec government to protect that distinctiveness; how extensive those powers actually would have been was widely disputed. In turn, Québec was to have acceded to the constitutional arrangements, including the new Canadian Charter of Rights and Freedoms, which were imposed on it in 1982 without its consent by Ottawa and the other nine provincial governments.[1]

Meech Lake needed to be ratified by the federal parliament and all ten provincial legislatures three years after its initial adoption. At the time of the June 1990 deadline, two provinces, Manitoba and Newfoundland had not ratified. And so the accord died.[2]

The three-year debate over Meech brought to the fore two longstanding regional cleavages in Canada. The first—and far deeper—is between

Québec and the rest of the country. The second is between "central Canada" (Ontario and Québec) and the peripheries (the four Western provinces and the four Atlantic provinces).

When the accord was agreed to by Prime Minister Mulroney and the ten provincial premiers, fairly easy passage was expected. But strong opposition developed in English Canada, especially out of concern that the "distinct society" clause would weaken the protection of the Charter of Rights and Freedoms, and from irritation that Québec was being treated differently. This concern deepened when the Québec government exercised its already existing constitutional right to "override" the charter, and reenacted legislation banning outdoor signs in any language but French. The original legislation had been found by the Supreme Court of Canada to be in violation of the charter; use of the "override" by Québec removed this constitutional impediment. By 1990, public opinion polls showed strong majorities of English Canadians opposed to the accord. Canadian Indians also protested that Meech Lake did not address their concerns. In fact, an Indian member of the Manitoba legislature blocked consideration of the accord until the clock ran out. Desperate measures by the Mulroney government to save the accord were to no avail, including a marathon week-long negotiating session held in Ottawa behind closed doors by all eleven governments.

The determination of French-speaking Canadians to protect their language and culture on an overwhelmingly English-speaking continent has been a permanent theme since the British Conquest of Canada in 1763. Indeed, the Canadian Confederation of 1867 was arranged, in part, in order to accommodate this determination: it established the Province of Québec with a French-speaking majority and recognized its distinctive legal and educational systems.

Québec underwent a period of fairly rapid change during the 1960s, in what is called its *révolution tranquille* or "quiet revolution." The Québec government played a central role in the quiet revolution, acting as the "principal engine" of economic and social development for French-speakers, who mostly came to see themselves as Québécois first and Canadians second. Around the Québec government grew a "state middle class" of public servants, teachers, and others.

Members of this state middle class, along with others, (most notably intellectuals and artists) embraced the independence movement, centered in the Parti Québécois (PQ). The PQ, which won the Québec elections of 1976, proposed to the people of Québec in a May 1980 referendum that it be granted authority to negotiate Québec independence. But the "non" side took 60 percent of the vote. (The French-speaking vote split evenly.) Federalist forces invoked feelings of loyalty towards Canada and fears that Québec would suffer economically if it became independent.

Thereafter, it was widely assumed that any prospect for Québec independence was dead for years, and for a generation. But Québec has just undergone a second round of quiet, yet dramatic change in the 1980s, this time with the burgeoning private sector in the lead (often working hand in hand with the Québec government). French-speaking business people, the so-called *garde montante* or "new guard," have presided over a sometimes astonishing modernization of Québec's economic institutions, largely fueled by exports, especially to the United States. In consequence, no Canadian province was more enthusiastic about the Canada-U.S. Free Trade Agreement of 1988 than Québec. Few people foresaw that the self-confident new guard, like the state middle class before it, could be sympathetic to arguments for Québec sovereignty—until the Meech Lake imbroglio made that evident.

The "distinct society clause," and the constitutional arrangements associated with it in the Meech Lake accord came to constitute the absolute minimum for Québec's acquiescence to Canada's current federal arrangements. The accord thus took on enormous symbolic importance, even beyond the legal and political impacts it might have had. Premier Robert Bourassa of Québec (head of the Québec Liberal Party) described Meech as a "test" for "the acceptance of Québec as a distinct society by the rest of Canada, or the acceptance of Québec, period."[3]

Thus, in the eyes of Québec, English Canada failed the test. "We are at a critical point in our history," Bourassa said in a televised address on 23 June 1990. "The decision to reject the Meech Lake accord calls into question our political future."[4] Quite unlike the contentious situation in 1980, the collapse of Meech Lake in 1990 precipitated remarkable agreement among most Québécois that Québec's relationship with Canada must be reshaped. Residual loyalty to Canada has been badly damaged by the perception that English Canada, in failing to ratify Meech, refused to recognize the distinctiveness of Québec society. While economic access to the rest of Canada is still important, the new guard has its sights still set on export opportunities elsewhere. There is a good deal of confidence that a sovereign Québec would not suffer economically, especially within the context of North American free trade. Proponents of a strong role for the Québec government in protecting the French language and Québec culture continue to argue that authority must be transferred from Ottawa to Quebec City.

Québec seems firmly headed in the direction of sovereignty. Public opinion polls consistently have shown a very high percentage of Québécois supporting such a step. In March of 1991, both the Bourassa government and the Parti Québécois opposition agreed that a referendum on independence would be held in autumn 1992 *unless* the Canadian federal government and the governments of all the other provinces are able to propose to Québec a fundamental restructuring of the federal system. Bourassa's Liberals, for their part, have firmly indicated that nothing short of a sweeping transfer of a very wide range of powers from Ottawa to Québec City would allow them to continue championing Québec's remaining in Canada and to hold a referendum not on sovereignty, but on the proposal emanating from the rest of Canada. Two special committees of the Québec legislature are to be created during 1991: one to prepare the way to independence, the other to consider any final proposal from the rest of Canada.

Canada's peripheries also nurse historic grievances. Over 60 percent of Canada's population is located in Ontario and Québec, as is most of its wealth. With most of the seats in the federal House of Commons also allocated to central Canada, citizens of Atlantic, and especially western Canada have long believed that Ottawa tends to ignore their interests in favor of the two central provinces.

Atlantic Canada (Newfoundland, Prince Edward Island, New Brunswick, and Nova Scotia) is poor, and dependent on transfer payments from the richer provinces, administered by Ottawa. So it has thus been very leery of steps to weaken federal authority. But Western Canada (British Columbia, Alberta, Saskatchewan, and Manitoba) is economically better off, especially British Columbia and Alberta. The west strongly supported Free Trade with the United States, partially in the (correct) belief that the agreement would reduce the federal government's ability to favor central over western Canada, particularly in the energy sector.

Politically, western discontent has manifested itself in two ways in recent years. The west, especially Alberta, has championed the creation of a more powerful Canadian Senate, along the lines of the U.S. Senate, in which it could limit further the power of the federal government to favor Ontario and Québec. It has also tended to support third parties. The newest, the Reform Party, recently won a seat from Alberta in the federal House of Commons and is poised to take more in the next general election. The Reform Party calls for a restructuring of Confederation, again with a view towards weakening Ottawa's authority.

After the collapse of Meech Lake, the premier of British Columbia, Bill vander Zalm, warned that his province would have to consider political sovereignty if Québec chose that option. Quite unlike Québécois, however, the emotional and political allegiances of western Canadians are firmly with Canada. As the next round of constitutional discussions opens, in whatever form, the west will be torn between its own decentralizing agenda and a desire to keep the country together.

It is far from clear that Canada outside of Québec will want to—or be able to—respond to the Québec call for one final proposal which could head off a vote on independence. Among many English Canadians the urge to save the country will, of course, be strong and the

Mulroney government can be expected to spare no effort. But English Canadians will resent Québec's strategy of "holding a knife against the throat of English Canada." Public opinion polls have shown that many, if not most English Canadians, are weary of the constitutional struggles and opposed to giving the Québec government new powers, even if refusal to do so would precipitate independence.

Time is very short. Finding agreement between the federal government and the provincial governments before the Québec deadline of autumn 1992 will be very difficult. This is especially the case inasmuch as the nine provinces outside Québec will probably insist on dealing not only with Québec's demands, but with their own agendas (including such matters as a new Senate) and with the concerns of the native peoples. Can the country's constitutional structure really be remade in eighteen months?

Further complicating matters, the federal government is in a weak political position. Prime Minister Mulroney is deeply unpopular across English Canada. Jean Chrétien, the new leader of the federal opposition and of the Liberal Party of Canada (who was, coincidentally, chosen on the day Meech died) is from Québec. But his old-style, anti-Meech, views of federalism are unpopular there, and his party is divided. There is a strong chance that no party will win a majority in the next federal election (which must be held by late 1993), with seats going to Mulroney's Conservatives, Chrétien's Liberals, the New Democratic Party, the Reform Party in the west and the *Bloc Québécois* which supports Québec sovereignty and which emerged from defections from the ranks of both major parties in the Commons.

Potential outcomes of the current crisis over the next five years include (organized to reflect impact on defense, not in order of probability):

1. *The constitutional status quo.* Given the sentiment in Québec, this is highly unlikely.

2. *Canada remaining together, but with a general decentralization of federal authority to the provinces in the economic and cultural realms.* This is a strong possibility, in that it could meet the demands of different regions. It would be objected to by many English Canadians, especially in Ontario and in Atlantic Canada, who would favor the retention of a relatively strong federal government for English Canada.

3. *Canada remaining together, but with substantial authority devolved to Québec alone in the economic and cultural realms.* This is also a possibility, in that the majority of English Canadians and possibly Québécois might support such an accommodation in order to keep the country together, if only in name. But it raises at least two potentially intractable problems: representation of Québec within a federal government which would have limited authority over it, and the demands of the other provinces.

4. *Québec becoming "sovereign," and negotiating an association with Canada which includes leaving defense in the hands of the Canadian government.* This would obviously be emotionally painful for English Canada and could come at some economic cost to Québec. But ironically, it might be easier to negotiate a clean break with one province than to give it special status within the Canadian Confederation or to arrange general decentralization. In other words, better a well arranged divorce than a marriage in name only.

Most Québécois, like most Canadians, are uninterested in defense issues. Arguments in favor of Québec sovereignty have focused on economics and culture. So it is not inconceivable that Québec, although sovereign, might leave defense in the hands of the Canadian government.

The line between this option and option (3), it can be seen readily, is thin. So the actual outcome might not fit neatly into either category.

5. *Québec becoming sovereign, with or without an economic association with Canada, and opting for the establishment of Québec armed forces.* Many of the arguments used to structure Canadian defense policy could be applied to a sovereign Québec: Québec armed forces would protect the sovereignty of Québec's territory, airspace and possibly waters, and could undergird Québec diplomacy through the provision of token forces, while a Québec defense budget could be used as a form of economic subsidy, especially to the aerospace industry located in the Montreal area.

During the summer of 1990 the usefulness of armed forces for still another purpose, that of lending assistance to civil authorities, was brought home dramatically to Québécois. Units of the Canadian army were sent in to prevent further violence when Mohawk Indians erected barricades at two locations in the province, including the approach to a bridge into Montreal. A provincial policeman was killed in one skirmish. By the time barricades were down and the army withdrawn, many Québécois seemed to be asking whether a sovereign Québec might need to maintain small-scale forces precisely for such emergencies.

Thus the possibility of an independent Québec opting for armed forces cannot be ruled out. The PQ calls for such a course. Its current position paper on sovereignty advocates the establishment of:

> moderate armed forces (*une armée de taille modérée*), equipped with conventional, non-nuclear forces, which would have the tasks of territorial protection and assisting the population in a natural disaster. A sovereign Québec will offer its forces for participation in United Nations peacekeeping operations.
>
> (Québec) will maintain its commitments to NATO and NORAD, defensive alliances permitting the maintenance of a climate of stability and security which enhances disarmament initiatives.[5]

Still, this does not necessarily mean that Québec armed forces would include all combat elements (army, navy, and air force), as will be discussed below.

6. *The breakup of the country into more than two sovereign states.* This possibility, which would raise numerous problems for the United States, cannot be ruled out summarily, given the two cleavages. Nonetheless, it is highly unlikely because English Canadians, in the wake of the departure of Québec, would in all probability strive to redefine their country as overwhelmingly English-speaking, yet still distinct from the United States.

IMPACTS ON CANADA-U.S. DEFENSE RELATIONS

Perhaps it is not gratuitous to say, before dealing with the impacts of the various options, that Americans, when thinking of these matters, should strenuously avoid the memories of their own country's Civil War. The chances of Canada breaking up or threatening to break up in a climate of domestic violence are all but nonexistent. To be sure, sporadic violence by extremists cannot be ruled out. But almost all Canadians understand that force will play no role whatsoever in keeping their country together.

The first four potential outcomes, in which defense would remain in the hands of the Canadian government, would have little or no impact on Canada-U.S. defense relations.

The sixth outcome—which, to repeat, is highly unlikely—would in all probability necessitate a simple, yet drastic step of which little can or needs to be said: the United States would have to undertake itself all operations essential to the security of North America, including those located in Canada. For it is hard to imagine that several Canadas would be able to manage, pay for, or coordinate coherent armed forces.

The fifth outcome, in which Québec opts for the establishment of its own military would obviously have a direct impact on the Canadian Armed Forces. Officers and enlisted personnel would have to decide their allegiances. Military facilities and equipment in Québec (and perhaps a portion of them in Germany) would be transferred to the newly sovereign Québec state.

It is conceivable that either Canada or Québec, or both, or neither, would decide to maintain small token forces in Germany as part of a multinational force or earmark forces for the reinforcement of Europe. Canada, as a signatory of the North Atlantic Treaty could remain a NATO member without forces in Europe. The allies would have to decide whether they would welcome Québec membership, and under what conditions.

As many Québécois learned to their surprise during the Mohawk crisis, the complete infrastructure for a small army is already located in Québec in the form of the 5ième Groupe-brigade du Canada. While there are Canada-U.S. plans to deal with small-scale conventional attacks on North America (seizure of radar stations, etc.) the probability of such an event has always been so very low, and the forces earmarked to deal with it so small that the disruption of the Canadian army would have little impact on North American security.

It probably can be assumed that the Canadian navy, because of its basing in British Columbia and Atlantic Canada, would remain, intact, in Canadian hands. The loss of very roughly one quarter of Canada's tax base would obviously have an impact on the country's defense budget. So the navy's hopes for continuing with its current program of building new ships and submarines would probably suffer. While the United States might have to assume a greater role in the seaward defense of North America, the bilateral and NATO arrangements for cooperation with the Canadian navy should remain intact. Québec, for its part, might be content with a very limited naval force of small vessels to patrol the Gulf of St. Lawrence; coast guard or police vessels might do.

In this fifth case the most difficult issue to deal with, from the U.S. perspective, would be air defense, if Québec opted for its own air defense force. As outlined in chapter VI, the air defense of eastern Canada is conducted by aircraft based at Bagotville, Québec, with several aircraft from Bagotville on alert at Goose Bay, Labrador. All are controlled by Canadian NORAD region headquarters at North Bay, Ontario. The Forward Operating Location (FOL) for northern air defense operations in eastern Canada is also located in Québec, at Kuujjuaq. The numbers are not large: 441 Squadron, which is responsible for eastern Canadian NORAD operation has about twelve CF-18s; it is backed up by 433 Squadron with about another twelve aircraft. In the wake of the 1985 North American air defense modernization agreement, there are no air defense radar stations located in Québec.

But problems would emerge readily. How would Québec man, train, and maintain what would be, in effect, a small piece spun off a larger air force? Whose aircraft would be responsible for air defense operations in Atlantic Canada?

Thorny command and control issues would also arise. Would Québec build its own air defense control center, or would it propose that North Bay become a joint Canada-Québec control center? If Québec opted for its own center, would Canada be obliged to create duplicate facilities in Atlantic Canada?

Finally, and inevitably there would be the NORAD issue. Québec, it can probably be safely assumed, would be eager for close relations with both the United States and Canada. It would thus be prepared to accept an accommodation of the current Canada-U.S. arrangements whereby information is shared between the continent's air defense forces and aircraft fly across the border in accordance with jointly prepared plans and operational understandings. Yet it might be very difficult for the United States to accept the tri-nationalization of NORAD, including the admission of Québec officers to Colorado Springs, given the very small contribution Québec would make and given the centrality of NORAD in the integrated assessment of attack.

If Québec were simply given a role at North Bay, where Canadian and Québec operations were controlled, NORAD might continue as a Canada-U.S. entity. But more likely some of the "other, less integrative options" discussed in chapter VII might prove attractive to all three countries, especially the United States. In particular, USSPACECOM would permanently assume the role of providing integrated assessment of attack. Canadians would leave Colorado Springs. USSPACECOM would be provided information by either a continental air defense command (perhaps located at Langley Air Force Base), or directly from United States and Canadian/Québec, or United States, Canadian and Québec air defense commands, all of which would coordinate their plans and operations.

Given these complications, should Québec independence come and should Québec opt for armed forces, clearly the interests of North American defense would be served by a decision taken by Québec to leave air defense in the hands of the United States and Canada. It is thus conceivable that in the course of full independence negotiations, Québec might be persuaded to restrict itself to an army.

NOTES

1. Not surprisingly, much has been written about Meech Lake. For an overview, see Michael Behiels, *Meech Lake Primer* (Ottawa: University of Ottawa Press, 1989).
2. See Andrew Cohen, *A Deal Undone: The Making and Breaking of the Meech Lake Accord* (Vancouver: Douglas and McIntyre, 1990).
3. *Globe and Mail* (Toronto), 1 July 1989, D1, D8.
4. *Le Devoir* (Montreal), 24 June 1990, 13.
5. "La souveraineté: Pourquoi? Comment?" Montréal: Service des communications du Parti Québécois, 1990. Unofficial translation.

X

Summary and Recommendations for U.S. Policy Toward Canada

SUMMARY

Canadian defense policy is in disarray. Eventually, the Mulroney government or its successor will have to come to grips with the full implications of April 1989 and face the commitment-capability gap: barring a very unlikely decision to restore substantial growth to the defense budget, Canada can no longer sustain the same range of military commitments in North America and Europe it has had since 1951. The current demands of Canadian sovereignty protection, and the opportunity afforded by the NATO arms reductions, coupled with an extremely low Canadian defense budget will lead to Canadian retrenchment in Europe. This will be the case even should no new needs arise to commit any Canadian defense resources in North America.

Yet those new needs may well arise, in two areas:

1. Should the United States decide in the 1990s that further modernization of the North American air defense system is necessary, in order to plug current detection gaps, or deal with "stealthy" threats or (least likely) complement a BMD system, Canada will feel compelled to enhance its own air defense efforts affecting its own territory and in its own airspace.

2. Should the Canadian government find its lack of under ice capability in the Arctic intolerable in the face of U.S. and Soviet operations there, and the development of Canadian hybrid submarine technology irresistible, it will decide to devote resources to sending Canadian submarines into those waters.

The driving force behind a Canadian concentration on home-based defense roles will not be the need to defend Canada. No such need exists, due to the presence of the United States. This is reflected in the low level of Canadian defense spending. Rather, it will be sovereignty protection in the "push-resistant" sense. The Canadian government cannot turn over all defense efforts undertaken within Canada to the United States, especially in the Arctic.

—189—

As Canadians come to see, over the next decade, their armed forces more and more as sovereignty protection forces, strategic differences with the United States may be highlighted. Canadians and Americans have not seen eye to eye on nuclear deterrence and Canadians cannot be expected to welcome a U.S. decision to deploy a BMD system.

All this holds out the unhappy and less than coherent prospect of Canada's concentrating its meager defense resources on home defense in cooperation with the United States, while at the same time trying to put political distance between Canadian efforts and those of the United States.

WHAT SHOULD U.S. POLICY TOWARD CANADA BE?

United States defense interests in Canada will continue to be threefold: (1) the United States needs access to Canadian airspace, waters and territory for U.S. strategic defense forces; (2) the United States seeks to share the financial burden of defense with Canada; and (3) the United States seeks from Canada the commitment of effective armed forces deployed to cooperate with those of the United States in the joint defense of the continent, and with the allies in Europe.

In the light of the conclusions summarized above, the following sections offer recommendations for U.S. policy towards Canada in pursuit of these three interests. It then concludes with first, a discussion of policy should Québec decide to become independent, and second, one general recommendation for U.S. policy.

(1) Access to Canadian Airspace, Waters, and Territory

Here U.S. interests are the most secure. To be sure, lurid scenarios about the future of Canada-U.S. defense relations can easily be concocted. In these, the Canadian government attempts to close the waters of the Arctic Archipelago to U.S. submarines in order to protect Canadian sovereignty and restrict the ability of the U.S. Navy to execute the Maritime Strategy. Or Ottawa refuses to permit more than a small number of U.S. air defense aircraft to enter its airspace, in order to prevent its use in the pursuit of flexible nuclear options. Or Ottawa makes it firmly known that it will forbid the deployment of elements of a U.S. BMD system on its territory.

All of the steps above have been proposed recently by a number of Canadian commentators. But it is exceedingly unlikely that the Canadian government would ever act upon any of them. Such a step would be unprecedented and the full consequences unpredictable. Thirty-five years ago at the height of the bomber age the Cabinet Defence Committee was given a blunt and still applicable warning by the Department of External Affairs: "it may be very difficult indeed for the

Canadian government to reject any major defense proposals which the United States Government presents with conviction as essential for the security of North America."[1]

Furthermore, Canadian governments have always seen North air defense efforts and ASW efforts as meeting both U.S. and Canadian security needs. Any differences here have been over the nature and extent of those efforts.

BMD, however, is different. Only in the case of BMD could a situation arise where Ottawa would disapprove of deployment itself, although here, too, if the United States ever were to "present with conviction" a proposal to deploy elements of a BMD system in Canada of which Canada disapproved, Ottawa would find it hard to resist.

But this truly is a worst case scenario. BMD deployments may never materialize. Or they might materialize within the context of the one case where Canadians would not disapprove: sanctioned by a U.S.-Soviet arms control agreement.

Moreover, the U.S. government today is in a position to allay for at least a decade the greatest of Canadian territorial worries concerning BMD. As discussed in chapter V, Canadian concerns, while understandable, are misplaced with respect to any of the first-phase BMD systems being considered. Accordingly:

- *The U.S. Department of Defense should publicly confirm that none of the elements of a first-phase BMD system would require basing in Canada.*

Yet, it must be stressed, the issue of U.S. operations in Canada is far from irrelevant. The real question is not whether U.S. forces will always be admitted to Canada, but rather what the impact of U.S. air and naval forces (and of a hypothetical BMD effort) will be on the decisions Canada takes concerning the commitment of its own forces to North American defense.

(2) Sharing the Financial Burden of Defense with Canada

Here the prospect is very poor. The Mulroney government undertook the cuts of April 1989 in the full knowledge that there was very little the United States effectively could do in reaction. U.S. leverage in this area remains minimal, ultimately because of the U.S. "involuntary guarantee" of Canadian security. The cuts in the defense budgets of other NATO countries will also generate strong pressures in Canada to further cut, or at least not substantially increase, the Canadian budget.

The option is theoretically available of freezing Canada out of allied military and arms control discussions until it pays its "dues." But there is no inclination on the part of either Washington or the European allies to play hard ball on this issue with a fellow NATO member. Short of that kind of allied coercion, all there remains is jawboning and appeals to equity and fairness, not the most powerful of policy instruments.

> • *The president, the secretary of state and the secretary of defense should, in their regular meetings with their Canadian counterparts, continue to express unhappiness over the abysmal level of Canadian defense spending, far below the NATO average.*

Once a year members of Congress and members of the Canadian Parliament meet as the Canada-U.S. Inter-Parliamentary Group for a frank and fairly freewheeling discussion of the relationship between the two countries. For the Canadians, this tends to be an important gathering; senior members of the various party caucuses usually attend. In this forum, as well, the issue of Canadian defense spending should continue to be raised.

> • *The U.S. members of the Canada-U.S. Inter Parliamentary Group should reiterate U.S. concerns over the deplorable state of Canada's defenses. While recognizing Canada's fiscal problems, they should not hesitate to ask their Canadian counterparts to consider the simple morality of Canada's taking, in effect, a free ride on the backs of its allies, even in an era of arms reductions. Perhaps they might cite as well the observation of the Chief of the Canadian Defence Staff that "to have a dividend you must first risk capital . . . the amount of capital Canadians have risked in defence over the past twenty years has not guaranteed much of a dividend."* [2]

(3) The Commitment of Effective Canadian Armed Forces, Deployed to Cooperate with Those of the United States

As Canada shifts towards a home-based military posture, and away from a trans-Atlantic one, the United States can have significant influence, in pursuit of its own interests. Any American heavy handedness, it certainly bears repeating, is bound to be counterproductive. Rather, the U.S. government is in a position to encourage Ottawa in certain directions, and also where possible, alleviate Canadian concerns about the nature of American defense policies and plans.

The protection of Canadian sovereignty is not inherently incompatible with U.S. defense interests. To the contrary, up until now at least, the two have been largely complementary. For example, a CF-18 out of Goose Bay, Newfoundland, sent aloft to intercept a *Bear*-H over the Atlantic protects Canadian sovereignty and serves the defense interests of both the United States and Canada. A *Tribal*-class destroyer out of Halifax on ASW patrol in the CANLANT region similarly fulfills both tasks.

Thus, ironically, inadvertent threats by the United States to Canadian sovereignty sometimes serve U.S. defense interests. They precipitate Canada's paying for and manning defense efforts the United States would otherwise have to pay for and man in Canada. In fact, as seen so often in the preceding pages, Canada has frequently been motivated to undertake defense missions at home lest they be performed entirely by Americans.

But it is not always so simple. Nor will it be in the future. Canadian sovereignty protection and U.S. defense interests are not necessarily identical. Sovereignty protection, as it is understood in Canada, places a premium on the *presence* of Canadians, rather than on the fulfillment of a defense mission. To be sure, when presence and defense mission are identical, everyone, Americans and Canadians, may be content, as in the case of that CF-18 over the Atlantic or that destroyer in it.

Nonetheless, the Canadian emphasis on sovereignty protection can pose two long term future problems for the United States. First, Canada can devote its very scarce military resources to presence rather than military mission, knowing that the United States can be counted on, in the final analysis, for defense. The *Arcturus* aircraft will be a classic example. It will display the maple-leaf flag on its side in flights over the Arctic, where Canadian sovereignty concerns run high, but serve no defense interest except to free more capable aircraft for other missions. Second, the need to establish a sovereign presence can also motivate Ottawa to give the Canadian military a defense mission—but one the United States would rather reserve for itself. This was the case, of course, with the projected Canadian SSN missions in the Arctic.

Both forms of Canadian sovereignty protection could become problems for the United States over the next decade. Out of concern over U.S. nuclear strategy, and should deployment ever occur over a U.S. BMD system, Canada may decide to limit the extent of its participation in North American air defense, emphasizing presence rather than defense. And it may develop hybrid submarines for Arctic ASW.

Out of these concerns, four general principles emerge for the conduct of U.S. policy towards Canadian defense policy. (1) The United States must recognize that as it commits air defense and naval defense force to North America, this will create strong sovereignty protection incentives for Canada. (2) The United States should continue to encourage Canada to deploy defense forces meeting U.S. interests; this encouragement should include access to the relevant U.S. technology and plans. (3) In areas where the deployment of Canadian forces for sovereignty purposes are at odds with U.S. interests—in other words, in Arctic waters—the United States should explore ways of meeting Canadian sovereignty concerns. (4) The United States should continually be aware of, and where possible attempt to alleviate Canadian concerns over the implications for Canada-U.S. defense cooperation of U.S. nuclear strategy and BMD deployments.

These general principles can be applied to the three areas of Canadian defense deployments: Europe, maritime defense and North American aerospace defense.

Canada in Europe. In one way or another, there will be a substantial reduction of the Canadian military presence in Europe. Such a presence, even at the most limited token levels, will be in the interests of European stability in the 1990s. The best way to secure this would be through the establishment of a multinational force involving Canada.

- *The United States should support the establishment of a multinational NATO force in Germany which involves a small Canadian contribution, on the order of perhaps as few as 1000 personnel.*

Ottawa may be tempted to limit its military involvement in Europe to such a contribution. Yet Canada could usefully continue to contribute, as well, to the reinforcement of the NATO Northern Flank, especially in the light of the increasing nervousness of the Norwegian government as Soviet forces are withdrawn from Eastern Europe and deployed in the Soviet homeland.

- *The United States should encourage Canada to retain its commitment to send from Canada a battalion-group to the NATO Northern Flank as part of the Allied Mobile Force-Land. It should also ask Ottawa to consider reviving some or all of its larger commitments to reinforce Norway that it abandoned in 1987, as a substitute for the current Canadian forces in Germany.[3]*

Maritime Defense. On the naval side the United States will encourage Canada to continue to concentrate on its traditional ASW roles in the North Atlantic, which mesh well with the U.S. Navy's roles and attempt to dissuade it from investing in expensive, untried technologies for Arctic ASW. For such dissuasion to be fully effective, the United States must seek to alleviate Canadian Arctic sovereignty concerns.

Unfortunately the one step that would do the most—resolution of the dispute over the legal status of the Northwest Passage—appears at the moment to be entirely out of reach, given the diverging legal interests of the two countries in the region. A second and therefore key step would be to work more closely with officers of the Canadian navy in the Canadian Arctic. This will be painful for the U.S. Navy. But it will be far less painful than the prospect reemerging over the next decade of the unwelcome diversion of Canadian resources to Arctic ASW.

- *The U.S. Department of Defense should explore ways of sharing more extensive information with the Canadian navy concerning the movement of U.S. (and to the extent available, Soviet)*

*submarines through Canadian Arctic waters. Possibilities would
include the formation of a U.S. Navy-MARCOM Working Group
on the Arctic or the admission of Canadian naval officers to the
COMSUBWESTLANT operational staff. The existence of any new
such arrangements should be made public, so that the Canadian
government can be seen as attending to Canada's Arctic interests.*

* *The United States and Canada should also explore the possibility
of U.S. SSNs being sent from time to time on Canadian sovereignty
patrol missions in Arctic waters. During the course of such missions, the U.S. boats could be placed under the operational control (limited as necessary) of the Commander, MARCOM, at
Halifax and carry Canadian naval officers on board. These arrangements would be similar to the ones that now exist for U.S.
AWACS aircraft with Canadian officers on board to operate in
Canadian airspace under the operational control of the air
defense commander at North Bay, Ontario, except that the joint
naval arrangements would extend only to selected, intermittent
voyages. Here, too, the existence of any new such arrangements
should be made public.*

* *The U.S. Department of Defense should review whether U.S. ASW
operations would be enhanced by the placement of a fixed, under-
ice detection system in the waters of the Canadian Arctic Archipelago with a view towards entering into discussions with the
Canadian Department of National Defence on the possibility of
jointly operating such a system, much as Canada is involved in
the operation of the Atlantic SOSUS system.*

Canada has been diverting naval resources from their Atlantic concentration to the Pacific, motivated as much by the need to stake a claim
to access to U.S. information as by the need to deal with the Soviet
threat. Accordingly,

* *The U.S. Department of Defense should review current policy
on the sharing of ASW information with Canada in the Pacific,
especially as it pertains to information from the Pacific SOSUS
system.*

Finally, it should be observed that two steps which extend far beyond
U.S. policy towards Canada would have a beneficial impact on U.S.-
Canadian naval relations, especially in the Arctic. The first of these
would be an agreement between the United States and the Soviet Union
limiting sea-launched cruise missiles. Second, as Prof. Joel J. Sokolsky
of the Royal Military College of Canada has urged:

Canada can do little with regard to the strategic antisubmarine warfare
aspects of the USN's "maritime strategy" and the possible impact upon

strategic stability and arms control, but the U.S. should recognize that Canada and other allies have concerns about the future of the Arctic region. The Bush administration should review the feasibility of mounting a significant challenge to the Soviets in their own backyard.[4]

North American Air Defense. Effective Canadian air defenses serve U.S. interests. There are three potential barriers. The first is technology.

- *The United States should continue to involve Canada as fully as the Canadian government wishes in the development of advanced air defense technology under the aegis of the Air Defense Initiative, and encourage Canada to devote resources to the development of space-based radar. It should also take pains to ensure that regardless of the evolution of command relations at Colorado Springs, the Canadian air force continues to have access to U.S. plans and technology for space-based air defense systems.*

The second arises from the political difficulties the Canadian government will continue to face concerning the relationship between air defense and any possible, future U.S. BMD system, especially within the NORAD-USSPACECOM arrangements. Fortunately, some of these can be alleviated at the time of NORAD renewal in 1991.

- *The United States and Canada should renew the NORAD agreement in 1991. Because there is no prospect that NORAD, as opposed to USSPACECOM, would ever be charged with the operation of a U.S. BMD system, nothing would be lost militarily and much could be gained politically if the 1991 agreement specified that it was the intent of both the United States and Canadian governments never to place any active strategic defense systems, other than those for air defense, under NORAD's control. Alternatively, the U.S. government could make a more informal statement to this effect. At the time of NORAD renewal, official U.S. spokesmen should also publicly echo the conclusion of the Canadian parliamentary committee at the last renewal that "Other, less integrative arrangements are conceivable and functioned quite satisfactorily until 1957. This option is always available to Canada, should it feel uncomfortable with directions taken in the United States."*
- *Finally, because of the persistent confusion in Canada concerning the current arrangements, U.S. officials should cooperate fully with their Canadian colleagues at renewal or thereafter to ensure that the NORAD-USSPACECOM relationship is once again fully and exhaustively explained.*

The last potential barrier is the relationship between North American air defense and U.S. nuclear strategy. It may eventually prove to be the most intractable. Given the differing strategic approaches of

Canadians and Americans, the Canadian government may in the future feel compelled to limit the extent of Canadian air defense operations in a further modernized North American system. As long as the United States continued to enjoy access to Canadian territory and airspace, this would be incompatible with U.S. interests only in that Canada would not be bearing as heavy a load in continental air defense operations as it might.

In the recent past, the nature of current U.S. nuclear strategy has often been distorted and exaggerated in Canada, creating even greater difficulties for the Canadian government in justifying air defense cooperation with the United States. While recognizing that there are real differences between the Canadian "apocalyptic" consensus and the current U.S. flexible approach, the U.S. government can at the very least minimize some of the difficulties Ottawa may face, by attempting to dispel any reoccurrence of the persistent feeling in Canada that the United States takes too lightly the potential consequences of a central nuclear exchange. There may be no problem in the 1990s. However, it may become necessary if the retention of flexible nuclear options by the U.S. appears to Canadians as dangerous and unnecessary.

- *U.S. officials should be prepared to emphasize, should it be necessary, to a Canadian audience that no government is more cognizant of the potential horrors of nuclear war than the United States, that the United States has no expectations that it could ever win a nuclear war, that U.S. strategy remains firmly based on the deterrence of attacks on itself and its allies, that the retention of some flexibility in U.S. nuclear planning remains prudent, and that Canada plays a critical role in the protection of the U.S. nuclear deterrent.*

IF QUEBEC OPTS FOR INDEPENDENCE

Since the establishment of the Québec independence movement in the late 1960s, the U.S. government has followed a wise and prudent policy that is still applicable:[5]

- *As Québec and the rest of Canada debate the future of their relationship, the U.S. government should continue to stress that, while it hopes Canada will remain united, this is a matter for Canadians to decide without any U.S. interference.*

Should the debate in Québec and the rest of Canada actually produce a Québec decision to opt for independence, it then will be more than legitimate for the United States to pursue its interests as the actual negotiations over the restructuring of the Canada-Québec relationship are underway. As discussed in the previous chapter, North American air defense would be complicated by an active Québec role.

> • *Should Québec clearly opt for independence, the United States should encourage it to leave North American air defense in the hands of the United States and Canada.*

The United States will have an interest, though, in involving an independent Québec in the planning and discussion of North Atlantic and North American security matters.

> • *If an independent Québec is established, the United States should support its candidacy to be a signatory to the North Atlantic Treaty, and should seek with both the Canadian and Québec governments ways to incorporate Québec in discussions of North American security.*

TALKING DIRECTLY TO CANADIANS

A persistent theme in this book has been public Canadian confusion over or misunderstanding of U.S. policies and plans. There has been confusion over U.S. nuclear strategy, over procedures for the deployment of U.S. nuclear weapons to Canada, over the NORAD-USSPACECOM arrangements, over the relationship between air defense modernization and BMD, and over the implications of BMD for Canadian territorial sovereignty. Behind all this confusion, and the dark suspicions it sometimes engenders, lies the curious way Canadians receive—and sometimes do not receive—information they regard as credible about their defense relationship with the United States.

Senior U.S. officials almost never comment on that relationship. In fact, no U.S. secretary of defense or secretary of state has made extensive, well-prepared, trenchant comments on the subject for decades.[6] Not only are they, of course, busy with other matters but they apparently have felt that the subject is best left to their Canadian counterparts. In one real sense this may have been wise, for it has prevented any of the counterproductive scenes imaginable where Canadians felt they were being told what to do by the pushy Americans.

Unhappily, the information does not get through from Canadian sources, for two reasons. First, as was discussed in chapter III, Canadian officials often shy away from the sensitive subject of nuclear strategy. Second, and still more unhappily, Canadian officials often lack credibility at home. The "real" sources, the Canadian press and public generally believe, are Americans. Under these circumstances, offhanded remarks by senior U.S. officials, such as Caspar Weinberger's concerning "launchers" in Canada, take on unwarranted significance.

Complicating the problem is a lack of sophistication among the Canadian press concerning defense issues, reflecting, in large part, the general national lack of interest in the subject. No Canadian newspaper has a fulltime defense correspondent. Further complications arise from the eternal Canadian suspicion of U.S. entangling designs. Accordingly,

> • *The U.S. government should—cautiously—take advantage of opportunities to explain to Canadians U.S. defense policies affecting Canada and U.S. perceptions of Canada-U.S. defense relations. Unobtrusive, yet effective occasions are available for this purpose. For example senior defense officials could accept invitations from Canadian universities, defense associations, or research organizations to speak on the subject.*

Rather than just the usual bromides to be found in the usual official U.S. speeches at Canadian-American gatherings, celebrating the undefended Canada-U.S. border and the like, U.S. officials could usefully lay some public groundwork for the next decade of partnership between the two countries for the joint defense of the continent they share.

NOTES

1. Defence Liaison (1) Division, Department of External Affairs, "Continental Radar Defence," 3 October 1953, Brooke Claxton papers, vol. 102, Public Archives of Canada, Ottawa.
2. General A.J.G.D. De Chastelain, " 'The Art of Prudent Walking': Coming to Grips with Detente—An Update from a Canadian Military Perspective," *Canadian Defence Quarterly* 19, no. 6 (June 1990): 13.
3. Although somewhat dated, for details of such a posture see chapter 4, "Toward a New Canadian Defense Posture: Imperatives for Change and Leadership," in *Canada and Collective Security: Odd Man Out,* ed. Joseph T. Jockel and Joel J. Sokolsky (New York: Praeger and Georgetown Center for Strategic and International Studies, 1986).
4. Joel J. Sokolsky, *Defending Canada* (New York: Priority Press, 1989), 59.
5. For a perceptive history of U.S. policy toward Québec, see Jean-François Lisée, *Dans l'oeil de l'aigle: Washington face au Québec* (Montréal: Boréal, 1990).
6. In fact, it may well be that no such comments have been made since the Second World War. I have never encountered any evidence to the contrary.

Bibliography

NOTE: Two Canadian research organizations publish bibliographies especially useful to the study of Canada-U.S. defense relations. The Canadian Institute for International Peace and Security in Ottawa has assembled *Canada and International Peace and Security: A Bibliography (1985–1989)*. The Canadian Institute of International Affairs in Toronto has published a series of volumes under the title *A Bibliography of Works on Canadian Foreign Policy*. The first volume covers 1945–70; at the moment the most recent deals with 1981–85.

For current developments, the *Defence Newsletter,* issued monthly by the Centre for Foreign Policy Studies of Dalhousie University in Halifax, is indispensible.

Allison, Graham T., Albert Carnesdale, and Joseph S. Nye. *Hawks, Doves and Owls: An Agenda for Avoiding Nuclear War.* New York: W. W. Norton, 1985.
Angell, David R. "NORAD and Binational Nuclear Alert: Consultation and Decisionmaking in the Integrated Command." *Defence Analysis* 4 (June 1988): 129–37.
Asker, James R. "Congress Raises ABM Treaty Concerns on Strategic Defense Development." *Aviation Week and Space Technology* 132, no. 26 (25 June 1990): 30.
Atwood, Margaret. *Second Words: Selected Critical Prose.* Toronto: Anansi, 1982.
Aviation Week and Space Technology. "New Soviet Bombers, Fighters Heighten Alaska's Role." 130 (9 May 1989): 43–45.
———. "Politics Holds Key to Pace of Strategic Defense Research." 132, no. 12 (19 March 1990): 62–63.
———. "Political Review, Technical Tests Will Set Course of SDI Research." 130 (20 March 1989): 61.
———. "Washington Roundup . . . Blackjack Cruise." 128 (28 March 1988): 15.
Bagnal, James. "British Boat Must Navigate Past Obstacles" and "Cost Key Factor for Adjustments to French Sub." *Financial Post* (8 February 1988): 42.
Barnes, Fred. "Pebbles Go Bam-Bam." *New Republic* (17 April 1989): 12–15.
Barnes, Thomas G. " 'Canada, True North:' A 'Here There' or a Boreal Myth." *The American Review of Canadian Studies* 19, no. 4 (Winter 1989): 369–79.

Barrett, John. "Arms Control and Canada's Security Policy." *International Journal* 42, no. 4 (Autumn 1987): 731–68.

Beattie, C. E., and K. R. Greenway. "Offering Up Canada's North." *Northern Perspectives* 14, no. 4 (September–October 1986): 5–8.

Behiels, Michael. *Meech Lake Primer.* Ottawa: University of Ottawa Press, 1989.

Bobbitt, Philip. *Democracy and Deterrence: The History and Future of Nuclear Strategy.* New York: St. Martin's Press, 1988.

Bracken, Paul. *The Command and Control of Nuclear Forces.* New Haven and London: Yale University Press, 1983.

Brebner, J. Bartlett. *Canada: A Modern History.* Ann Arbor: The University of Michigan Press, 1971.

Breemer, Jan S. "The U.S. Navy Plans for a Differrent Type of Cold War." *Sea Power* 27, no. 9 (August 1984): 25.

Bromke, Adam, and Kim Richard Nossal. "Trudeau Rides the Third Rail." *International Perspectives* (May/June 1984): 3–67.

Brooks, Linton F. "Naval Power and National Security: The Case for the Maritime Strategy." *International Security* 11, no. 2 (Fall 1986): 58–88.

——— . "Nuclear SLCMs Add to Deterrence and Security." *International Security* 13, no. 3 (Winter 1988–1989): 169.

Bulletin of the Atomic Scientists "U.S. and Soviet nuclear weapons under development, 1988." (October 1988): 56.

Bundy, McGeorge. "Strategic Deterrence Thirty Years Later: What Has Changed?" *The Future of Strategic Deterrence, Papers from the 21st Annual Conference of the IISS.* Adelphi Paper no. 160, London: International Institute for Strategic Studies, 1980.

Byers, R. B. *Canadian Security and Defence: The Legacy and the Challenges.* Adelphi Paper no. 214, London: International Institute for Strategic Studies (Winter 1986).

Byers, R. B., John Hamre, and G. R. Lindsey. *Aerospace Defence: Canada's Future Role?* Toronto: Canadian Institute of International Affairs, Wellesley Papers 9, 1985.

Byers, R. B., and Michael Slack (eds). *Strategy and the Arctic.* Polaris Paper no. 4. Toronto: Canadian Institute of Strategic Studies, 1986.

Canada. Department of External Affairs. *Canada Treaty Series.*

——— . "Statement by Prime Minister on Air Defence Policy." 20 February 1959. *Canadian Weekly Bulletin* (5 March 1959): 6.

Canada. Department of National Defence. *Canada's New Submarines.* Ottawa: 1988.

——— . *Challenge and Commitment: A Defence Policy for Canada.* Ottawa: 1987.

——— . *SSN Fact Sheets.* Ottawa: 1988.

——— . *White Paper on Defence.* Ottawa: March 1964.

Canada. House of Commons. *Debates.* Ottawa: 1957–90.

——— . Standing Committee on External Affairs and National Defence. *Minutes of Proceedings and Evidence.* Ottawa: 1980–86.

——— . *NORAD 1986.* Ottawa: February 1986.

——— . Standing Committee on National Defence. *Minutes of Proceedings and Evidence.* Ottawa: 1986–90.

Canada. Minister of National Defence. *White Paper on Defence: Defence in the 70s.* Ottawa: 1971.

Canada. Secretary of State for External Affairs. *Foreign Policy for Canadians.* Ottawa: 1971.

Canada. Senate. Standing Committee on Foreign Affairs. Subcommittee on National Defence. *Canada's Maritime Defence.* Ottawa: May 1983.

———. *Proceedings.* Ottawa: 1981–84.

———. Special Committee on National Defence. *Canada's Territorial Air Defence.* Ottawa: January 1986.

Canadian Institute of International Affairs. "Challenge and Commitment: Comments on the Defence White Paper." *Behind the Headlines* 45, no. 1 (September 1987).

Canadian Institute for Strategic Studies. "Moving To Fortress North America?" *Strategic Datalink* no. 14 (May 1988).

———. "The 1989 Federal Budget—The Death of Defence?" *Strategic Datalink* no. 12 (May 1989).

de Chastelain, General A.J.G.D. "The Art of Prudent Walking: Coming to Grips with Detente—An Update from a Canadian Military Perspective." *Canadian Defence Quarterly* 19, no. 6 (June 1990): 11–14.

Chircop, Aldo E., and Susan J. Ralston (eds). *Canadian Arctic Sovereignty: Are Canadian and U.S. Interests Contradictory or Complementary? Proceedings of the 1986 Ronald St. John Macdonald Symposium.* Halifax: International Insights Society, Law School, Dalhousie University, 1987.

Cimbala, Stephen J. (ed). *Strategic Air Defense.* Wilmington, Del.: S. R. Books, 1989.

———. *The Technology, Strategy and Politics of SDI.* Boulder and London: Westview Press, 1987.

Cohen, Andrew. *A Deal Undone: The Making and Breaking of the Meech Lake Accord.* Vancouver: Douglas and McIntyre, 1990.

Collins, John M. *U.S./Soviet Military Balance: Statistical Trends, 1980–1987 (As of January 1, 1988).* Washington: Congressional Research Service Report 88-425 S, 15 April 1988.

Conant, Melvin. *The Long Polar Watch: Canada and the Defense of North America.* New York: Harper and Brothers, 1962.

Cox, David. "A Review of the Geneva Negotiations, 1989–1990." *Background Paper.* Ottawa: Canadian Institute for International Peace and Security, 32 (May 1990).

———. "Canada's Defense Debate." *Washington Quarterly* 10, no. 4 (Autumn 1987): 99–112.

———. *Trends in Continental Defence: A Canadian Perspective.* Ottawa: Canadian Institute for International Peace and Security, Occasional Paper 2, 1986.

Crickark, F. W. "An Anti-Submarine Warfare Capability in the Arctic: A National Requirement." *Canadian Defence Quarterly* 16, no. 4 (April 1987): 24–30.

———. "The Canadian Navy: New Directions." *NATO's Sixteen Nations* 33 (special issue) (January 1988): 50–64.

David, Charles-Philippe. *Debating Counterforce: A Conventional Approach in a Nuclear Age.* Boulder and London: Westview Press, 1987.

Delaney, William P. "Air Defense of the United States: Strategic Missions and Modern Technology." *International Security* 15, no. 1 (Summer 1990): 181–211.

Dickey, John Sloan. *Canada and the American Presence: The United States Interest In an Independent Canada.* New York: New York University Press, 1975.

Doran, Charles F. *Forgotten Partnership: U.S.-Canada Relations Today.* Baltimore and London: The Johns Hopkins University Press, 1984.

Dosman, E. J. (ed). *The Arctic in Question.* Toronto: Oxford University Press, 1976.

Dulles, John Foster. "The Evolution of Foreign Policy." *Department of State Bulletin* 30, no. 761 (25 January 1954): 107–10.

Dzuiban, Col. Stanley W. *Military Relations between the United States and Canada, 1939–1945.* Washington: Office of the Chief of Military History, Department of the Army, 1959.

Eayrs, James. *Canada in World Affairs, October 1955 through June 1957.* Toronto: Oxford University Press, 1959.

————. *In Defence of Canada: Growing Up Allied.* Toronto: University of Toronto Press, 1980.

————. *In Defence of Canada: Peacemaking and Deterrence.* Toronto: University of Toronto Press, 1972.

————. *Northern Approaches: Canada and the Search for Peace.* Toronto: Macmilland Company of Canada, 1961.

————. "The Road from Ogdensburg." *Canadian Forum* (February 1971): 364–66.

Epstein, William. "New Stance Tarnishes Canada's Reputation." *Bulletin of the Atomic Scientists* 3, no. 8 (October 1987): 11.

"Fleets of the Future." *Canada's Navy Annual.* Calgary: Corvus Publishing Group 1986.

Foley, Theresa M. "Bush Defense Strategy to Reshape SDI Program." *Aviation Week and Space Technology* (30 January 1989): 18–20.

Friedman, Norman. "Stealth Technology, SDI and the Cruise Missile." *Military Technology* (October 1985): 122–26.

Frye, Northrup. *Divisions on a Ground: Essays on Canadian Culture.* Toronto: Anansi, 1982.

Furtado, Francis J. *U.S. and Soviet Land-Attack SLCM Programs: Implications for Strategic Stability.* ORAE Memorandum 129. Ottawa: Department of National Defence, Operational Research and Analysis Establishment, June 1990.

Gordon, J. King (ed). *Canada's Role as A Middle Power.* Toronto: Canadian Institute of International Affairs, 1965.

Gottemoeller, Rose E. "Finding Solutions to SLCM Arms Control Problems." *International Security* 13, no. 3 (Winter 1988–1989): 175–83.

————. *Land-Attack Cruise Missiles.* Adelphi Paper no. 226. London: International Insitute for Strategic Studies, Winter 1987–88.

Grant, Shelagh D. *Sovereignty or Security? Government Policy in the Canadian North, 1936–1950.* Vancouver: University of British Columbia Press, 1988.

Gray, Colin S., and Keith Payne. "Victory is Possible." *Foreign Policy* 39 (Summer 1980): 14.

Griffiths, Franklyn (ed.) *Politics of the Northwest Passage.* Kingston and Montreal: McGill-Queen's University Press, 1987.

Guerrier, Stephen W., and Wayne C. Thompson (eds). *Perspectives on Strategic Defense.* Boulder and London: Westview Press, 1987.

Gwyn, Richard, and Sandra Gwyn. "The Politics of Peace." *Saturday Night* (May 1984): 19–32.

Haglund, David (ed). *Canada's Defence Industrial Base: The Political Economy of Preparedness and Procurement.* Kington: Ronald P. Frye, 1988.

——— . "The Canadian SSN Program and the Nonproliferation Question." Kingston: Centre for International Relations, Queen's University, Occasional Paper 29, (October 1987).

Haydon, Commander Peter T. *The Strategic Importance of the Arctic: Understanding the Military Issues.* Ottawa: Department of National Defence, Directorate of Strategic Policy Planning, Strategic Issues Paper 1/87, March 1987.

Hayward, Daniel. *The Air Defence Initiative.* Ottawa: Canadian Centre for Arms Control and Disarmament, Issue Brief no. 9, 1988.

——— . "Hybrid Submarine Technologies." Canadian Centre for Arms Control and Disarmament, *Arms Control Communique,* no. 53 (12 September 1988).

Heeney, Arnold D. *The Things That Are Caesar's: The Memoirs of a Canadian Public Servant.* Toronto: University of Toronto Press, 1972.

Hertzman, Lewis , et al. *Alliances and Illusions: Canada and the NATO-NORAD Question.* Edmonton: Hurtig, 1969.

Hill, Roger. "Unified Canada-U.S. Defence Production: A Hazardous Road." *Peace and Security,* (Summer 1989): 4–6.

Hobson, Sharon. "Canada's Space-based Radar Project." *Jane's Defence Weekly* 7, no. 6 (14 February 1987): 226.

Holmes, John. *Canada: A Middle-Aged Power.* Toronto: McClelland and Stewart, 1976.

——— . *The Shaping of Peace: Canada and the Search for World Order,* vol. 2. Toronto: University of Toronto Press, 1982.

Holst, Johan Jorgen (ed). *Deterrence and Defense in the North.* Oslo: Norwegian University Press, 1985.

Honderich, John. *Arctic Imperative: Is Canada Losing the North?* Toronto: University of Toronto Press, 1987.

Hunt, Lieutenant-Colonel G. D. "Reinforcing the NATO North Flank: The Canadian Experience." *Canadian Defence Quarterly* 16, no. 4 (Spring 1987): 31–38.

Jockel, Joseph T. *Canada and NATO's Northern Flank.* Toronto: York University Centre for International and Strategic Studies, 1986.

——— . *No Boundaries Upstairs: Canada, the United States and the Origins of North American Air Defence.* Vancouver: University of British Columbia Press, 1987.

Jockel, Joseph T., and Joel J. Sokolsky. *Canada and Collective Security: Odd Man Out.* The Washington Papers. New York: Praeger, 1986.

Joffre, Joseph. "Peace and Populism: Why the European Anti-Nuclear Movement Failed." *International Security* 2, no. 4 (Spring 1987): 3–40

Kaufman, William W. *Glasnost, Perestroika and U.S. Defense Spending*. Washington, D.C.: The Brookings Institution, 1990.

——. *A Thoroughly Efficient Navy*. Washington, D.C.: The Brookings Institution, 1987.

Kennedy, Tim. "Missiles, Space and Aviation." *National Defense* 75, no. 459 (July/August 1990): 14.

Kirton, John (ed). *Canada, the United States and Space*. Toronto: Canadian Institute of International Affairs, 1986.

Kissinger, Henry A. *White House Years*. Boston: Little Brown, 1979.

Lamb, John, and Tariq Rauf. "When Choosing Nuclear Submarine Take Arms Control Seriously." Ottawa: Centre for Arms Control and Disarmament: *Arms Control Communiqué* no. 49 (16 May 1988).

Langdon, Frank, and Douglas Ross. "Towards a Canadian Maritime Strategy in the North Pacific." *International Journal* 42, no. 4. (Autumn 1987): 848–89.

"La souverainet: Pourquoi? Comment?" Montréal: Service des communications du Parti Québécois, 1990.

Latham, Andrew, and Michael Slack. "Security Policy at the Crossroads: What Direction for Canada in Europe?" *Canadian Defence Quarterly* 19, no. 6 (Summer 1990): 23–29.

Lise, Jean-Franois. *Dans l'oeil de l'aigle: Washington face au Québec*. Montréal: Boréal, 1990.

Lynch, David J. "U.S. Considers Defense Shield." *Defense Week* 7, no. 25 (23 June 1986): 12.

Macdonald, Brian (ed). *Airwar 2000*. Toronto: Canadian Institute of Strategic Studies, 1989.

——. "A Nuclear Navy for Canada." *Strategic Datalink*. Canadian Institute of Strategic Studies, 1987.

——. "The White Paper, The Army Reserve and Army Reform." *Canadian Defence Quarterly* 17, no. 4 (1988): 9.

Mann, Paul. "Superpowers Agree to Arms Cuts, but SS-18, Other Disputes Go on." *Aviation Week and Space Technology* 132, no. 24 (11 June 1990): 66–67.

Manson, General Paul. "Consolidation in Europe: Implementing the White Paper." *Canadian Defence Quarterly* 17, special number (1 February 1988): 21–30.

MccGwire, Michael. *Military Objectives in Soviet Foreign Policy*. Washington, D.C.: The Brookings Institution, 1987.

McLin, Jon B. *Canada's Changing Defense Policy, 1957–1963*. Baltimore: The Johns Hopkins University Press, 1967.

McNamara, Robert. "The Military Role of Nuclear Weapons." *Foreign Affairs* 62, no. 1. (Fall 1983): 59–80.

Meyer, LTC Dierck. "Enhancement of NATO's Military Integration: Multinational Formulations for Central Europe." *The Martello Papers*. Kingston: Queen's University Centre for International Relations, 1990.

Morton, Desmond. "Defending the Indefensible: Some Historical Perspectives on Canadian Defence 1967–1987." *International Journal* 42, no. 4, (Autumn 1987): 627–44.

Mosley, Leonard. *Dulles: A Biography of Eleanor, Allan and John Foster Dulles*. New York: The Dial Press/James Wade, 1978.

Motolla, Kari (ed). *Arctic Challenge: Nordic and Canadian Approaches to Security and Cooperation in an Emerging International Region.* Boulder and London: Westview Press, 1988.

Mustin, Vice-Admiral Henry C. "The Sea-Launched Cruise Missile: More than a Bargaining Chip." *International Security* 13, no. 3 (Winter 1988–89): 184–90.

The Name of the Chamber was Peace. Toronto: Samuel Stevens and Company, 1988.

Nitze, Paul H. "The Case for Cutting Strategic Arms." *Washington Post* 21 June 1988, A19.

North Atlantic Assembly. Civil Affairs Committee. *Interim Report of the Sub-Committee on Public Information on Defence and Security: The Netherlands, Turkey and Canada.* Brussels, September 1987.

O'Connor, Brigadier-General Gordon J. "Effective Reserves: The Challenge of the Total Force Army." *Canadian Defence Quarterly* 18, no. 5 (April 1989): 19–24.

O'Rourke, Ronald. "Canadian Nuclear-Powered Submarine Program: Issues for Congress." Congressional Research Service. *Issue Brief,* no. IB88083 (15 July 1988).

——— . *Nuclear Escalation, Strategic Anti-Submarine Warfare and the Navy's Forward Maritime Strategy.* Congressional Research Service Report no. 87-138F, 27 Feburary 1987.

"OTH-B Radar Station Nears Completion." *International Defense Review* 20, no. 3 (1987): 341.

Page, Robert. *Northern Development: The Canadian Dilemma.* Toronto: McClelland and Stewart, 1986.

Peace and Security. "The Federal Budget: Defence and Foreign Policy: A Media Roundtable." Summer 1989, 9.

Pearson, Geoffrey. "On Fireproof Houses: Canada's Security." *Points of View* no. 4. Ottawa: Canadian Institute for International Peace and Security (December 1988).

Pearson, Lester B. "The Development of Canadian Foreign Policy." *Foreign Affairs* (October 1951): 17–30.

——— . "A Look at the New Look." Canada. Department of External Affairs, *Statements and Speeches* 54/16 (15 March 1954).

——— . *Mike: The Memoirs of the Right Honourable Lester B. Pearson,* vol. 2. Toronto: Signet, 1975.

Pearson, Michael, et.al. "The World is Entitled to Ask Questions: The Trudeau Peace Initiative Reconsidered." *International Journal* (Winter 1985–1986): 129–58.

Pharand, Donat. *Canada's Arctic Water in International Law.* Cambridge: Cambridge University Press, 1988.

Pickersgill, J. W. (ed). *The Mackenzie King Record, 1945–1946,* vol. 3. Toronto: University of Toronto Press, 1968.

Pike, John. "The Strategic Defense Initiative and Canada," staff paper. Washington, D.C.: Federation of American Scientists, 17 March 1986.

Postol, Theodore A. "Banning Nuclear SLCMs: It Would Be Nice If We Could." *International Security* 13, no. 3 (Winter 1988–1989): 201.

Regehr, Ernie. *Arms Canada: The Deadly Business of Military Exports.* Toronto: James Lorimer and Company, 1987.

Regehr, Ernie, and Simon Rosemblum (eds). *Canada and the Nuclear Arms Race.* Toronto: James Lorimer and Company, 1983.

Richelson, Jeffrey. "PD-59, NSDD-13 and the Reagan Strategic Modernization Program." *The Journal of Strategic Studies* 6, no. 2 (June 1983): 125–46.

Robinson, Basil. *Diefenbaker's World: A Populist in Foreign Affairs.* Toronto: University of Toronto Press, 1989.

Rosemblum, Simon. *Misguided Missiles: Canada, the Cruise and Star Wars.* Toronto: James Lorimer and Company, 1985.

Ross, Douglas. "Canadian-American Relations and the Strategic Defense Initiative: A Case Study in the Management of Strategic Doctrinal Incompatibilities," paper presented for the 1987 Pearson-Dickey Conference, Montebello, Quebec, 4–6 November 1987.

Rubin, James R. "Sea-Launched Cruise Missiles: Facing Up to the Arms Control Challenge." *Arms Control Today* (April 1986): 4.

Sakitt, Mark. "Submarine Warfare in the Arctic: Option or Illusion." Stanford: The Center for International Security and Arms Control, May 1988.

Schadwick, Martin. "Canada and North America Air Defense: New Technology, Old Issues?" *Defense and Foreign Affairs* 15, no. 5 (May 1987): 69–72.

———. "NORAD, Sovereignty and Changing Technology." Occasional Paper no. 3. Toronto: Research Programme in Strategic Studies, York University, 1985.

Scheer, Robert. *With Enough Shovels: Reagan, Bush and Nuclear War.* New York: Vintage Books, 1983.

Schelling, Thomas C. "What Went Wrong with Arms Control." *Foreign Affairs* 64, no. 2 (Winter 1985/1986): 230.

Shragge, Eric (ed.). *Roots of Peace: The Movement Against Militarism in Canada.* Toronto: Between the Lines, 1986.

Simpson, Jeffrey. "Canada Roused by Military Plan." *Bulletin of the Atomic Scientists* 43, no. 8 (October 1987): 9–10.

Slocombe, Walter. "The Countervailing Strategy." *International Security* 5, no. 4 (Spring 1981): 18–27.

Sokolksy, Joel J. *Defending Canada.* New York: Priority Press Publications, 1989.

Stares, Paul B. *Space and National Security.* Washington, D.C.: The Brookings Insitution, 1987.

Stavridis, James. "Creating ASW Killing Zones." U.S. Naval Institute *Proceedings* 113/10/106 (October 1987): 42.

Steinbruner, John D. "Nuclear Decapitation." *Foreign Policy* 45 (Winter 1981–1982): 18–28.

Sutherland, R. J. "Canada's Long Term Strategic Situation." *International Journal* 17, no. 3 (Summer 1962): 199–223.

Taggart, P. J. "Canada's Blind Spot." U.S. Naval Institute *Proceedings* 113/3/1009 (March 1987): 145–49.

Thomas, Vice-Admiral Charles M. "A Message from the Commander of Maritime Command." *Canada's Navy Annual.* Calgary: Corvus Publishing Group, 1988, 8.

Thomas, Valerie. "False Obstacle to Arms Control." *New York Times* 13 July 1989, A23.

Towell, Pat. "Bush's Revisions of SDI May Augur Policy Shifts in Future." *Congressional Quarterly* (29 April 1989): 976–80.

———. "Political Struggles Over SDI Set to Enter a New Phase." *Congressional Quarterly* (April 1989): 702–6.

Trudeau, Pierre Elliott, and C. David Crenna (eds). *Lifting the Shadow of War.* Edmonton: Hurtig, 1987.

The True North Strong and Free? Proceedings of a Public Inquiry into Canadian Defence Policy and Nuclear Arms. West Vancouver: Gordon Soules Sook Publishers, Ltd., 1987.

Tucker, Michael. *Canadian Foreign Policy: Contemporary Issues and Themes.* Toronto: McGraw Hill Ryerson, 1980.

———. "Trudeau and the Politics of Peace." *International Perspectives* (May/June 1984): 7–10.

Tugwell, Maurice. *Peace with Freedom.* Toronto: Key Porter Books, 1988.

U.S. Congress. House Committee on Armed Services. *Defense Department Authorization and Oversight,* Hearings before the Committee on H.R. 1872, DoD Authorization of Appropriations for FY 1986. 99th Cong. 1st sess. 1985.

———. Full Committee Hearing on *Continental Air Defense.* 97th Cong. 1st sess. 22 July 1981.

U.S. Congress. Office of Technology Assessment. *SDI: Technology, Survivability and Software.* 1988.

U.S. Congress. Senate Committee on Armed Services. Hearings, *Department of Defense Authorization for Appropriations for FY 1987,* 99th Cong. 2nd sess. part 1, 1986.

U.S. Department of Defense. "Report of the Advisory Panel on Submarine and Antisubmarine Warfare to the House Armed Services Subcommittees on Research and Development and Seapower and Strategic and Critical Materials (unclassified edition)," 21 March 1989.

———. Strategic Defense Initiative Organization. *Report to Congress on the Strategic Defense Initiative.* April 1987.

U.S. General Accounting Office. *Drug Control: Issues Surrounding Increased Use of the Military in Drug Interdiction.* GAO.NSIAD-88-156 (executive summary), April 1988.

———. *Drug Smuggling: Capabilities for Interdicting Private Aircraft are Limited and Costly.* GAO/GGD-93, June 1989.

U.S. President. *Public Papers of the Presidents of the United States, Ronald Reagan.* 1981–89.

———. *Weekly Compilation of Presidential Documents.* 1981–90.

———. Commission on Strategic Forces. *Report of the President's Commission on Strategic Forces.* April 1983.

Vlahos, Michael. *Strategic Defense and the American Ethos: Can the Nuclear World Be Changed?* SAIS Papers, no. 13. Boulder and London: Westview Press, 1986.

Walsh, Don. "Is It Time for the SS<u>n</u>?: Hybrid Reactor Boats Could Augment the Navy's Seawolf Fleet." *Sea Power* (April 1989): 4.

Watkins, Admiral James D. "The Maritime Strategy." In The Maritime Strategy, supplement to the January 1986 edition of the U.S. Naval Institute *Proceedings*.

Weston, W. C. "L'importance stratégique de l'espace pour les besoins militaires futurs du Canada." *Etudes Internationales* 19, no. 3 (September 1988): 493–99.

Whittington, Michael S. (ed). *The North*. Studies of the Royal Commission on the Economic Union and Development Prospects for Canada. Toronto: University of Toronto Press, 1985.

Zaloga, Steven. "Tuplev's New Strategic Bomber: Tu-160 Blackjack." *Jane's Soviet Intelligence Review* (September 1988): 14.

Index

Security to the North: Canada-U.S. Defense Relations in the 1990s

Production Editor: Julie L. Loehr
Design: Lynne A. Brown
Copy Editor: Martha Bates

Text composed by Lansing Graphics, Inc.
in Cheltenham ITC Book 10/11.6

Printed by Thomson-Shore
on 60# Glatfelter Thor White

Bound on Holliston Crown Linen 13745 Country Blue—
stamped with General Roll Leaf semi-gloss foil, pigment #P650

DATE DUE